BECOMING A WOMAN OF STRENGTH

Ruth Barton speaks to the deepest desires and most crippling temptations women face. She opens the way for a transforming journey of calling and connectedness. It is a valuable, much needed book that will help women draw close to God and live to their fullest potential.

—Drs. Les and Leslie Parrott
Authors of *Saving Your Marriage Before It Starts*

In a day when Christian men are being challenged en masse to act more like men, it is encouraging to find a book that advocates the biblical premise that both women and men should be Christ-like. This admonition could easily remain in the realm of sanctimonious, ethereal fluff. But this book is a substantive, gut-level, practical and well-researched piece of writing that deals with real life issues from a vibrantly biblical perspective.

To women and men who are confused by the welter of conflicting definitions of their own gender, roles, and sexuality that is currently thrown at them, the author offers excellent, biblically grounded guidance for the development of authentic Christian womanhood. I predict that this work will become a classic textbook for Christians in quest of wholesome, God-honoring, biblically accurate answers to some of the most urgent personal issues of the day.

—Dr. Gilbert Bilezikian
Professor of Biblical Studies Emeritus at Wheaton College

This is a book filled with wisdom, truth-telling, encouragement, and practical help for today's Christian woman struggling with issues of marriage and parenting, identity and work as she seeks to know and follow Jesus. I found it enjoyable reading as well as challenging.

—Roberta Hestenes
President, Eastern College

Becoming a Woman of Strength

14 Life Challenges for Women—and the Men Who Love Them

R. Ruth Barton

Harold Shaw Publishers
Wheaton, Illinois

Copyright © 1994 by R. Ruth Barton

All rights reserved. No part of this book may be reproduced or transmitted in any form or by any means, electronic or mechanical, including photocopying, recording, or any information storage and retrieval system without written permission from Harold Shaw Publishers, Box 567, Wheaton, Illinois, 60189. Printed in the United States of America.

ISBN 0-87788-063-8

Cover design by David LaPlaca

Library of Congress Cataloging-in-Publication Data
Barton, R. Ruth, 1960-
    Becoming a woman of strength : 14 life challenges for women—and the men who love them / R. Ruth Barton.
    p. cm.
    Includes bibliographical references.
    ISBN 0-87788-063-8 (pbk.)
    1. Christian women—Conduct of life. 2. Decision-making—Religious aspects—
Christianity. I. Title.
BJK1610.B38 1994
248.8'43—dc20   94-12458
                                                            CIP

99 98 97 96 95 95 94

10 9 8 7 6 5 4 3 2 1

Contents

Preface

One can never wrestle enough with God if one does so out of pure regard for truth. Christ likes us to prefer truth to him, because before being Christ, he is truth. If one turns aside from him to go toward the truth, one will not go far before falling into his arms.

Simone Weil, Waiting for God

Book writing has been likened to childbirth, and rightly so. This "child" grew quietly at first, with only the most subtle signs that anything was happening. But then it started to kick and punch with questions about what it meant to be a Christian, what it meant to be a woman, and what it meant to be both at the same time.

At times the child within would sleep and I would go about the business of serving God in the "acceptable" ways, but it would always wake again, demanding that I pay attention. And so I have, as time has gone by, paid more and more attention to the wrestlings within, allowing the questions to speak louder, allowing Truth (rather than dogma) to lead and nurture spiritual life. Sometimes I have been frightened because Truth has taken me in different directions than others in my life have gone. But I know that one cannot refuse to seek the truth and still remain faithful to the God of all truth, the Christ who is truth personified, and the Holy Spirit whose main job it is to lead us into truth—right here, right now.

As it became more obvious that I was "pregnant" with a message, the folks at Shaw Publishers said, "We think you have a book in you!" They offered the tools, the professional support and flexibility necessary so that the work of labor and delivery could begin. For their role in the birthing process I am very grateful.

I found that one of the biggest differences between birthing a child and birthing a book is that, in childbirth, once labor has truly begun there is no turning back. What is within will emerge and take on a life of its own, no matter how frightening or painful the process. However, with a book one can always decide at some point that birthing is too scary or too threatening to life as the author knows it. One can always decide, "I am going to keep this inside; I cannot let this go out into the world. Besides, the world has too many books already. It doesn't need mine." One can always turn back from the tedium of the labor or the paroxyisms of pain.

I faced my share of these solitary moments when, although surrounded by people, I realized that the decision to continue obeying God in this task was mine alone. How grateful I am for his strength in allowing me to see this project to its completion and for the activity of the Holy Spirit that I felt with such certainty as I worked. The effort has been worth it for that experience alone.

But still, it is a frightening task to write a book about the things that matter most to you: the issues with which you have struggled the most deeply, the truths that have been hardest to learn and tell, the desires that are rooted in the deepest parts of your soul. It is even more intimidating to write about the life of Christ and what it means to follow him wholeheartedly (as I did in the final chapter) while being so aware of one's own shortcomings.

I console myself by assuring you, the reader, that we teachers teach the lessons we most need to learn and write the words we most need to have spoken to ourselves. I will return again and again to the words I have written here, for my own instruction and encouragement in going deeper with God. I write about the Christ-life, not because I have learned to implement it perfectly or consistently, but because Christ's ways are right and true no matter how much I stumble in my attempts to follow in his footsteps.

One of the most excruciating aspects of writing this book was understanding its limits. Every chapter presents a separate topic on which entire books have been written. (That is why you will find resources listed at the end of each chapter.) The challenge was to take a large amount of research on each topic and somehow distill it into what I understood to be its essence. Obviously this process was very subjective and I had to make many difficult choices about what to include and what to leave out. Most of the time I bypassed the obvious in order to give attention to aspects of these important issues that are addressed less frequently in Christian circles. I trust that the reader can be tolerant when she or he thinks "But she forgot to mention . . . !"

The most meaningful compliment I ever received as a writer came from a friend after she read an article of mine on the subject of fighting for your marriage. She said, "My husband and I lay in bed one night, read your article, and then talked about it. We had never talked before about some of the things you mentioned, but it was so good that we did. Thanks!" She never told me whether they agreed with me or if they thought the article was well-written; she just let me know that it opened up new avenues of communication between them and it made a difference in their marriage. That was really my deepest desire for that article.

My desire for this book is very similar. Of course I would love it if people read it and agreed with me. But I would love it even more if men and women would read this book together and allow it to open up communication between them about things they have never discussed before, truths about themselves and the world they have never seen before, and ways of relating that invite the strengths of all to flourish.

If you think about it, there really are very few "women's issues"; most of them are "people issues" at the core. Which of us—male or female—isn't affected by materialism, sexuality, children, today's abundance of choices, the struggle for self-esteem and purpose, and the lifelong task of becoming like Christ? These are challenges that women and men must face together. "For the enormous problems that face the world today, in both the private and public sphere, cannot be solved by women—or men—alone. They can only be surmounted by men and women side by side."*

R. Ruth Barton
Wheaton, Illinois
1994

*Ann Morrow Lindberg, *Gift from the Sea* (New York: Pantheon Books, 1975), p. 132.

1

The Power of Choice

As women today, you face tough choices. You know the rules are basically as follows: If you don't get married, you are abnormal. If you get married but don't have children, you are a selfish yuppie. If you get married and have children, but work outside the home, you are a bad mother. If you get married and have children and stay home, you've wasted your education.

Hillary Rodham Clinton, Commencement address, Wellesley College

This may be a dream come true but when it all comes down, it's an awful lot to do.

Amy Grant, "Hats"

A recent article in the *Chicago Tribune Magazine* discusses the fact that, as Americans, we have reached a time when "choice, rather than freeing the individual, has become so complex, difficult, and costly that it has become overchoice."[1] And who is most affected? The modern woman, of course!

It used to be that a woman's life pattern was pretty simple: she went to school, got married, stayed married to the same man—for better or worse—and raised children. There were widely accepted standards of conduct and morality so that she knew what was expected. But today "a woman can do anything. She can be traditionally feminine and that's alright; she can work, she can stay at home; she can be any way she wants with a man. But whenever there are the kinds of choices there are today, unless you have some solid base, life can be frightening."[2]

As exhilarating as it has been to have more freedom and more options, there is the downside. Social scientists point out that "choices do not necessarily make life easier—they often make life more difficult because they produce guilt, self-doubt and stress."[3] Why? Because with increased options come increased possibilites for mistakes. Today's women live with the weightiness of this reality all the time.

To top it off, since we are the first generation of women to have such a variety of options, we often lack immediate role models who have successfully negotiated the twists, turns, and pitfalls that characterize the road ahead of us. It is no wonder we sometimes feel like we are travelling in uncharted territory.

Choice: A God-Given Prerogative

There is nothing wrong with having choices. In fact, God built into his perfect world the opportunity to choose, as evidenced in the instructions to Adam and Eve:

> And the LORD God commanded the man, saying, "From any tree of the garden you may eat freely; but from the tree of the knowledge of good and evil you shall not eat, for in the day that you eat from it you shall surely die." (Genesis 2:16-17, NASB)

It was a simple test of obedience—an opportunity for the first man and woman to develop their moral natures, to exercise their spiritual muscles, to choose loyalty and obedience to God even in the face of another alternative. And although the choice they eventually made was a poor one, with dire consequences for the human race, the process that Eve went through in making her choice holds instruction for us today.

Eve's Choice

We don't know how Eve was informed of God's instruction regarding the tree of knowledge. It is possible that God spoke with Eve about it himself or that Adam relayed the information to her. Whichever the case, Eve had an accurate understanding of God's instruction (Genesis 3:2-3) and the stage was set for the first man and first woman to make their first choice.

Eve's choice to take specific action was, as it often is for us, a process in which smaller and less tangible choices became the foundation for a decision that had very concrete and far-reaching results.

She listened to the voice of temptation.

In this case, the voice of temptation was that of Satan himself, disguised as a beautiful and fascinating creature. He drew her into conversation by asking a question in which he deliberately misquoted God's initial instruction and cast doubt on God's goodness: "Indeed, has God said, 'You shall not eat from any tree of the garden?' "

Eve was one-on-one with Satan with no apparent help from Adam, who was right there with her (3:6).

To her credit, Eve started out strong by stating clearly and accurately what God had said (3:2-3). Satan, however, got more bold with his tactics and began to contradict God directly. He called God a liar ("You surely shall not die!") and accused him of withholding something very good from her ("For God knows that in the day you eat from it your eyes will be opened, and you will be like God, knowing good and evil" Genesis 3:5, NASB).

Eve listened. And she began to contemplate what Satan said: *Could it be true? Could this be a cruel hoax perpetrated by a God who wants me to believe he is good while he is actually withholding the best? Am I missing out on something wonderful?* And then she gazed longingly at the forbidden fruit. It appealed to her physical appetites and to her sense of beauty and artistry. And it appealed to her human pride, promising to make her more than God had created her to be.

She chose to believe the voice of temptation.

Knowing God as she did—much better than she knew this fascinating creature—and knowing his love and the beauty of all that he had created for her, Eve chose to believe the voice of temptation, even though it was the opposite of what God had said. Once she had chosen whom she was going to believe, she was on a slippery slope.

She acted upon her belief.

By an act of her will Eve reached out, took the fruit and ate it. She also offered some to her husband who took it without any argument at all. (At least Eve had tried to put up a fight!) Their choices forever altered the course of the human race.

At any point in the process Eve could have chosen differently and avoided the horrible chain of events her choice precipitated. But once she took her first bite, that domino effect was in motion and she would have to live with the results.

She experienced guilt and shame for the first time, emotions that were uncomfortable, at best, after the complete freedom and peace she had experienced up until that time. Her choice altered her relationship with God, causing her to attempt to hide from the One who knew and loved her best. Never again would she and Adam enjoy face-to-face talks with God, for now they had to be dismissed from the garden for their own protection (3:8, 22-24). Tension was introduced into the marriage relationship for the first time as Adam and Eve each blamed the other for their own personal choices (verses 12-13).

In addition to the immediate effects of Eve's and Adam's choice, there were more long-lasting consequences for them and for humanity as a whole. Women were cursed to experience intense pain in childbirth; men were cursed to a lifetime of hard work with uncooperative ground in order to provide for their families. The pattern of sin and death, which didn't exist until that moment, became an ongoing reality for the entire human race. And this reality meant that we would need a Savior, necessitating Christ's death for our salvation many years later.

That's quite a grocery list of consequences—far more serious than the consequences of any choices we make today! However, as devastating as those consequences were, Eve's wrong choice was not the end of the world for her. Rather than giving up, she lived to understand and prove by her life that God never deserted her or stopped loving her. In fact, he was right there with her planning for solutions, working to redeem her sinful choice. Eve went on to find the courage to live with the consequences of her choice, to give birth to children, and to become the mother of the human race. Perhaps one of the most important lessons here is one of hope: that although we have tremendous power through our personal choices to alter the course of our own and others' lives, we need not be paralyzed by fear. God is more powerful still to redeem even the poorest of choices if we turn to him.

Choice and the Modern Woman

Comedienne Lily Tomlin once said, "If I had known what it was like to have it all, I might have settled for less." Don't you think that's the way Eve felt? She had so much, but when she chose to go for the chance to have it all, she found that "having it all" was not all she had hoped it would be. God's intention was not to withhold something good but to protect her from the knowledge and the reality of good and evil. It was a reality she could have done much better without, but now she would face the pain and disillusionment that accompanied her poor choice.

It seems that women today experience similar feelings of ambivalence about some of the choices we have made. As an entire generation, we have witnessed and, in some cases, experienced the power of choice. In the 60s we burned our bras (the editorial "we"—I wasn't wearing one yet!) and fought for equal rights. In the 70s we experienced the initial euphoria of getting out there to prove what we could do. But in the 80s the euphoria wore off and we began to experience a new realism about the choices we had made.

Supermom was seen for the myth that it is.

The physical exhaustion women experienced from managing a home and career helped us to see our limitations. One woman who is chief financial officer of a Fortune 500 company put it this way: "I used to think I could work and raise a family. I realize now that it's hard just to do my job well."[4]

We experienced mixed emotions.

One woman says "I've cried on my way to work many times" as she describes how her two-year-old often cries, clings to her, and asks why she has to have a job.

Another woman comments:

I have mixed feelings about myself and what I'm doing. I'm proud of what I've accomplished, and I know I never would have been able to get this far if I hadn't focused on my goals as my first priority. But in doing that I had to say no to my friends and family a lot. I couldn't really be there for people when they needed me because my career and schooling always had to come first. So while I feel proud of my accomplishments, I don't feel good about myself as a friend."[5]

Some have become disillusioned.

Another woman, writing for *Newsweek*, observes:

Feminism made women disposable. So today a lot of females are around 40 and single with a couple of kids to raise on their own. Child support may pay for a couple of pairs of shoes but in general, feminism gave men all the financial and personal advantages over women. What's worse, we asked for it. The reality of feminism is a lot of frenzied and overworked women dropping kids off at day-care centers. If the child is sick, they just send along some Tylenol and rush off to an underpaid job they don't even like. Mopping floors and folding laundry after midnight, they live on five hours of sleep and it shows in their faces."[6]

Judith is disillusioned in another way.

I feel split down the middle. Society is telling me to get a job and make something of my life; my mother is telling me to stay home with my children; my husband is saying he needs me to work so we can pay the bills. I have no freedom to do what is right. There are so many people giving me their input as to what they think I should do with my life, that I'm distracted from figuring it out myself."[7]

We've learned that choosing one thing often means taking away from something else.

An executive vice president of another Fortune 500 company recognizes that there has been a price to pay in order for her to get where she is: "I don't take care of the house. I don't cook. I don't market. I don't take my children to the malls and museums. And I don't have close friends. I am frequently too tired to tell my husband about my day, listen to him tell me about his day or play with the children."[8]

It's no wonder that sometimes it seems better to settle for less! I can't help but wonder how these women will feel about their choices twenty years down the road. In fact, I wonder the same thing about myself.

Choice and Me

I am not describing this scenario to be disparaging about equal opportunity or women working outside the home. I am glad for the progress we have made in terms of equality for women and grateful to those who have fought for rights that belong to women as human beings created in the image of God. However, I do want to demonstrate—through the words of these women—that all choices have consequences. We are mortals in bodies that have limits, and every time we choose to spend our time and energy one way, it means there is less for something else. When we choose to put our financial resources toward one thing, those resources are unavailable for other things. When we choose one response to a situation, we automatically eliminate other responses. This is the nature—the power—of choice, and we need to be prepared to live with the consequences.

It can be truly frightening when we stop to think about the power we have as women, through decisions we make every day, to alter the course of our lives, our relationships, and the lives of others—for better or worse! I realize that the choices I am making today regarding professional commitments, ministry in the church and community, how tired and overextended I let myself become, whether I respond out of love or anger, whether I keep growing and confronting my selfishness and wrong thinking . . . all of these personal choices will powerfully affect my husband, my children, and others around me. And I don't want to live with regrets, do you? So how do we sift through our options and choose wisely?

Our choices will not always be as clear-cut as the one Eve faced in the garden of Eden. Situations are rarely that black and white. However, there are some choices that, if made on a daily basis, will keep our lives headed in the right direction.

We can choose to make our decisions based on an understanding of values and purpose.

There is no way to negotiate the decision-making process successfully without a clear idea of what you want to accomplish with your life and what matters most to you.

A well-defined value system can help us be aware of what is most important to us in any given situation and then choose to live out of that awareness. For instance: during the writing of this chapter when I was away from the computer for a moment, my two-year-old spied the lovely red on/off switch right at her eye level and decided to push it. My heart sank and my stomach turned over as I realized that I had probably lost all of my work on the book so far. How did a well-defined value system help me in choosing my response?

After my initial yelp (which was enough to scare her anyway!), I remembered that in my saner moments I had decided that people are more important than things—even my writing.

(If you know anything about writers, you know that that's saying a lot!) Fortunately, because I had been working on the subject of "choices," even in the midst of this frustrating moment when the computer screen went blank I was very aware of what I consider valuable (my little girl feeling loved even when she makes a mistake), and I was able to wrap my arms around her and say "Haley, I'm sorry for scaring you. You are much more important to me than my book. But you are never supposed to touch that button without asking Mommy first. Do you understand?"

I am not always that controlled; sometimes the emotions of the moment get the best of me. But I am developing an ongoing awareness of a well-defined value system. And I have the ability (as we all do) to make choices according to my values, whether I am dealing with large ethical questions or the smaller, daily responses to those around me.

Similarly, a sense of purpose can help us make powerful choices to use our lives for God rather than wandering aimlessly through life, allowing people and circumstances to pull us this way and that. Several years ago I had the opportunity to serve on staff at our church as Women's Ministry Director. It was a wonderful opportunity in which my lifelong love of the church, my passion for women's ministry, and my spiritual gifts found expression. For a year I poured my heart into building this ministry from scratch—and loved every minute of it. The only problem was, I had a newborn baby, a five-year-old, a seven-year-old, and a husband who were all wishing I would pour more of my heart into them.

Toward the end of the first year I began to realize that even though I claimed my role as wife and mother was one of God's most important purposes for me, I wasn't always making scheduling choices that reflected that purpose. I also hit that brick wall called humanness; I realized that I couldn't squeeze any more energy out of this body. There was no more time, no more emotional stamina, no more of me to go around. No matter how much I wanted to be able to do it all and do it right now, I was limited—like everyone else—by twenty-four-hour days and a very human body and mind. So I cried, and raged, and tried to finagle things, but it was time to say "Not now, maybe later" to women's ministry. Now, as a freelance writer and speaker, I am able to evaluate each opportunity on a case-by-case basis and work it in and around my family responsibilities.

It takes time to search out our own values and purpose and learn to use them as a solid base from which to make our choices. The more we weigh our options against what really matters in life, the more natural this process becomes. And as we mature and become more sure of ourselves in this area, we will finally gain freedom from the guilt and uncertainty that plague us when we go first one way and then another.

But where do we start? This question brings us to the second foundational choice necessary for keeping our lives going in the right direction.

We must choose who we are going to listen to.

These days there are a lot of voices sounding so intelligent and reasonable that they can be very persuasive. Movie stars on their second and third marriages are anxious to tell us how to have a happy marriage. We listen with rapt attention as sports figures share their secrets of success only to find out later that their personal lives are fraught with sexual immorality, gambling, and substance abuse. Psychologists and other "experts" speak with authority on every issue from morality to childrearing and yet often end up rethinking and/or recanting later in life. To say nothing of friends and family—all of whom have their own bit of advice about how to be successful in life.

Of course some of these sources do have valuable advice to offer. But it is still up to us to monitor those influences and view them critically. This well known passage in Philippians impresses me with the importance of thinking critically about what we allow into our minds and how we process it: "Whatever is true, whatever is honorable, whatever is right . . . let your mind dwell on these things" (4:8, NASB). We must also choose carefully those we will learn from and emulate: "The things you have learned and received and heard and seen in me, practice these things" (4:9, NASB).

It is possible to track major influences in our lives if we're willing to give it a little thought. Periodically I ask myself questions like:

- How much time do I spend watching television, listening to music, reading books, and watching movies that reflect a mindset lacking spiritual values? If I am constantly filling my mind with them and failing to view them critically, they can become major influences in a wrong direction.
- How much time am I spending listening to God by reading and meditating on his Word? Am I at a point in my relationship with him where I can recognize his truth and his voice even when I am one-on-one with temptation?
- What about my friends? What is the direction or outcome of their lives, and is that what I want for myself? Do I spend time with people who are influencing me toward a lifestyle and system of priorities that reflect what I believe as a Christian?
- Whose advice do I solicit and take most seriously as I make my choices? Do I go to someone who will automatically agree with me or to someone who will help me listen to God?

The Ultimate Choice

As we listen to all the voices that are out there, it will ultimately come down, as it did for Eve, to choosing who we are going to believe. We, too, will have to decide if we are going to believe the voice of temptation or the voice of God.

Margaret is a woman who just recently chose to believe the voice of temptation. She knows the Lord and knows his instruction regarding marital fidelity, and yet she chose to have an affair with a co-worker. Somehow she became convinced that life with this man would be better than the life she had with her husband,

and she has acted on that belief. Not only did she have the affair, she divorced her husband so she could be with her lover, altering forever the course of her own life, her husband's life, and the lives of their young children. She believed the myth of the greener grass.

Melissa on the other hand, when faced with a similar temptation, made the choice to view it as an alarm, warning her of weak spots in her marriage. She requested a transfer at work so as to avoid regular contact with her "friend" and chose to get counseling with her husband. Recently, they have begun to invest more time and energy into their marriage and feel that their relationship is stronger than ever. What a difference Melissa's choice has made for her and for her family!

I don't know much about the process that Margaret went through in making her choice, but I can't help wondering, Who was she listening to? Where were godly friends who could challenge her to listen to God's voice above the noise of her own passion and desire? What was she allowing into her mind at the time—books and media that inflamed her desire and presented infidelity as a pleasing option? Or the Word of God, which is living and active and able to judge the thoughts and intentions of the heart?

We've all heard the voice of temptation at one time or another, and in all probability we will hear it again. But as we learn to monitor the influences in our lives and hear God's voice, he will guide us and give us the opportunity to demonstrate with our lives that his ways are perfect.

This doesn't mean that there won't be any detours or delays or wrong turns. Sometimes upon looking back, we may feel that there was a better option than the one we chose. Possibly—because we are human and fallible—we didn't see it clearly, or even know it was there. In such cases we can remind ourselves that a few missteps here and there do not take us completely off a course that is generally well set.

When the Options Seem Limited

Even as we talk about all the options women have today, many times we feel that our own personal choices are rather limited. In fact, there are seasons in our lives when we feel "stuck" and don't have all the choices we would like to have—concerning income level, how we are treated by our husbands, educational opportunities, type of home, looks or body shape, number of children, and so on. Mothers of young children go through periods when the most basic choices—when they can eat, sleep, or go to the bathroom—are determined by someone else's schedule and needs! Most of us must deal at some point with situations that narrow our range of options, such as a dead-end job, a difficult marriage, demanding toddlers, or singleness. We cannot always choose our circumstances *but we can always choose our response to our circumstances.* Even when some of our choices are being made for us, we can choose to obey God in our attitudes and actions. These are perhaps the most powerful choices we will ever make, and no one can take them away.

Victor Frankl, a Jewish psychiatrist, discovered this truth for himself during his imprisonment in the death camps of Nazi Germany during World War II. In the midst of deprivation, humiliation, torture, and the tragic deaths of his family members he became aware of what he later called "the last of the human freedoms"—the freedom to choose his responses no matter what the Nazis did to control his environment or harm his body. "In the midst of the most degrading circumstances imaginable, Frankl . . . discovered a fundamental principle about the nature of man: Between stimulus and response, man [and woman] has the freedom to choose" (brackets mine).[9]

The circumstances of most of us bear little resemblance to the prison camps of Nazi Germany, and yet we have no less responsiblity to choose our responses, not based on what is going on around us but on the character that God is developing in our lives. Between the stimulus (the tenth childish interruption in fifteen minutes, the condescending comment of a colleague, the undeserved anger of a husband, the inner frustration of a life with too much in it) and my response, there is always a very important choice to be made. And these choices speak eloquently about who we are and what the outcome of our lives will be.

In later chapters we will take a closer look at Bible women and contemporary women who made powerful choices that enabled them to keep growing despite limitations and adversity.

What's Ahead? More Opportunities to Choose

In a special issue of *Time* magazine entitled "Women: The Road Ahead," one writer comments that "the future looms with so many choices that the freedom it promises can be frightening."[10] From President to jail inmate to police chief to heads of major corporations to bishops to moms single by choice—all options are open to women in the 90s.

As we've already noted, there is nothing wrong with having options. But, as women heading into the year 2000, we must be careful who we listen to and who we believe. We want to make sure that we "have it all" by the right definition. In the end, it is our everyday choices that will determine the outcome of our lives.

FOR DISCUSSION

1. Tell about a choice you've made that turned out to be a right choice. What helped you make that choice? Or, tell about a choice that turned out to be a wrong choice. What were the consequences of that choice? What could have helped you make a better one?

2. What are some of the main influences in your life right now as you make choices? How do you feel about the direction these influences are encouraging you to take?

3. What are some of the choices you are facing right now? What ideas from this chapter might help you in making these choices?

For Further Study
Tucker, Ruth. *Multiple Choices*. Grand Rapids, Mich.: Zondervan, 1992.

Notes
1. William Ecenbarger, "The Bane of Democracy," *Chicago Tribune Magazine* (March 10, 1991), p. 25.
2. Barbara Walters in *The Quotable Woman* (Philadelphia: Running Press, 1991), p. 15.
3. Ecenbarger, p. 25.
4. Jaclyn Fierman, "Why Women Still Don't Hit the Top," *Fortune* (July 30, 1990), p. 58.

5. Linda Tschirhart Sanford and Mary Ellen Donovan, *Women & Self-Esteem* (New York: Penguin Books), p. 219.

6. Kay Ebeling, "The Failure of Feminism," *Newsweek* (November 19, 1990), p. 9.

7. Alice Slaikeu Lawhead, *The Lie of the Good Life* (Portland, Oreg.: Multnomah Press, 1989), p. 54.

8. Fierman, p. 58.

9. Stephen Covey, *The Seven Habits of Highly Effective People* (New York: Simon & Schuster, 1989), pp. 69-70.

10. Nancy Gibbs, "The Dreams of Youth," *Time Special Issue* (Fall 1990), p. 12.

2

Looking for Love in All the Wrong Places

I want first of all to be at peace with myself. I want a singleness of eye, a purity of intention, a central core to my life to help me carry out these activities and obligations as well as I can. I want, in fact, to live "in grace" as much of the time as possible. By grace I mean an inner harmony, essentially spiritual, which can be translated into outward harmony. I would like to achieve a state of inner spiritual grace from which I could function and give as I was meant to in the eyes of God.

Anne Morrow Lindberg, 1955

Because of my husband's death I am faced again with woman's recurring lesson. To quote my own words, "woman must come of age by herself—she must find her true center alone." The lesson seems to need relearning about every twenty years in a woman's life.

Anne Morrow Lindberg, 1975

Amidst an avalanche of information on family dysfunction— abuse, alcoholism, drug addiction, and neglect—award-winning songwriter and performer Gloria Gaither has offered a refreshing book entitled *What My Parents Did Right*. She opens the book with thoughts about how her own parents prepared her for a full and fruitful life by teaching strong moral values, building her self-esteem, and imparting their faith.

[My mother] had eyes for catching us when we were up to something good and for ferreting out some hidden talent or latent ability in us. When no one else could see it, when others

17

saw only an awkward clumsy kid, Mother saw beyond the unpredictable growth spurts and adolescent acne to some great rainbow of promise circumventing the obvious.

Our home was filled with great thinkers, teachers, missionaries, evangelists and theologians. Mother made sure my sister and I sat by these great men and women at the table and were involved in their deep conversations... My parents were verbal about their relationships with God, with each other, with us as children, and with others. "I love you" was heard daily . . . In our home, we could ask any questions without being belittled and question any answer without being condemned. Failure was allowed but we were always expected to try. I don't remember my parents ever talking down to us, but instead they included us in family decisions and important discussions. . . . My greatest deterrents from wrong and encouragements towards right was my parents' trust. They believed in me and in my good judgment.[1]

Today Gloria enjoys a rich and rewarding life that is full of a deep relationship with God, healthy relationships with family, and the opportunity to make a difference with her unique gifts and spiritual calling. Here is one example of life as God intended it to be. It is the life that Jesus described in so many different ways when he was here on this earth—the abundant life mentioned in John 10:10 and the fruitful life described in John 15:16.

Our souls need the encouragement of stories like Gloria's because they help us to reach for God's ideal even when reality falls short. Sadly, there are many women for whom the experience of being loved and highly valued is not the norm. A recent report by the American Psychological Association revealed that for one in every four women, the experience of being female in contemporary culture is cause for severe depression.[2]

Studies of women have repeatedly shown disturbing patterns: lack of self-esteem, an inability to feel powerful or in control of one's life, a vulnerability to depression, a tendency to see oneself as less talented, less able than one really is. The myriad of studies that have been done over the years give the distinct impression of constriction, a crippling, a sense of being somehow not quite as good, not quite as able, not quite as bright, not quite as valuable as men . . . Certainly there are many women who have escaped this blight, who have lived full and happy lives, but when you leaf through the studies you can sense, floating in the air, ghosts of unborn dreams, unrealized hopes, undiscovered talents. The tragedies are the "might have beens," and they are the most poignant.[3]

Feeling "Less Than": A Common Female Experience

While it is true that women and men alike share basic human needs for identity and self-worth, there is much evidence that for women these commodities, which are so crucial to living a full and functional life, can be very hard to come by. Unless a woman has been extraordinarily sheltered, her experiences in the family, church, educational institutions, business world, government, medical profession, even the general public, systematically rob her of the essentials of self-esteem.

Once a girl develops an understanding of language, it is definitely communicated to her that she is less significant than boys. A girl may have learned this simply by the absence of strong, autonomous, competent female figures in the male-dominated culture that she gradually discovers during her unfolding childhood. Within her family she may have learned she was insignificant by the way her family listened more attentively during dinner conversation to males than females, or the way her brothers were encouraged to take their ideas and career plans seriously while girls were told it didn't really matter what they did.[4]

Consider some other common female experiences:

- A woman remembers, "The boys in our church youth group used to razz us about our "inferiority" to them. They knew we didn't respect them much at the time but looked forward to the day when perhaps some of us would be married (God forbid!) to some of them and then we'd have to answer to their beck and call."[5]

- A woman applies for admission to a Ph.D. program in computer science at a major university. Her qualifications (Graduate Record exam score, G.P.A. and the like) were far superior to those of the two men who applied at the same time. But they were admitted, and she was not. The professors told her they did not want to waste their time on a woman because she was likely to "get married and have children." (This really did happen—in 1992!)

- A single woman who is vice president in charge of Finance and Accounting in her professional life finds that instead of being included in a broad range of social and ministry opportunities in her church, she is relegated to "singles activities" reminiscent of the high school youth group. Meanwhile, her male counterparts are recruited for all manner of teaching and leadership roles. She wonders if she will ever be viewed as a full-fledged adult this side of marriage.

- A young mother spends all of her waking hours knee-deep in diapers and dishes, wondering if she has any capacity left for intelligent thinking or adult conversation. On occasion she does accompany her husband to a business function where her worst fears are confirmed. Once her husband's associates find out she is an at-home mom, they lose interest and focus almost exclusively on her husband.

- Many women attend church year after year and never hear significant teaching or messages given by other women. More than a few begin to wonder, "Don't women have anything to say that would be valuable to the congregation?"

- A woman works for her company for twelve years in a secretarial-type position that pays $12,000 a year. Despite repeated requests to move into a sales position that would pay considerably more, her boss (who makes $100,000 a year) tells her, "No, we need you where you are now."

- A woman who has been thin all of her life finds that she cannot lose the weight she gained during pregnancy. She avoids mirrors most of the time but when she does happen to see herself, she can't help comparing herself unfavorably with images of the perfect women she sees in magazines and on T.V. To make matters worse, her husband often comments about the attractiveness of the women he sees and muses out loud, "I wonder how she keeps herself in such good shape?"

- A woman who has chosen to stay at home to raise her children rather than working outside the home finds that she cannot get a credit card, apply for a mortgage, or buy a car without her husband's signature. Through divorce or the death of her spouse she realizes how dependent and vulnerable she had become.

- Over the years, a woman puts her husband through graduate school, works beside him to start his own business, manages the home and raises the children, accompanies him to business functions and gives numerous dinner parties. She looks forward to a time in the future when she and her husband can spend time relaxing, travelling together, and enjoying the fruit of their labors. Instead, just as the youngest child is preparing to leave for college, her husband leaves her for a younger woman. Rather than enjoying some long-awaited companionship in her middle years, she finds herself shattered and alone.

- A woman works in a religious organization for fifteen years and watches as positions in upper management are always filled by men—some of whom are less qualified than she is. When she questions why this would be so, the president agrees with her in theory about needing women in these positions but nothing changes.

These are *not* isolated incidents. Each one is a real-life experience carefully chosen from long lists of similar experiences. In other countries the situation for women is even worse. A recent cover article in *U.S. News and World Report* entitled "The War Against Women" documents how women are being used and abused in country after country around the world. The author boldly states that, according to the 1993 U.N. Human Development Report "there is still no country that treats its women as well as its men."[6]

- In the new Russia, women applying for office jobs are often told that their duties include sleeping with the boss. A typical want ad reads, "Not older than 25; bright appearance, long legs compulsory."
- In China, India, and other nations where sons are still valued more highly than daughters, ultra-sound is now being used to determine the sex of babies so that females can be aborted or poison can be administered at birth.
- In some Islamic countries, rape *victims* are charged and imprisoned for adultery. Those who try to fight such inequities receive death threats, have their passports revoked and their writings banned.
- In parts of Africa, the Middle East, and Asia genital mutilation, a custom in which all or part of a girl's outer genitalia is removed, is still practiced. Female circumcision (removal of the hood of the clitoris), clitoridectomy (removal of the clitoris), or genital infibulation (removal of the clitoris and labia, stitching the vulva together, leaving only a small opening for urine and menstrual flow) are procedures performed without anesthesia, causing severe medical problems and removing almost any possibility for sexual pleasure.
- In India, bride burnings, dowry-murders, "stove burstings" (so-called "domestic accidents" in which a young wife is killed) are common forms of domestic violence that take the lives of many women whose families cannot keep paying for their protection. In countries where dowries can add up to ten times a man's annual income, dowry extortion is very common and there is little protection for the women who are being used as merchandise.

- In industrial nations, women's pay still averages two thirds that of men's, mainly because women are clustered in low-wage "women's jobs." In the United States for instance, year-round full-time working women earned 71 percent of the male wage in 1992 and women high school graduates earned slightly less than did men who dropped out of school before ninth grade.[7]

Facing Our Oldest Enemy

How are we to interpret the meaning of these realities? What is the impact on a woman's self-esteem when she takes an honest look at them?

For starters, we can begin to understand that the problem women have with knowing who we are and what we are worth is rooted in systems much older and larger than ourselves. Beliefs about ourselves have been shaped by ideas, principles, rules, and procedures that have governed the world in which we live. Significant—and seemingly insignificant—events whisper to us day in and day out, "See, you are not quite as good as . . . You don't matter quite as much." We are not untouched by the demeaning experiences of women struggling for the essentials of self-esteem and worth here and in other countries. We feel the pain of being "put down" and having to fight for basic human rights as a population group in general. We may find that we are shocked by articles such as the one quoted from in *U.S. News & World Report*, but the fact is, we are so used to being seen and treated as "less than" that many times we hardly distinguish the discrimination from other hard realities in life.

Whether the abuse and disrespect of women is overt (as in the "less enlightened" countries just described) or more subtle (as we still observe here in the United States), the universality of the female experience of being "less than" is astounding. As I have delved more deeply into the experiences of women across barriers of race and time, I have become convinced that women's extraordinary struggle for dignity, equality, and worth is not only systemic in nature but *is a direct result of the enmity that came between Satan and the woman in the Garden of Eden so long ago* (Genesis 3:15). Ever since that day women have been a particular target of Satan for all manner of discrimination, abuse, and inhumane treatment, from Bible times to the present. The introduction of shame, blame, and domination into human relationships as a result of sin became a perfect tool of Satan to destroy the human family by causing one grouping of people to set themselves up as better than another grouping—men over women, whites over blacks, Nazis over Jews.

Our efforts to gain equality and a sense of worth are not a new struggle born out of the feminist movement or some "liberal" theology. It is a battle that has been raging throughout human history. When we seek to restore to women (or anyone else who has been discriminated against) the dignity and equality that God intended when he created us, we are, in a very real sense, engaged in battle against Satan himself. We echo Old and New Testament prophets alike when we denounce the evil and sometimes invisible systems that govern our world because Satan is still active in the affairs of humankind. It is described in Ephesians 6:12: "For our struggle is not against enemies of blood and flesh, but against the rulers, against the authorities, against the cosmic powers of this present darkness, against the spiritual forces of evil in the heavenly places" (NRSVB).

Although we've been hearing for years that the problem is men ("male chauvinist pigs"), the Christian woman must never lose sight of our real enemy—Satan—and the many subtle ways evil has infiltrated men's and women's reactions to each other.

The High Cost of Low Self-Esteem

There is a price to be paid when self-esteem is lacking for any of us in the human family.

Cherry Boone began struggling with anorexia nervosa when she was a young teen, using her mother's diet pills to help her lose weight and stay up all night to write A+ term papers. By the time she was 16 she was jogging four miles a day, skipping breakfast and lunch, and counteracting her eating binges by vomiting and taking laxatives. Less than two years into her marriage her weight had dropped to 80 pounds and she was hospitalized. Realizing that her life was in danger and that they needed to take drastic measures, she and her husband moved out of state in order to focus on their marriage and her eating disorder. Today Cherry Boone O'Neil understands that "my eating disorder was precipitated by things such as low self-esteem and perfectionism. I was always the 'good girl' but never felt that I measured up. When I started to lose weight, I received praise from everyone, which encouraged me to continue."[8]

Cherry is not the only one. Today, some 3.1 million women suffer from eating disorders and an estimated 6 percent of serious cases die.

On another front, a journalist and correspondent-turned-author describes her insatiable desire for love from older men. Although married she says

> My unconscious drive was specifically directed at men old enough to be my father, men who were what I had never known my father to be, who were gentle, approachable, who would spend time with me and talk to me, advise me, think I was special—and who were Christian. . . . The only thing which ever ended these relationships was a geographical re-location of some kind. But as surely as night followed day I would start another one the minute the right person came along, and I knew I would, as I had done for twenty years but I never knew why. I spiritualized these relationships: he was the spiritual mentor; I was the protégeé; I didn't know how else to explain them to myself. Each relationship seemed more intense than the last and in each case the size of my world would shrink down to the size of the person I could not do without.[9]

The writer, Briar Whitehead, is not alone. Relationship addiction—characterized by a pattern of trying to find our identity and fill our emptiness of soul through relationships with others—is a common addiction among women.

Another woman who grew up as a missionary kid in China tells of making herself sick when she came to the States and tried to fit in with popular western ideas about what a woman could and should be. Although Kari had a strong and effective witness to students on the secular college campus where she was teaching, some of her associates in the Christian organization with which she was affiliated thought she should give up her teaching post when it came time for her to get married. Not wishing to be divisive, Kari did just that, but her heartbreak at having left her teaching post and the deep friendships she had with her students caused tension during the early years of her marriage.

> I was beginning to listen to the common teaching that a woman's chief role is to be a support to her husband in his ministry, be a homemaker and raise children to follow the Lord. I was a woman at war with myself. While I tried to agree with my conscious mind to a view that limited a woman's contribution to the kingdom, my subconscious revolted within me. . . .
>
> Overcome with grief over the ministry I had left and trying to fit into the role of a submissive homemaker, I felt myself losing my identity. Who was I? For the first time in my life, I developed the "I'm just a woman" syndrome. When I could no longer look at myself as a precious disciple and disciple-maker, a friend of Jesus Christ, I became sick. Many months were spent in bed with an undiagnosed fever. After the fever subsided, I went into a deep depression. Guilt feelings about having left my first love (Christ) swept over me—some from God and some based on false regret.[10]

Kari is among many who have experienced this kind of crisis. I can't tell you how many women I meet who have no sense of who they are and what their mission is apart from their roles (or potential roles) as wife and mother. But I can tell you of the despair that many of them have experienced or will experience when the season of filling these roles is past—either through divorce, death of a spouse, or kids leaving the nest—when all that is left is an aching void where a fully developed Christ follower should have been.

Self-destructive behaviors. Relationships that don't work. Children of God who are not fully available for kingdom work. These are just some of the costs of low self-esteem. As these true stories have illustrated,

> Our level of self-esteem affects virtually everything we think, say and do. It affects how we see the world and our place in it. It affects how others in the world see and treat us. It affects the choices we make—choices about what we will do with our lives and with whom we will be involved. It affects our ability to both give and receive love. And it affects our ability to take action to change things that need to be changed. If a woman has an insufficient amount of self-esteem, she will not be able to act in her own best interest. And if a woman has no self-esteem at all, she will eventually become overwhelmed, immobile and eventually will give up.[11]

Exactly What Is Self-Esteem?

Self-esteem can be described as how much we like, approve, or respect the person that we know ourselves to be. It is a sense of our proper dignity and value and our ability to take satisfaction in the contribution we make to this world. To me, this is one of the most striking aspects of the godly woman described in Proverbs 31. Not only is she busy with fulfilling work in her home and beyond, but she takes a great deal of delight in her work (verse 13). She moves with a purposefulness in life that lends strength and dignity to her character. She knows that what she is contributing to her family, her business, and her community is valuable. "She senses that her gain is good" (verse 18, NASB).

Many women today do not move through life with the strength that comes from the sense of well-being, purpose, and competence that this woman exhibited. Why? Because unfortunately the essentials of self-esteem are often hard for women to come by. Or, if they do have a sense of who they are, it is who they are as lived through someone else.

For instance, a woman may find that she has a tendency to identify herself most clearly as "so-and-so's wife" or "so-and-so's mother." Or she may feel that her purpose in life is merely to support her husband in the purposes of his life or to help her children find their niche—rather than finding one of her own. She may be lulled into a false sense of security because she has a man to take care of her, naively believing that she has no need of any other skills besides those associated with housekeeping and children. Or she may be accustomed to accepting the values of her parents, pastor, or husband, without ever asking her own hard questions and searching out God's answers for herself.

Know how much you are worth.

This lack of identity is not in keeping with Christ's intention for us as women. As his conversation with the woman of Samaria in John 4 demonstrates, all of the elements of personhood that make for wholeness and abundant life are things that Christ brings to the sisters as well as the brothers in the family of God. First of all, he wants us to know how much we are worth. In the words of psychologist Larry Crabb, "each of us fervently wishes for someone to see us exactly as we are, warts and all, and still accept us. The thought that someone can remain warmly committed to us even with all our faults exposed is utterly inconceivable—yet we long for that experience. We long to be in a relationship with someone who is strong enough to be constant, someone whose love is untainted by even a trace of manipulative self-interest, someone who really wants us."[12]

We are most fortunate if this message was communicated consistently within our families from infancy onward but, sadly, this is not always the case. All children are at risk for finding themselves in a family that does not know how to instill in them a sense of their value, but, as we have already described, female children face an even greater risk than male children of growing up without this certainty.

The Samaritan woman of John 4—we'll call her Samara since her name is not given—had additional reasons to believe that she wasn't worth much, that no one could possibly love her. Not only was she of the lesser sex,[13] she was also of a lesser race,[14] and she was a woman known for her blatant immorality. She had had five husbands and at the time she met Christ, she was living with a man to whom she was not married.

It is not hard to imagine the disillusionment that Samara must have carried with her as she came to Jacob's well on the day when her path crossed that of Christ himself. Imagine having been through five marriages and working on a sixth! I'm sure she experienced quite a range and intensity of emotion: anger, sadness, disillusionment, feelings of being used and misunderstood. The fact that she chose to draw water in the heat of the day rather than in the cool of the morning suggests that perhaps she was so depressed and ostracized that she avoided contact with those who might demean her. She was fully aware of how people viewed her, so much so that she expressed surprise that Jesus would even initiate conversation with her: "How is it that you, a Jew, ask a drink of me, a woman of Samaria?" (John 4:9, NRSVB).

But Christ demonstrated that there was no damaging favoritism with him. Just by beginning an intelligent conversation with her and treating her as an equal, Jesus communicated her significance. Most men would not have been willing to risk their reputation by being found in conversation with a woman such as this (in Jewish custom it was considered inappropriate for a man to talk with his own wife in public, let alone a "loose" woman). Christ, with a surprising lack of concern about appearances, chose to walk right into Samaria that day and initiate a conversation with a woman who was "less than" in every way that mattered to the people of that day.

Even so, Christ did not treat Samara as though she were beneath him or as someone who needed to be pulled out of the sewer and saved. Instead, he treated her as one with whom he could dialogue on an equal level. In the course of the conversation Jesus affirmed her intelligence and ability to understand spiritual truth by discussing theology with her. He revealed new truth that was, as far as we can tell, unknown to anyone else—including the disciples![15] Throughout the conversation Jesus answered her thoughtful and intelligent questions with respect and sensitivity to what was behind those questions: a deep spiritual hunger.

Later on, when the disciples came to offer him lunch, he made it clear that talking with Samara was the most important thing he could be doing at the moment—even more important than eating. He said, "My food is to do the will of him who sent me and to complete his work." The value that Christ placed on Samara was unaffected by the fact that he knew her deepest, darkest secrets. What an amazing first this must have been for her, and how life-changing it was!

Know who you are as an individual and as part of a community.

Another key to a woman's self-esteem is knowledge of herself as an individual who is unique and separate from others, balanced by a sense of how she fits into her community. Many women lack self-esteem precisely because they know so little about themselves.

Women have historically been denied the opportunities for self-discovery that many men take for granted. As a result, many women we interviewed had great difficulty describing themselves at all. "Shot full of holes," "full of gaps," "blank—not much self there," are just some of the phrases these women used to describe themselves. A woman who sees herself as a blank has virtually no chance of experiencing self-esteem.[16]

For example, one mother of three, in the middle of a drawn-out, antagonistic divorce from an abusive husband, was encouraged to take some time off in order to refresh herself and regroup for ongoing legal battles and the constant care of her very troubled children. When asked, "What are some things that *you* enjoy doing?" she honestly had no idea. For twenty years she had accommodated her husband's every whim, in addition to providing the only real parenting for their children. Her situation of being "sucked dry" is more common than we would like to think.

Others, rather than seeing themselves as total blanks, have a tendency to identify themselves by the roles they play (such as wife and mother), their career, or their sex appeal. All of these have been society's way, at one time or another, of defining us as women. The problem is that *these aspects of life are changeable and temporary*—as any woman whose marital status has changed, who has lost a job, or has gone through the aging process would attest. As important as these parts of life are at different times, they are inadequate as a way of defining ourselves.

It is safe to say that Samara had very little sense of herself apart from her continued attempts to find the right man. In this way she was not all that different from many women today who share a common tendency to feel that they haven't gotten a life until they've gotten a man. In one provocative book entitled *Why Do I Think I Am Nothing Without a Man?* the author makes this statement:

> Women, for all their gains in the working world, still tend to get their refuge, self-esteem and pride more from the home, the family, the man they landed. Thinking you are nothing without a man is a problem women share regardless of marital status—and also regardless of age, nationality, income, upbringing, professional standing, religion, personal appearance. You don't have to live alone to think you are nothing without a man. You don't have to be divorced, widowed or never married. You can be living with a man or married and

think that without this man you would be lonely, socially inhibited, emotionally and sexually barren.[17]

These are very strong words, but my experiences working with girls and women in many different settings leads me to believe that they are true. I have known women who have dropped out of school to follow a man around; women who have rushed into marriage with the wrong man just so they wouldn't be alone; women who have given in to sexual pressure out of fear of losing a man; women who are so tied to the home and to their man's schedule that they are not even free to go out for lunch with a friend; women who live their lives so completely for their man that they wouldn't consider inconveniencing him by taking a class or a part-time job that would keep them challenged and growing.

I have known women who spend a lifetime adapting to their husband's life and calling—enduring financial hardship so he can go to school, holding down the fort at home while he travels, managing the household while he spends long hours working, studying or ministering, being tolerant of the stress all of this places on a marriage and family—never thinking of asking for the same opportunities for themselves. Somehow they feel that the privilege of having that kind of support in life goes with being male, not female.

How has this happened? Why do we think that we are worth so little that we allow our identities to be overshadowed by others? Mary Stewart Van Leeuwen draws our attention to God's prediction in Genesis 3:16 that men and women, in their own unique ways, would have a tendency to misuse the dominion and "one-fleshness" that was built into humanity at creation. Just as men have a tendency to twist responsible dominion into wrongful domination, the peculiarly female sin is to preserve relationships at all cost—even if the cost is her own lack of responsible action in the world.

The woman's temptation is to avoid taking risks that might upset relationships. It is the temptation to let creational sociability become fallen "social enmeshment." [Thus] one of the main problems of today's counselling psychologists is accounting for women's constant tendency to avoid developing personal self-sufficiency for the sake of preserving even pathological relationships with the opposite sex.[18]

Yes, men and women were created to be together and flourish in the blessedness of loving relationships. However, even though we may be looking forward to or are presently enjoying a relationship with a man, *we cannot let our love and desire for a man overshadow our love and commitment to serving God as fully developed human beings.* For me to live my life for my husband and adapt to him in such a way that I do not have a life of my own that is lived for God, my Creator and Jesus, my Savior and Lord is the sin of idolatry.

The sure foundation of my self-esteem is knowing that before, during, and after life with my husband, children, career, or even a youthful and physically able body, I am created to reflect God's character, to love him and to have honest, intimate communication with him. God's purposes for my life include and at the same time go far beyond my roles as wife, mother, or career woman. My identity is rooted in the fact that God has invested gifts and resources in me to make a unique contribution to my family but also to the larger world for his glory. I work in partnership with him as I receive with a grateful heart the gifts and resources he has given me, develop them, and use them to make a positive contribution in this world. I honor him as I become all he created me to be, reaching out in love and service to my physical family, my spiritual family, and the larger human family.

Coming into a personal relationship with Christ further clarifies the "who am I?" question, as Samara discovered. When she met Christ he made it clear that it was not her relationship with a man that defined her. He encouraged a realistic assessment of herself when he gave her the opportunity to face her sin and her failure to relate in a healthy fashion with men (John 4:16-17). But Christ was quick to point out the true source of her identity: "It's who you are and the way you live that count before God. Your worship must engage your spirit in the pursuit of truth. That's the kind of people the Father is out looking for: those who are simply and honestly *themselves* before him in their worship" (John 4:23, TM).

No longer would she be defined by gender, race, marital status, or desirability to men. Once she placed her faith in Jesus, realizing that he was the Messiah for whom she had been waiting (John 4:29), she received a spiritual identity that transcended all other roles and relationships. She, along with all of us who have put our faith in Christ, "are the ones chosen by God, chosen for the high calling of priestly work, chosen to be a holy people, God's instruments to do his work and speak out for him, to tell others of the night-and-day difference he made for you—from nothing to something, from rejected to accepted" (1 Peter 2:9-10, TM).

These and many other Scriptures define Christian women and men first and foremost in terms of their priestly function. To ascribe the function of "priest" or "called ones" to men in one way and to women in another robs us of the core our identity. We dare not lay down this, our true identity, for any human being or system that would seek to define us as anything less than full-fledged priests and disciples. If we do, we will be very empty indeed.

The challenge for women today is to take responsibility for the adult task of defining ourselves, not in relation to gender roles, careers, or sex appeal but in relation to the identity, worth, purpose, and enabling that come from God himself. (For further discussion of this subject, see chapter 4, "How Does God View Women?")

Understand God's purposes for your life.

In relating with Samara, Christ provided her with yet another essential of self-esteem: the opportunity to live purposefully and have impact. When the disciples returned from town with lunch, the Bible says "they were astonished that Jesus was speaking with a woman." Rather than expressing their shock out loud they stood there gaping until Samara hurried away—probably, in part, to escape their curious stares. Knowing their thoughts, Jesus began to point out that they were sitting right in the middle of a community that was ripe for responding to the message of the true Messiah. Indeed, while they were sitting there talking about the possibilities, Samara was already out there getting the job done. With great urgency she left her waterpot and went back to the city to tell everyone she knew, "Come and see a man who told me everything I had ever done! He cannot be the Messiah, can he?"

And the people came! Because of Samara's witness, many of the Samaritans in that place believed in Christ. They asked him to stay a little longer so Jesus stayed two more days, giving many more people a chance to hear him speak and to entrust their lives to him. By the time he left they were able to say to Samara, "It is no longer because of what you said that we believe, for we have heard for ourselves, and we know that this is truly the Savior of the world" (John 4:39-42, NASB). She had instigated a major evangelistic campaign because she had been called and enabled by God himself.

I never fail to experience a thrill when I read this part of Samara's story because it answers my own deep longings to see myself as one who has been placed on this earth and drawn into relationship with Christ to accomplish something meaningful and lasting. My soul resonates with the truth that "We have been made with a capacity to move purposefully in a direction, to join God in his purposes. We are far more than senseless parts of a preordered system that fatalistically moves us along. Therefore, in our innermost being, we thirst to be a part of the eternal plan, to make a lasting difference in our world. *We long for impact.*"[19]

Christ knew that Samara needed more meaning for her life than women's work and chasing after men. We all do! And so that is what he brings. He didn't wait for Samara to work out the right marital status, to be discipled, to join a church, or to get an education. He walked into Samara that day and chose a woman right where she was in life to bring a whole community to himself. How fresh! How like our wonderful Lord! Samara's story has motivated me over the years to open myself to the possibilities of purposeful living—even those purposes that, to others, seem inappropriate or out of the ordinary. The process of learning to live according to God's purposes is so rewarding, so meaningful, and so crucial that I devoted an entire chapter to discussing its practical implications (chapter 3).

Develop skills for functioning in the real world.

Closely connected with the need to know that our lives have purpose is the concept of competence—having the skills necessary to survive, thrive, and accomplish God's purposes. The need for competence presents a real challenge for women in our society:

> Women have been encouraged to become competent in very limited activities centering around home and family, putting women in what might be called a no-win situation. She has become competent in a skill that is socially devalued. (The idea that any idiot can stay home and raise kids is patently untrue, but it comes close to what our achievement-oriented society really believes about being a wife and mother.) She is being programmed for planned obsolescence. By the time a woman is forty, her child-rearing skills will be of little use, her children will be grown, and she still has nearly forty years or so to live.[20]

I am not saying that women should abandon competency in areas of home and family; all of us, men included, have areas of responsibility pertaining to our home life in which we must develop skill and competence. However, women in our society have not been encouraged to achieve outside the home or to be independent. This is another detriment to healthy self-esteem. Any woman should be confident that her skills are valuable in her society, and that she has the ability and know-how to provide the sole care for herself and her children, should she be called upon to do so.

One of the blows to a woman's self-esteem I have observed most regularly occurs around the time a woman begins contemplating what she is going to do with herself once her children are in school, off to college, or married. Often at this time in a family's life more income is needed because of college bills, weddings, etc. and so it is decided that a woman will go back to work. (The need to be able to generate income comes even sooner for a woman whose circumstances change due to divorce, death of her spouse, or her husband's unemployment—eventualities to which none of us are immune.) If a woman has not finished her education or has let her credentials and marketable experience lapse, she may find that her options are limited to low-paying jobs outside her fields of interest and abilities. Thus, she lacks the sense of self-worth that comes from spending one's best energies in work that is meaningful and challenging. In many cases, a woman faces this situation while her husband is enjoying the satisfaction and challenge of a well-established career in his chosen field.

Another painful reality women must face is the high divorce rate. And even if their marriages do survive, women tend to outlive their husbands by an average of fifteen years. Consequently, *the American woman who cannot support herself is either an actual or potential victim of financial stress and poverty.* Thus, a woman's need to broaden her range of skills so that she can support herself with meaningful work is crucial—not only for her self-esteem but also for the provision of physical necessities.

Out of sensitivity to these realities and out of a desire not to see the woman they love placed in such a vulnerable position, men need to give the women in their lives the same kind of support that they themselves expect for their career and ministry goals. This does not mean that family priorities have to fly out the window, as I will discuss more fully in chapter 10. Particularly if she has the support of an enlightened husband, a woman can remain committed to her family and still carve out some time for further schooling, job experiences that keep her skills current and her foot in the door of a meaningful career/ministry, or volunteer work that will contribute to a well-rounded résumé.

For myself, working out a balance between being available to my family while putting some time into my development as an author, speaker, and minister has been crucial to self-esteem. There is a feeling of well-being that comes from knowing that I am doing what is right for my family and that I haven't missed out on being an integral part of their lives. *But I also need to know that in addition to that connectedness with family, the part of me that stands before God alone and fits into his larger plan is continuing to develop and grow.* I also need to know that when the ability to generate income becomes a necessity I will have options that I enjoy and that reflect God's calling on my life. Because of the commitment Chris and I share to continue investing in these aspects of my life, I do not have inordinate fears about future possibilities—something happening to Chris, or his job, or our children leaving the nest. Rather, I feel confidence and enthusiasm about the future, knowing that God's purposes for me will always remain and that I have been prepared for them. Women who value themselves—and the men who value them—will insist upon this essential of self-esteem.

Gain realistic information about how the world works.

We as women also need to understand how the world outside our homes functions. And we need a coherent set of ethics and values to guide us as *we* function in this world. A few years ago I sat down with an elder from our church to discuss some of the problems the church was having. At one point in the conversation he said very matter-of-factly, "The church is a system so you just have to know how to work the system." I nodded my head sagely, as though I fully understood, but inside I felt a twinge of panic. I didn't even know what "a system" was, let alone how to "work it"! I wasn't even sure it was right to define the church in those terms but I did realize, *Hey! This man has information about how the world works (in this case, the world within the church) that I don't have. If I want to be part of the process of change around here, I had better figure this thing out.*

As a result of that conversation I began talking with my husband about how things worked in his career at the bank. Sure enough, although he didn't use the word *system*, I learned that he had made conscious efforts over the years to figure out who he needed to have on his side to get things done, what to say, how to say it, when to say it, and to whom, how far he could push an opinion before being labelled a troublemaker, how different kinds of behavior would be perceived by "the powers that be," and what kinds of career moves and contacts would be beneficial. As he grew in his understanding of the system in which he was functioning he got better at working within it to his own advantage.

Although I had always been impressed by my husband's insight and skill in these areas I assumed that because *I* didn't have them, they were just part of his personality. I was accustomed to approaching situations with guns blazing, telling "the truth, the whole truth, and nothing but the truth, so help me God" and letting the chips fall where they may. If that failed, I could just withdraw to the safety of my home where people had to take me as I am.

Now I realize that the information my husband had accumulated, his skill in these "worldly matters" and my lack of the same had less to do with personality and more to do with the kinds of opportunities men and women typically have. "Unfortunately, many of us women were given very little useful information about the world—information about how to go about building a career or how to use the legal system, for example."[21] And, I might add, information about how to protect oneself from being taken advantage of, how to buy and take care of a car, how to invest money and plan for a financial future, how to read and understand the fine print on documents we sign . . . the list goes on.[22]

Work from a reliable system of ethics and values.

The world is made up of different systems—your own family system (or way of doing things), the legal system, welfare, educational, and religious systems, etc. People who know how to work within these systems will be better off in them. There is a fine line, however, between participating in a system in ways that are healthy and for the good of all and "working the system" in dishonest, selfish, or manipulative ways.

This is where we rely on ethics and values. A clear sense of what is right and wrong and what matters most in life will determine how we use the information and skills that we have. A person who has a strong moral ethic will work within the system in ways that are honest. She will be complimentary when she honestly has something good to say but will refuse to fall into the trap of flattery for the sake of getting ahead. To the best of her ability she will tell the truth even when the truth is unpopular, but she will know how to pick her time and place. A woman who values all persons will use her knowledge of how the world works not only for her own good but also for the good of others. The Bible calls this being "shrewd as serpents, and innocent as doves" (Matthew 10:16, NASB).

There may be times when a woman realizes that a system in which she has been participating stands for something that goes against her ethics or values. She may begin to see that in a particular system women or blacks are discriminated against, dishonesty is required in order to get ahead, or people are manipulated and used. In this case her ethics and values may guide her to take a stand or to leave the system altogether.

There is a confidence that comes from knowing that we are increasing our understanding of the world in which we live, that we are not depending on someone else to do "the hard stuff" for us, and that even in the difficult and sometimes confusing dilemmas that we face, we are hammering out a set of ethics and values that are grounded in God's Word. Without these abilities, without this foundation of ethics and values to guide us, we will tend to live our lives timidly, full of uncertainty, afraid to make a move.

Finding All We Need in Christ

In 1987 both of my grandfathers died within just a few months of each other. They went peacefully in their sleep, having known and loved the Lord; our families rejoiced in the fact that they were now with him. However, their deaths had a great impact on me because they brought into focus one of the most profound facts of human existence: our ultimate separateness from other human beings. As a young wife and mother I watched my grandmothers approach the caskets to gaze at their husbands' beloved bodies one last time. Even though they knew that the bodies were not persons, those bodies had housed precious souls, enabling them to be touched and known and loved. And just before the casket was closed for the last time, Grandma Haley turned to my Dad, her eldest son, and asked, "How do you say good-bye?"

That is a good question, isn't it? My grandparents had travelled over fifty years of their journey together. How do you bring closure to a relationship, a way of living, that has been so rich? How do you say good-bye to one with whom you have travelled so far? As I watched this unfolding drama from my front row seat, I could not avoid the realization that someday it could very well be me approaching a casket, struggling to say my good-byes.

These events are inevitable and we will all stand before the casket one day trying to figure out how to say good-bye to those we have loved the most. No matter how greatly we have loved or how deeply we have committed ourselves, that parting of the ways will come.

That day I realized that there was only one way I would want to say such a good-bye: with my hand in the hand of the only One who can say, "I will go the rest of the way with you. I will never leave you nor forsake you." It became clear to me then that if my identity, my worth, my purpose, my values, my ability to survive in this world had all been derived from the person whose body was in the casket, the good-byes were going to be all the more devastating.

I do not describe this scenario to be morbid or to scare anyone away from the intimate relationships for which we were created. Rather, I paint this picture of life, death, and change as a backdrop against which Jesus' offer to be the primary and permanent source for the filling of our deepest needs becomes all the more precious. He offers to bring love and meaning to our lives—even after we have said our most difficult farewells.

The Lesson of a Lifetime

Learning to find all we need in Christ begins with understanding how much he loves and values us. Samara caught glimpses of that love and worth the day she met him at the well. But the ultimate expression of his love—his willingness to lay down his life in payment for our sin—was still in the future. We have seen expressions of his unconditional love that Samara did not have the opportunity to see. We know that if any one of us had been the only one needing salvation from sin, he still would have given his all.

But that is only the beginning. Each of us needs to cultivate our relationship with Christ as if it were only the two of us because, chances are, there will come a time when this is truly the case. *We cannot afford to invest our human relationships and endeavors with the meaning that only a relationship with the eternal God can provide.* That is why reading and studying the Scriptures for ourselves, allowing them to confront society's stereotypes and reshape our thoughts about ourselves, our purposes, and our values is so crucial. Then we can discipline ourselves to see ourselves as God sees us and root our self-esteem in his truth.

One woman has written down brief statements that reflect what she has learned about God's view of her and she repeats them to herself daily:

- I am complete in Christ.
- I am a worthwhile person just as I am.
- I stand before God alone as a whole person.
- I have talents and abilities that God gives because he expresses himself through me.
- I can love others and give good things to them because God's love is poured out in my heart.
- I have self-esteem and integrity on my own because I am just as God intended me to be.[23]

We, too, need to make our own discoveries about ourselves based on a careful study of God's Word and attentive listening to his voice, reminding ourselves often of the truth that we find. Women still have many experiences in society that can drag them into the pit of feeling "less than" if we don't have truth with which to combat it. Media presentations of women as empty-headed sex objects who lack self-respect and dignity, men who verbally or physically abuse their wives, churches that limit women in the use of their gifts, companies where there are no women (or a token one or two) on the board of trustees and in upper management, countries where women still lack basic human rights . . . these can be death to our self-esteem if we believe their meanings rather than truth that we have learned from God.

In addition, past messages about our worth (or the lack of it) inform the way we view ourselves today. Family and religious systems that were characterized by shame, sexism, abuse of women and children, conditional love based on performance, or an inability to express love contribute significantly to a woman's feeling of powerlessness and worthlessness. Christ, through the presence of the Holy Spirit (or the Helper as he is called in John 15 and 16), will go with us as we sort through these early messages. *We do not confront the past for the purpose of blaming others or making excuses for ourselves; we do so in order to uncover the lies that are misleading us and to enter more fully into the truth.* It is only then that we can be free from sinful self-absorption and self-deprecation and give to God and others from the fullness he intends.

Of course, we do not learn these lessons once and for all. There have been and continue to be times when I must come back to the most basic of life's lessons. My grandfathers' funerals were occasions when I faced, in a new way, the reality that even though one is married, there are ways in which life is still a solitary journey. In those moments I needed to come back and hear God say, "I will never leave you or forsake you." There have been times when people or circumstances have seemed limiting and I have had to learn to come back to God and ask, "Who are you calling me to be? What do you want me to do?" There are times when I have failed and feel that my usefulness to God is over. I need to listen to him speak in that moment saying, "My love for you and your usefulness to me are not conditional upon your performance. I didn't wait for perfection from Samara before I gave love and the chance to make a difference, and I'm not waiting for perfection from you."

Learning to find all we need in Christ is truly the lesson of a lifetime. It is tempting to oversimplify and overspiritualize the problem many women have with self-esteem, thinking that if we just tell ourselves over and over again how much God loves us then pretty soon we will be convinced. However, as foundational as this knowledge is, some of the essentials of self-esteem are very practical in nature, as I have sought to demonstrate in this chapter. God knows about these practical needs as well as the spiritual ones. He can be trusted to lead us in acquiring what is essential at the right time and in the right ways if we are open to his leading.

FOR DISCUSSION

1. Describe yourself in some way that would give others a good sense of who you are. How do feel about the person you have just described?

2. What early experiences shaped your feelings about yourself? When did you feel that you were significant or insignificant? When did you feel unique and separate from others? When did you feel "part of the group"? When did you first start to realize that you could make an impact on the world?

3. Were you encouraged to become competent so that you could take care of yourself, or were you led to believe that someone else would take care of you?

4. What kind of information were you given about how the world works, and what experience did you have in learning to use that information? Did you have a clear idea of what was right and wrong?

5. Which of the essentials of self-esteem are you deficient in right now? What kinds of experiences could you structure in order to begin acquiring these?

6. In the quote at the beginning of this chapter, Anne Morrow Lindberg says that "woman must come of age by herself—she must find her true center alone." Do you agree or disagree with this statement? Why or why not?

7. Are you prepared for the time when you may have to journey on with Christ alone? If not, what steps would you like to take to prepare?

For Further Study

Duckworth, Marion. *Celebrate Who You Are*. Wheaton, Ill.: Victor Books, 1990.

Littauer, Florence. *Wake Up, Women!* Dallas: Word Publishing, 1994.

Malcolm, Kari Torjesen. *Women At The Crossroads*. Downers Grove, Ill.: InterVarsity Press, 1982.

Miller, Jean Baker. *Toward a New Psychology of Women*, 2nd ed. Boston: Beacon Press, 1976.

Rivers, Caryl, Rosalind Barnett, and Grace Baruch. *Beyond Sugar and Spice: How Women Grow, Learn, and Thrive*. New York: G.P. Putnam's Sons, 1979.

Van Vonderen, Jeff. *Tired of Trying to Measure Up*. Minneapolis: Bethany House, 1989.

Ward, Ruth McRoberts. *Self-Esteem: Gift from God*. Grand Rapids, Mich.: Baker Books, 1984.

Notes

1. Gloria Gaither, ed., *What My Parents Did Right* (Nashville: Star Song, 1991), pp. 12-15.

2. *Chicago Tribune*, quoted in *Marriage Partnership* (Summer 1991), p. 27.

3. Caryl Rivers, Rosalind Barnett, and Grace Baruch, *Beyond Sugar and Spice* (New York: G.P. Putnam's Sons, 1979), p. 25.

4. Linda Tschirhart Sanford and Mary Ellen Donovan, *Women and Self-Esteem* (New York: Penguin Books, 1984), p. 40.

5. Alice Slaikeu Lawhead, *The Lie of the Good Life* (Portland, Oreg.: Multnomah, 1989).

6. Emily MacFarquhar, "The War Against Women," *U.S. News & World Report* (March 28, 1994), p. 44.

7. Ibid., pp. 44-56.

8. Ron R. Lee, "She was Destroying Herself and He Couldn't Stop Her," *Marriage Partnership* (Winter 1993), p. 44.

9. Briar Whitehead, *Craving for Love* (Turnbridge Wells, Great Britain: Monarch, 1993), pp. 19-20.

10. Kari Torjesen Malcolm, *Women at the Crossroads* (Downers Grove, Ill.: 1982), pp. 40-41.

11. Sanford and Donovan, *Women and Self-Esteem*, p. 3.

12. Lawrence J. Crabb, *Understanding People* (Grand Rapids, Mich.: Zondervan, 1987), p. 112.

13. In Jewish culture women were viewed as little more than the "property" of fathers or husbands.

14. Samaritans were viewed by Jews as "leftovers" from Israel because they intermarried with foreigners after the chiefs and nobles had been captured during the Babylonian captivity. "Real Jews" despised Samaritans because they felt that the Samaritans had sold their birthright. Consequently, they had forced the Samaritans to build their own place of worship at Mt. Gerazim. Most Jews avoided contact with the Samaritans at all costs, choosing to go around Samaria rather than through it.

15. Jesus told her that God was abolishing the old way of worshipping, which was based on outward rituals. In its place, he was ushering in a new kind of worship that was not associated with any outward trappings but involved the spirit of the worshipper (John 4:23). This would be a radical shift!

16. Sanford and Donovan, *Women and Self-Esteem*, p. 12.

17. Penelope Russianoff, Ph.D, *Why Do I Think I Am Nothing Without a Man?* (New York: Bantam Books, 1981), p. 3.

18. Mary Stewart VanLeeuwen, *Gender and Grace* (Downers Grove, Ill.: InterVarsity Press, 1990), p. 46.

19. Crabb, *Understanding People*, p. 110.

20. Rivers, Barnett, and Barucy, *Beyond Sugar and Spice*, p. 18.

21. Sanford and Donovan, *Women and Self-Esteem*, p. 51.

22. For an excellent discussion of practical information women need to have, see *Wake Up, Women: Submission Doesn't Mean Stupidity*, by Florence Littauer (Dallas: Word Publishing, 1994).

23. Marie Chapian, *Staying Happy in an Unhappy World* (Old Tappan, N.J.: Fleming H. Revell, 1985), p. 37.

3

Living Life on Purpose

I believe that what woman resents is not so much giving herself . . .
as in giving herself purposelessly. . . . Purposeful giving is not as
apt to deplete one's resources; it belongs to that natural order of
giving that seems to renew itself even in the act of depletion. The
more one gives, the more one has to give—like milk in the breast.

Anne Morrow Lindberg

The hardest thing about being a homemaker," I have wailed on
many occassions, "is the repetitiveness of the tasks! Almost
everything I do in life has to be done over again within hours or
days. It all seems so pointless!"

My own personal symbol of futility is the kitchen floor. It's
white (I picked it out so I can't blame anyone else for that) and
is just beautiful when it is clean. But the problem, of course, is
that no sooner have I cleaned it (usually on my hands and
knees after having planned my whole day around it) than
someone spills on it. I know that *never* is a very big word,
but this never fails.

The inevitability of it all has made this a family joke, and on
my good days I can laugh along. However, on my bad days I
begin to babble incoherently about the futility of my life; what
does life matter when you spend your days doing things that
have been undone by the time your husband gets home? What
do I have to show for the exhaustion I feel at the end of the day?
Why do I bother? It can go on and on. For sanity purposes, I have
been known to wash the floor in the late afternoon and then insist
that we all go out for dinner so that the floor stays clean for at
least several hours. Anything for a sense of accomplishment!

Let's face it: With all the options open to women today, our lives are still often filled with the mundane, the ridiculous, the difficult, even the tragic. Sometimes it is hard to feel that life has purpose when you spend most of your days scraping Play-Doh™ off the floor, cleaning the bathroom, or working for a boss who doesn't recognize your potential.

And yet all of us, deep down inside, harbor a very human desire for meaning in life. We want our lives to count for something, something that will last longer than a few hours or a few days. As one poet put it: "Life without meaning is the torture of restlessness and vague desire—It is a boat longing for the sea and yet afraid."[1]

It is this longing and restlessness that God wants to fill up with his purpose.

Esther: A Woman Transformed by Purpose

Esther was a woman for whom the mundane and tragic aspects of life took on new meaning—as she saw it in the context of God's purposes. As a result of this new understanding, she was utterly transformed from a frightened and somewhat passive woman into one of strength, courage, and action.

Esther's story takes place in Persia (present-day Pakistan) during the reign of King Xerxes. The opening scene, described in Esther 1, reveals Xerxes treating all of his officials, noblemen, and armies to a lavish banquet that was the culmination of a six-month period in which he had displayed the wealth and splendor of his kingdom. The royal wine flowed freely and the men drank without restraint. At the same time his wife, Queen Vashti, gave a seperate banquet for the women in another part of the palace.

At the end of this seven-day banquet when Xerxes was "merry with wine" (in other words, he was drunk), Xerxes called Queen Vashti to come and display her beauty to his drunken guests (Esther 1:11). One can only imagine the state that the king and his male guests were in after drinking and partying for seven days straight. Some historians believe that the king was commanding Vashti to appear naked except for her crown, and most agree it was not a respectful request but a demeaning one. We can be sure that it was not the kind of situation in which any self-respecting woman would willingly place herself.[2]

When Vashti refused to display herself as the king had commanded, his wise men convinced him that the queen's behavior was a threat not only to the king's honor but to male supremacy in general. He decided to make a public example of her by banishing her from his presence and giving her position to one who was more worthy. Obviously, there were no women's rights in this setting; women were absolutely expendable and completely at the mercy of the men in their lives. It was into this setting that Esther came.

A Beauty Pageant with a Twist

When the king's anger subsided, he began to miss Vashti. His attendants, who didn't want to risk losing all the progress they had made for mankind, came up with another bright idea: "Let's distract Xerxes from what he's feeling by staging a beauty pageant!" So they gathered all the beautiful young virgins in the kingdom into a harem for the king so that he could choose a replacement for Vashti.

Perhaps Esther, an orphaned Jewish girl in the care of her cousin Mordecai, was shopping in the outdoor market, laughing with friends or working around her home when the king's men rode through town seizing beautiful girls. It is not hard to imagine her panic and fright as she was torn from her only family and taken against her will to the king's palace. Who knows if she even realized, as she was being dragged away, that she would spend the next full year getting ready for one night of sex with a heathen king. Esther 2:12-14 tell us that there was considerably more involved in the Miss Persia beauty pageant than in the pageants to which we are accustomed. After the young lady was brought into the harem, she spent twelve months getting ready—six months with oil and myrrh and six months with herbs and cosmetics. When her turn came, she would spend the night with the king and then return to the second harem of the concubines. She was then considered used merchandise, the equivalent of a slave kept for the purposes of sex, childbearing, and housekeeping. She could never approach the king again unless he called her by name. Some beauty pageant!

If Esther was like most Jewish girls, she had dreamed all her life of marrying and bearing children; perhaps she had even imagined that she would be the one chosen to be the mother of the Messiah. But now her prospects of a normal marriage and family life were ruined, for she would become forever the property of the king. Here was the trauma of kidnapping and rape, the loneliness of being torn from family, the disappointment of a difficult marriage, and the loss of her hopes and dreams—all wrapped up in one life-changing event. There wasn't much Mordecai could do but advise her not to tell anyone she was a Jew. (Maybe he thought she would receive better treatment if no one knew she belonged to the race that had once been held captive in that country.) But certainly his presence as he walked back and forth in front of the harem every day must have been a comfort and a strength to his young cousin.

Hope in the Midst of Tragedy

As dismal as Esther's situation was, God was there—in the harem, in the palace, and in the king's bedroom—working in all of his sovereignty and power to bring about his good purposes. As Esther spent the next year preparing to go to the king, she found favor with everyone who knew her. And when her turn came, "the king loved Esther more than all the other women; of all the virgins she won his favor and devotion, so that he set the royal crown on her head and made her queen instead of Vashti" (2:17, NRSVB). Although she was not yet aware of it, the king's love would become the key to the accomplishment of God's great purpose in that place.

After Esther was settled in her new position as queen, King Xerxes promoted a proud and evil man named Haman to a position above all the other palace officials. The king then commanded that everyone should bow down to Haman. Mordecai, consistent with his Jewish faith and practice, refused. "When Haman saw that Mordecai did not bow down or do obeisance to him, Haman was infuriated. But he thought it beneath him to lay hands on Mordecai alone. So, having been told who Mordecai's people were, Haman plotted to destroy all the Jews, the people of Mordecai, throughout the whole kingdom of Ahasuerus" (3:5-6, NRSVB).

Haman cleverly convinced the king that the Jews scattered throughout the country were a threat to his supremacy. So the king gave permission for Haman to send out this edict: on the thirteenth day of the twelfth month, the king's soldiers would be sent out into all the king's provinces to "destroy, kill, and to annihilate all Jews, young and old, women and children, in one day . . . and to plunder their goods" (3:13, NRSVB).

When Mordecai first got wind of Haman's genocide plot against the Jews, he realized immediately the significance of Esther's position. He sent her a message urging her to "go to the king to make supplication to him and entreat him for her people." At first Esther was hesitant to get involved, and with very good reason. She reminded Mordecai that "if any man or woman goes to the king inside the inner court without being called, there is but one law—all alike are to be put to death. Only if the king holds out the golden scepter to someone, may that person live. I myself have not been called to come in to the king for thirty days" (4:11, NRSVB).

Help in Decision Making

It was at this point that Mordecai, who must have been very wise, made an interesting suggestion. After expressing complete confidence in God's ability to deliver the Jews, he said to Esther, "Who knows? Perhaps you have come to royal dignity for just such a time as this?" (4:14, NRSVB). He didn't presume to tell her what God was calling her to do; he merely heightened her awareness with his insightful question. Perhaps he realized that

God's call on our lives is very personal and he alone must speak it to our souls.

As a result of Mordecai's comment, the light began to dawn for Esther on all that had happened to her. The trauma, the loneliness, the unusualness of her situation began to make sense. As she became conscious of what she had come to the kingdom for, a sense of purpose—not personal safety, probabilities, social norms, or convenience—began to inform her decision-making process. The knowledge that God had brought her to this time and place for a specific purpose transformed her from a frightened, hesitant woman making excuses in Esther 4:11 to the courageous woman who sent this message to Mordecai: "Go, gather all the Jews . . . and hold a fast on my behalf . . . I and my maids will also fast as you do. After that, I will go to the king, though it is against the law; and if I perish, I perish" (verse 16).

Meaning in the Mundane

After asking the Jews to fast and pray for her, Esther took several days to think of a plan and prepare her heart. Then she swung into action. First, she made herself beautiful, the mundane task of getting dressed taking on a new significance that day. Can't you just see her standing in front of her closet, trying to choose the royal robe that would please the king and cause his heart to be open toward her? I'm sure her heart beat fast and her fingers shook as she applied her make-up. Maybe she rehearsed what she would say to the king if she did get the chance to speak. Certainly she thought of Queen Vashti in those moments, questioning whether she too would be banished for standing up for her convictions. She had spoken bravely three days before but now the moment of truth had come. Would she have the courage to follow through?

But Esther did follow through. She used everything she had at her disposal—her brains, her beauty, her position, the king's love for her—and risked it all to accomplish the purpose for which God had brought her to that time and place. She went and stood in the inner court of the king's palace, positioning herself so that the king could see her. She didn't have to wait long, for "As soon as the king saw Queen Esther standing in the court, she won his favor and he held out to her the golden scepter that was in his hand. Then Esther approached the king and he said to her, 'What is it, Queen Esther? What is your request? It shall be given you even up to half my kingdom' " (Esther 5:3).

A Life that Counts for God

From there Esther implemented a wildly successful plan that resulted in Haman being hung on the gallows he had built for Mordecai and the Jews being delivered from the annihilation that had been planned for them. Mordecai was promoted to a position of authority second only to the king himself and used his position for the good of his people, while Esther continued to enjoy the love of the king and the privileges and responsibilities of queenship. To this day the Jews still celebrate the feast of Purim "as the days on which the Jews gained relief from their enemies, and as the month that been turned for them from sorrow into gladness and from mourning into a holiday" (9:22). What a thrilling story of the mighty way God used a woman who had been uniquely prepared for his great purposes.

Seeing Ourselves as Women of Purpose

It's clear that the sovereignty of God permeates the book of Esther; it was such an unlikely situation in human terms. But even so, Esther needed to consider the suggestion Mordecai raised for her that day. She had not yet begun to realize that God had been carefully orchestrating her life to bring her to that place at that time and for that purpose. He had put together a package in her life—beauty, intelligence, nationality, position, love—and now the time had come for her to put it to use.

The sovereignty of God permeates our lives as well although we don't always see it. *God is putting together a package in each of our lives, preparing us to make a unique contribution to his kingdom.* We, too, need to ask ourselves, "What have I come

55

to the kingdom for? Why has God brought me to this particular time and place?"

Approaching life situations in this way represents a radical shift in thinking for some of us. We are more accustomed to thinking, *But I'm so limited. God could never use me!* There are many factors that cause us to feel limited or inadequate: a lack of formal education, a late start in the Christian life, our marital status, financial limitations, young children or rebellious teens in the home, a lack of self-confidence, and so on. But these are only perceived limitations. So often, what we see as limitations are God's training ground for unique usefulness to him.

Joni Erickson Tada is one who has discovered that her limitations were inextricably interwoven with God's purposes for her life. As a young girl of seventeen, she was paralyzed from the neck down in a diving accident. Facing the rest of her life as a quadriplegic confined to a wheelchair, she raged against God and wished to take her own life. But as she allowed God to deal with her at her point of deepest pain, she found that the limitations of her disabled body propelled her into ministry to others who are disabled. She found that they listened to her in a way that they wouldn't listen to someone whose body was whole. Now she has an international ministry to this group of people who, up to this point, had been largely unreached for Christ. God brought her to a time and a place in a disabled body for a purpose.

Identifying God's Purposes

No matter what our circumstances, then, we still need to ask ourselves, "What have I come to the kingdom for?" Generally speaking we have all come to this time and place as servants of Jesus Christ, as investors of what he has given us. But we need to go beyond the general and get down to specifics: "What unique gifts, experiences, opportunities, and burdens is God blending together in my life to make me of special use to him?"

In *The Seven Habits of Highly Effective People*, Stephen Covey points out that when you begin with the end in mind "each part of your life—today's behavior, tomorrow's behavior, next month's behavior—can be examined in the context of the whole, in the context of what really matters most to you. By keeping that end clearly in mind, you can make sure . . . that each day of your life contributes in a meaningful way to the vision you have of your life as a whole."[3]

Paul said the same thing in different words:

> Live life, then, with a due sense of responsibility, not as those who do not know the meaning of life but as *those who do.* Make the best use of your time, despite the evils of these days. Don't be vague but grasp firmly what you know to be the will of the Lord. (Ephesians 5:15-17, PHILLIPS)

Purpose. A life purpose answers our larger questions about the meaning of life and the reasons for our existence. It reflects the overall vision God has given us for what he wants to do in and through our lives. Formulating a life purpose statement is not something that can be rushed, because it is forged as we search the Scriptures and listen to the Lord speak to us in a very personal way. It reflects what we are aiming for in life and will probably stay basically the same with minor variations and fine-tuning throughout our lives.

Priorities. Since a life-purpose statement is, by nature, rather general, it is also important to identify the specific priority areas through which these purposes will be accomplished: spiritual life, personal growth, family life, work, service in the church and the world. Then within these priority areas we can develop more specific purpose statements. If one of my larger purposes in life is to know God, I need to be more specific about what I am aiming for in this area. Do I need to learn to be quiet and just be in his presence? Do I want to develop a deeper prayer life? What character issues do I need to work on? In regard to my family, what exactly do I want my husband and children to receive from me and from our home life? As far as my contribution to my church and community is concerned, what gifts has God given me that need to be developed? How do those fit with the things

I'm burdened about? And what about friendships, intellectual challenges, and healthy living?

This is the place to dream the dreams that God is whispering to our hearts—even the ones that seem so far-fetched we're almost afraid to put them into words.

Planning. The process of identifying purposes and priorities doesn't guarantee that in reality we will spend our time and energy on those priorities. It is very easy to say "I want to be more responsive to my husband sexually" or "I want to be a writer" or "I want to be more involved in my children's education," but it is quite another thing to take steps to make it so.

Goals help us plan our priorities into the minutes and hours of our days; they are the steps that will take us to the end result. An effective goal is reachable, measurable, and realistic, taking into consideration our season of life and other factors that might effect our plans (i.e. health, transportation, finances, husband's schedule, etc.). If our goals are unrealistic, we set ourselves up for failure and discouragement.

For instance, one of the main purposes of my life is to serve God with my gifts. Since I understand that one of the ways I am to accomplish this is through writing, writing has become a priority. When the opportunity came along to write my first Bible studyguide, I said yes because I could see how it fit into God's purposes for my life, but I needed a realistic plan that would take into account my busy season of life. Since I had two young daughters, the only writing time I had was in the early mornings and in the afternoons while my older daughter was in pre-school and my younger daughter was napping. So, my goal for accomplishing this writing project was to write early in the morning five mornings week and during nap-time three afternoons a week. It would be easy to tell if I was accomplishing my goals from day to day. And I felt confident that working at that pace, I would finish the project in a year.

Discipline. It was a great plan, but there was one problem. Quite often when I took my older daughter to preschool, I would run into a friend who was fun to be with and enjoyed shopping, as I do. If either one of us said anything about shopping, we would throw responsibility to the wind and go. As you can imagine, this greatly hindered my work on the writing project (not to mention how hard it was on our budget!). I had not yet come to grips with the fact that saying yes to the goals and plans that would take me step by step toward God's purposes would also involve saying no to things that interfered. I finally realized that if I wanted the long-term satisfaction of seeing my work in print, I would have to give up the short-term pleasure of those spur-of-the-moment shopping trips. Every preschool day, I faced the choice between short-term pleasure and "making the best use of my time." Sometimes I succumbed to temptation, but I grew more consistent in sticking to my plan and eventually got the job done.

Delaying self-gratification is one habit necessary to saying no, but it's a difficult one to develop! And in saying no we sometimes risk the disappointment of others. They may even think we are wrong for not being available for the activities and projects they think are important. Many women have been conditioned to be "people pleasers" and, as such, find it very hard to hold on to their own priorities in the face of this kind of pressure. But we must remember that others don't necessarily know the purposes to which God has called us or the commitments we are juggling. When we give in to pressure (that comes from ourselves or from others) we are fitting into others' purposes rather than God's. Each one of us is responsible to God for what we do with the time and energy he has given us; people who are spiritually wise will trust him to move us to do what he is calling us to.

In *A Time for Risking*, Miriam Adeney comments that "Only those who turn down standard activities will have time and energy for priority affairs."[4] She offers this challenge:

For you, kingdom priorities might mean saying no to talking on the telephone so much. Or saying no to well-established committees in order to serve on more needy committees. Saying no to certain kinds of reading in order to do other, more crucial reading. Saying no to thinking so much about how you feel or about the way you look—saying no to your "pity parties." Kingdom priorities might mean monitoring your imagination and bringing every thought captive to Christ (2 Corinthians 10:5). It might mean limiting the time you spend thinking about fashion, shopping, romance, eating out, backpacking, gardening, skiing, soap operas, novels, gossip, or whatever catches your imagination, in order consciously to focus a certain amount of your thoughts on people's need for Jesus, on world hunger, on nuclear weapon dangers, on teenage mothers. Kingdom priorities may mean saying no to spending so much time with certain friends in order to spend time with friends who need you more. Or limiting your mindless conversations, in order consciously to make your conversations channels of grace.[5]

This is not to say that there should be no time for fun and relaxation; we need some of that or we will burn out quickly. But in the context of purposeful living, relaxation is even more delicious because we give it to ourselves intentionally. This too is part of our conscious choice to live our lives in the balanced and fruitful way that God intended.

Another helpful discipline is actually to chart out our purposes, priorities, and plans. There are many tools on the market designed to help with this process, but I have found that creating my own chart has helped me to solidify my thoughts and commitments. In addition to a written life purpose statement, I use a separate sheet of paper for each priority area (spiritual life, personal development, family, church, work, etc.) and then divide the paper into three columns. The first column contains my purpose statements (what I'm aiming for) in that area. The second contains my plan (specific goals and scheduling) and the third contains any disciplines involved (things I will need to say no to in order to say yes to what really matters).[6]

Saying Yes to God

Have you ever imagined what would have happened if some of the women in the Bible had said no to the purposes of God in their lives? What if Esther had said, "But Lord, I have myself set up pretty well here. Just look at me! I'm the queen and the king loves me. Why would I want to mess that up?" Or what if Deborah, when God called her to be a prophet, judge, and military leader in Israel, had responded like this: "But Lord, don't you know that women aren't supposed to do those sorts of things?" And what about Mary, the mother of Jesus? "But God, this is extremely inconvenient: couldn't you wait until after I get married? This is going to ruin my reputation and besides, I had a few things I wanted to do before I had kids!"

In any of these cases, history could have turned out quite differently. But these women did not allow themselves to be limited by the voices of cultural norms, personal convenience, or fear. Rather, they allowed God to put a package together in their lives and they responded when he called them to use it.

We may not be called to be Deborahs or Esthers, leading armies or thwarting great political schemes (although I wouldn't rule that out!). God may be putting our package together in such a way that we are uniquely prepared to confront injustice and immorality in our community, to mold a young life, to care unselfishly for aging parents, to serve Jesus by opening our home, or to speak with discernment to the church. Knowing that God is in control of preparing us for his purposes adds value to many aspects of life that would otherwise be mundane. The young mother who is scraping Play-Doh™ off the floor can see it the context of purpose—she has provided her child with an important tactile experience! A woman working in a job that isn't exactly a dream come true can take advantage of the character-building opportunities that are a part of the spiritual growth for which she is aiming. We can even clean the bathroom with an awareness that we are creating the atmosphere in our home that is important to us.

Of course, there will be other opportunities that require more courage: speaking out publicly about something important, home schooling our kids, running for public office, sharing Christ with a neighbor, or moving into the inner city in order to make a difference there.

Our challenge then is to say yes to the most important things, the things for which God has brought us to this time and place. In so doing, we make room in our lives for meaning and value, and we will feel God's pleasure upon us. Rather than the "torture of restlessness and vague desire," the wind of the Spirit will fill our sails and move us into the high sea of purposeful living. Will it be frightening? At times, yes. Will it be risky? More so than staying in a quiet harbor. Will it be exhilirating? You bet! Will it be fulfilling? Well, let's put it this way: It's the only way to live.

FOR DISCUSSION

1. What are some of the gifts, opportunities, burdens, and preparations that God is blending together in your life right now? Do you have a sense that God has brought you to this time and place for a purpose? (If your answer is no, don't force it. God will make it clear in his time.)

2. As you think about what God may be calling you to do, what are the limitations you face? How will you approach these areas?

3. What is your plan of action for accomplishing the purposes that God is impressing upon your heart? What will you need to say yes to and what will you need to say no to?

For Further Study

Adeney, Miriam. *A Time for Risking*. Portland, Oreg.: Multnomah Press, 1987.

Barton, R. Ruth. *Becoming Women of Purpose*. Wheaton, Ill.: Shaw Publishers, 1992.

Biehl, Cheryl. *I Can't Do Everything!* Sisters, Oreg.: Questar Publishers. 1990.

Covey, Stephen. *The Seven Habits of Highly Effective People*. New York: Simon & Schuster, 1989.

Notes

1. Edgar Lee Masters, "George Grey," *Spoon River Anthology* (1st edition 1915; New York: Penquin Books, 1992).

2. One commentator notes, "had the king been sober he would not have considered such a breach of custom, for he knew that Eastern women lived

in seclusion and that such a request as he made in this drunken condition amounted to a gross insult. For Vashti to appear in the banquet hall, though dressed in her royal robes and crowned, would be almost as degrading as for a modern woman to go naked into a man's party. What Xerxes demanded was a surrender of womanly honor, and Vashti, who was neither vain nor wanton, was unwilling to comply." Herbert Lockyer, *All the Women of the Bible* (Grand Rapids, Mich.: Zondervan, 1958), pp. 165-66.

3. Stephen Covey, *The Seven Habits of Highly Effective People* (New York: Simon & Schuster, 1989), p. 98.

4. Miriam Adeney, *A Time for Risking* (Portland, Oreg.: Multnomah), p. 61.

5. Ibid., pp. 56-57.

6. For a step-by-step workbook on purposeful living, see R. Ruth Barton, *Becoming Women of Purpose* (Wheaton, Ill.: Shaw Publishers, 1992).

4

How Does God View Women?

Dear God, Are boys better than girls? I know you are one, but please try to be fair.

from Children's Letters to God

We still laugh about the time our oldest daughter, then two and a half, traipsed into church during a worship service wearing a diaper on her head. She was trailing behind us as we slipped into our front row seats a few minutes late so we didn't realize that she was making this fashion statement until she had already caused a bit of a stir.

This was more than childhood silliness. Early in her young life she had observed that the women in our church (including her mother) wore head coverings, usually veils of some sort. To her, putting something on her head was part of what it meant to be a woman.

For me, having grown up in this kind of a church setting, being a woman meant wearing a head covering to symbolize my submission to men's authority—and much more. It meant not being allowed to speak in church gatherings. It meant knowing that even though I was supposed to be a priest (according to 1 Peter 2:5, 9), men were the only ones allowed to perform the priestly functions of teaching, leading worship, serving communion, or offering an audible prayer when the church gathered. It meant hearing letters from women missionaries read in church services but finding that when they were home on furlough they could not get up in these same gatherings and give a report. It meant listening while the men were exhorted to step forward and accept their God-given responsibility of teaching and leading, while watching the godly women I respected sit in numb silence.

All of these rules, spoken and unspoken, sent a powerful message to a young, spiritually sensitive girl who was trying to figure out what it meant to be female and be Christian. The message was not a very positive one.

A Growing Awareness

A small Christian liberal arts college in the midwest gave me the opportunity to experience, for the first time, an environment in which gender wasn't such a big issue. Women could speak and pray in chapel, serve as leaders in student government, and receive equal encouragement from their professors. At the same time, I found that my love for the church was growing and I served there in any way I could. I realized that there was nothing I wanted more than to spend my life serving God among his people. So, in addition to certifying to teach, I also took Bible, Greek, and Christian education courses with a view to "plugging in" to the church with greater effectiveness.

I emerged from college with great eagerness but soon discovered that, while my male peers were groomed to serve as preachers, teachers, and elders in my home church, women were relegated to a much more narrow sphere of ministry. When young men demonstrated desire or ability to teach and lead the congregation, it was cause for celebration; when a young woman shared these same desires she was viewed as rebellious. I began to wonder if God had made a mistake in entrusting a woman with my particular gifts and desires for ministry.

It was even more disturbing to see that women did not have much voice in church life at all. It was painful when the men would retreat to another room to discuss important spiritual matters, leaving the women to tend to the kitchen and the children. The belief that women (by nature of their female-ness) functioned best behind the scenes and men (by virtue of their male-ness) were best suited for up-front leadership didn't fit with my understanding of spiritual gifts and personality types. I couldn't help wondering, "Is the female perspective so devoid of value that Christian congregations can live without it?"

For many years I hid my struggle, alternating between self-blame (was it my own character flaws that kept me from being content with the traditional role carved out for women?) and anger at those who perpetrated such a discriminatory system. At the same time I kept serving in whatever capacity I was allowed: working with youth, teaching girls' Sunday school and women's Bible studies, directing vacation Bible school and women's ministries, playing piano, singing in the choir. While I enjoyed each of these ministry opportunities, I continued to experience a great deal of turmoil over women's lack of freedom to participate fully in different aspects of church life.

It was becoming a crisis of faith for me. After all, the church is God's church. Was this an accurate reflection of him? Was he really a chauvinistic father who allowed his sons to speak and participate in family decisions while barring his daughters from the same privileges? Was Eve's sin so much greater and more unforgivable than Adam's that the entire female gender must forever be treated with suspicion and controlling measures?

These were not the questions of a theologian; they were questions wrung from the heart of a daughter to her heavenly Father. I did not want to believe the conclusions at which some women were arriving; and yet they didn't surprise me. As one woman said, "I have read the Bible. The Christian slate is there for all to read and it cannot be wiped clean . . . for Christianity is a male religion, written by men, for men, with a male god."[1]

As irreverent as it seemed to question God on these matters, that was never the attitude that was in my heart. These questions were getting in the way of the most important relationship in my life and I needed to ask them. Fortunately, I knew God well enough to be confident that he was big enough and loving enough to help me find the answers.

A Time to Study

Finally, the time came for me to quit stewing and start studying. The women in my church invited me to develop material on contemporary women's issues for use in their weekly Bible study. For an entire year, I poured over the Scriptures from beginning to end, studying anything and everything that had to do with women. My heart was stirred by women in the Bible such as Abigail, Deborah, Huldah, Esther, and Priscilla,[2] who made an impact for God's kingdom in courageous ways that, even now, strike us as being outside the normal "woman's role." I marvelled at the freedom they found to follow the Lord's call on their lives. I found myself weeping with love for Jesus as I witnessed the respect with which he treated women. And through my study of spiritual gifts, *I began to discover that God gives gifts not based on gender but based on the work he has called us to do.*

What I was learning just didn't fit with the emphasis on the silence and subordination of women with which I had grown up. After that Bible study was finished,[3] I kept right on studying, and I've been studying ever since. Even now, I do not claim to have all the answers regarding this issue on which so many Christians disagree. But I can say that I know enough to be at peace with God, to be able to follow his call on my life with courage, and to teach my daughters what God says about being a woman. We all need to know at least that much.

Creation

I began my study with creation, for it is there that we get our first glimpses of what it means to be human beings created male and female. In Genesis 1 and 2 we see God's original and best plan for gender relations: a partnership model in which a man and a woman function together as a team of equals. In Genesis 1, we learn that God created humankind in two sexes—male and female—and that both were created equally in his image (verses 26-27). God blessed the man and the woman and gave them both the responsibility to be fruitful and multiply, to fill the earth, subdue it, and rule together over all living things (verses 28-29). When God surveyed all that he had made, including his newest addition of this "marriage team," for the first time in the entire creation story he commented that it was "very good."

Genesis 2 gives a more detailed account of the creation of man and woman. Verse 18 tells us God recognized that it was not good for man to be alone, and so he created woman—"a helper suitable for him." Traditionally, theologians have interpreted this passage to mean that woman was somehow subordinate to man because she was created to be his helper *(ezer)*. This is puzzling and disturbing because elsewhere in the Scriptures the same Hebrew word *(ezer)* is most often used in reference to God himself. For example, in Exodus 18:4 Jethro named his son Eleiezer because "the God of my father was my help *[ezer]*." And in Psalm 40:17, as in many other places, the psalmist refers to God as "my help *[ezer]* and my deliverer." It is also important to note that "ezer" is translated in other places in the Scripture as succorer, rescuer, deliverer, strength, and power.[4]

Furthermore, as Ruth Tucker points out, in contemporary usage the word *helper* most often connotes strength. A parent helps a child with his homework. A doctor is a helper to a patient. A rich nation is a helper to refugees. A person who is in distress psychologically or spiritually looks to a pastor or a counselor for help. "The one who helps is the one who has something to offer the one who is helpless or needs help. Adam needed help. He had no partner. God created a partner—a helper. There is no hint of either superiority or subordination."[5]

When God brought Eve to Adam, he was astounded and overjoyed to find someone who was like him: "This is now bone of my bones, and flesh of my flesh" (Genesis 2:23, NASB). But he also recognized and named the gender difference when he called her "Woman, because she was taken out of Man" (NASB). "For this cause" [because of their fundamental unity] the man is instructed to leave his own family and cleave or cling to his wife (verse 24).

Rather than pull a woman into the authority structure of the husband's family (as in the patriarchal system that developed later), Genesis teaches that the man is the one who should move away from his family toward his wife and cling to her in a new relationship that is characterized by interdependence. "Therefore a man leaves his father and his mother and clings to his wife, and they become one flesh" (2:24, NRSVB).

Paul expands on this interdependence in 1 Corinthians 11:11-12 when he points out that "in the Lord, neither is woman independent of man, nor is man independent of woman. For as the woman originates from the man, so also the man has his birth through the woman" (NASB). This interdependence is pictured in the phrase "and they shall become one flesh." There is nothing here to suggest that one is "over" the other. In fact, any introduction of hierarchy seems completely contradictory to the oneness and interdependence pictured here.

The Fall

The Fall caused terrible distortions in relationships between men and women. Eve's choice and Adam's choice to disobey God caused dire consequences for the human race. Among these was the introduction of sin and guilt, shame and blame into the male/female relationship. Many of us have been taught that Eve was somehow "more guilty" than Adam because she ate the fruit first and then offered it to him. However, Genesis 3:6 reveals that Adam was with Eve during her temptation, apparently offering no help. Eve was left to hold her own in conversation with the serpent and when she offered Adam the fruit, he took it without argument: "She also gave some to her husband, who was with her, and he ate" (NRSVB).

Paul's interpretation of this incident is that "it was not Adam who was deceived, but the woman being quite deceived, fell into transgression" (1 Timothy 2:14, NASB). The question comes to mind: which is worse—to sin knowingly or to be deceived? And if Paul is attributing "greater guilt" to Eve, how are we to interpret Romans 5:12-19 ("sin came into the world through one man" NRSVB) and other passages in which Paul ascribes primary guilt to Adam? This apparent contradiction can be resolved by recognizing that Adam and Eve were equally responsible for their personal choices in the Garden of Eden.

The consequences of the fall outlined in Genesis 3:14-19 are predictions of how things would be in a sinful world rather than a prescription or a commandment for how God wanted things to be. In no way did it mean that women were prohibited from finding ways to avoid the pain of childbirth or free themselves from wrongful domination by their husbands. By the same token, God predicted that men would have to work very hard to get the ground to bear fruit; but he did not prohibit them from finding ways to make work easier—which they have. More significantly, within this sad scenario came another prediction—a promise even!—that one day Someone would come who would break the power of the evil one (Genesis 3:15). That Someone has come and the church is still discovering how his life, death, and resurrection can redeem all areas of life—including relationships between the sexes.

The Life of Christ

In Old Testament days, the effects of sin in the lives of men and women were clearly seen. Women were viewed and treated as possesions—as "less than" men. Consequently, they were the victims of terrible abuse and violence (Genesis 16; Genesis 19:1-8; Judges 11:29-40; Judges 19). Even so, women like Miriam, Huldah, Abigail, Esther, and Deborah demonstrated that "you can't keep a good woman down." When a woman was the right person for the job, whether it was leading in worship, prophesying, exhorting, saving a nation from genocide, or leading into battle, God didn't hesitate to use her. And the results were pretty impressive.

This reality was all but lost on Jewish men who, at the time of Christ, were still thanking God regularly "that I was not born a woman." They were forbidden to teach the words of the law to a woman publicly.

When Christ came, he broke manmade rules for gender relations and made new ones that reflected more accurately God's heart toward women. That is why we see him talking to an immoral woman about theology, worship, the state of her relationships, and the state of her soul (John 4). That is why we see him pointing out to the men that a woman caught in adultery was no more guilty than they were (John 8:1-11), and why we see him receiving Mary's act of worship as much more meaningful than anything that was going on in the synagogues (John 12:1-8). That is why some of his best friends were women—women were last at the cross and first at the tomb (Mark 15:40-47). And he appeared first to a woman and gave her the joyful responsibility of informing the disciples that he was alive! (Mark 16:1-8).

Christ, who was God come to earth in human form, was untainted by the sexism that characterized the society in which he lived. He raised a new standard for men and women to follow in their relationships. The impact of his life on gender relations can be summed up in Galatians 3:27-28: "For all of you who were baptized into Christ have clothed yourself with Christ. There is neither Jew nor Greek, there is neither slave nor free man, there is neither male nor female; for you are all one in Christ Jesus" (NASB). These words are revolutionary from a cultural, political, and religious standpoint. The church is still in the process of applying these verses by dealing with the discrimination and partiality (all kinds) that exist in direct contradiction to the equality spoken of here.

The Early Church

After Christ's death, the disciples returned to Jerusalem to await the Holy Spirit. Acts 1:14 says that they "all with one mind were continually devoting themselves to prayer, along with the women" (NASB). When the day of Pentecost came, they were all together in one place and tongues of fire rested on each one of them. All of them were filled with the Holy Spirit and were speaking in tongues (Acts 2:4). When Peter got up to preach, he explained these events to those who were watching. He said that this was a fulfillment of Joel's prophecy that when God poured forth his Spirit upon all humanity, sons and daughters, men and women would prophesy (that is, speak forth the mind of God). And they did! (2:16-18).

As the early church grew, women worked right alongside the men in spreading the gospel and planting churches. In many cases it was a woman (such as Lydia in Philippi) who was the prime mover in getting a church started and hosting it in her home. Other women taught theology (Priscilla), served as ministers or deacons (Phoebe), prophesied (Phillip's daughters), and simply worked very hard (see Romans 16:1-16).

First Corinthians 12 puts into words what was already in evidence in the early church: To each one is given the manifestation of the Spirit (spiritual gift) without regard to gender. It was entirely consistent with Peter's assertion that "God is not one to show partiality" (Acts 10:34) and that we are all members of the royal priesthood called out of darkness by God to proclaim his excellencies (1 Peter 2:9-10).

Redemption

At the heart of the Gospel is a message of freedom for all who are oppressed (Galatians 5:1), and one doesn't need to look far to see that women have been greatly oppressed. Not only did Christ model a new kind of relationship between men and women; through his death he redeemed us from the oppressive effects of the curse (Galatians 3:13). *When we require women to pay over and over again for Eve's transgression with their silence and submission, we negate the full redemptive power of the Gospel.* Rather than becoming an example of relationships that have been redeemed, we model the reality of the curse. Rather than living out God's ideal (as seen in Genesis 1) so that our presence in society begins to transform it, we allow ourselves to be squeezed into the world's mold of sexism and discrimination.

But What About . . . ?

There are several Biblical texts that have, at times, confused us as we have sought to understand how men and women are to function together in marriage, ministry, and society. However, basic principles of Biblical interpretation teach us to interpret these passages in light of broad theological themes such as the ones we have just observed—themes rooted in creation, the character of God (his justice and impartiality), the life and teachings of Christ, the leading of the Holy Spirit in the early church, and general New Testament teaching regarding spiritual gifts and the priesthood of all believers.

A thematic approach to Scripture reveals that "more than a hundred passages in the Bible affirm women in roles of leadership, and fewer than half a dozen appear to be in opposition."[6] Yet we as Christians have built an elaborate system of belief and practice on a few passages. These passages have loomed so large that we have allowed them to color everything else we read. I am not suggesting we merely dismiss these passages because we do not understand them. They are still part of the Scriptures, and we must continue to wrestle with their true meaning. But we must resist the temptation to lift them out of the context of broader themes or elevate them to the point that they become more important than the overall message of the Scriptures.

With that in mind, let's take a look at the primary passage from which people infer that women are to be limited in the scope of their ministry. First Timothy 2:11-12 says: "Let a woman learn in silence with full submission. I permit no woman to teach or have authority over a man; she is to keep silent" (NRSVB). While an exhaustive study of this passage and related research is beyond the scope of this book, I would like to provide an overview of important new research that sheds greater light on this difficult passage.

Historical context. At the time that Paul wrote this letter to believers, Ephesus stood as a bastion of feminine supremacy in religion. The shrine of the great mother goddess Artemis (or Diana, as the Romans knew her) was located in Ephesus, and there she was worshipped as the mother of gods and men. It was believed that she was the originator of life and her presence or intervention guaranteed economic and political security.

It was in this religious climate that gnosticism, with its radical distortions of biblical stories, began to develop and infiltrate the church. One such distortion twisted the story of Eve to say that she was the one who brought life to Adam. Richard and Catherine Kroeger write: "According to gnostic thought, all matter was evil. The Creator, the God of the Hebrew Bible, was evil because he made the material world. The serpent was beneficent in helping Adam and Eve to shake off the deception perpetrated on them by the Creator, and Eve was the mediator who brought true knowledge to the human race."[7]

The veneration of Eve that grew out of this distortion dovetailed perfectly with the practice of goddess worship that was already firmly entrenched in the religious psyche of those living in the first century. It was a logical progression to mythologize and deify Eve as the mediator of truth and special hidden knowledge. Gnostics developed an entire belief system that claimed that mystic knowledge resided not only in feminine figures of sacred literature (such as Eve and Mary the mother of Jesus) but also in actual gnostic women who were willing to share their divine secrets. These secrets were often conveyed through the use of nonsense-repetitious syllables, riddles, and paradoxes that apparently made sense to gnostics themselves but were very difficult for anyone else to understand and refute.

Paul wrote to his young protégé, Timothy, for the express purpose of encouraging him to stay at the church in Ephesus to combat such false teaching: "I urge you . . . to remain in Ephesus so that you may instruct certain people not to teach any different doctrine, and not to occupy themselves with myths and endless genealogies that promote speculations rather than divine training that is known by faith." (1 Timothy 1:3-4, NRSVB). The church in Ephesus was not a healthy church; it was in crisis due in part to confusion about the woman's role as mediator of religious truth. Rules that were harsher than normal were needed to give these women an opportunity to learn and submit themselves to the true mediator of knowledge—Jesus Christ, as revealed in the Scriptures and the teaching of the apostles.

Key words. It is important that we understand the meaning of two key words: *hesuchia* (translated "silent" in many versions of 1 Timothy 2:12-13) and *authentein* (translated "to have authority" in verse 12).

According to widely respected Greek scholar W. E. Vine, the Greek word *hesuchia* denotes "quietness" or "tranquility arising from within."[8] He does not even list "silence" as a possible translation. Consistent with this definition, *hesuchia* is translated "quiet" in 2 Thessalonians 3:12 "Such persons we command and exhort to do their work quietly *[hesuchia]*" and 1 Timothy 2:2 ". . . so that we may lead a quiet *[hesuchia*, adjective form] and peaceable life" (NRSVB).

There is a world of difference between the absolute silence implied by the translations to which most of us have had access and the quiet tranquility that a more careful translation describes! We need to ask ourselves, Why would the translators make this kind of a word choice? What impact does a more accurate translation have on our understanding of the role of women?

The Greek word *authentein* presents us with a different kind of challenge. Although there are several other Greek words translated "authority" in the New Testament[9] this is the only time the Greek word *authentein* appears there. In cases like this it is common practice for translators to turn to secular literature of the same time period for further clues as to the meaning of such a rare word. However, in the case of the word *authentein*, it is not that easy; until this century, it was not found in any other works written around Paul's time! With this key word being so difficult to pin down, no wonder scholars have found the passage hard to understand.

Fortunately, recent scholarship has uncovered new information about this rarely used word. Greek scholars Richard and Catherine Kroeger offer a fascinating study of *authentein* based on their extensive research of ancient history and literature. By tracing this word through ancient documents, they have found that it had a wide range of meanings as follows:

1. to begin something, to be primarily responsible for a condition or action (especially murder)
2. to rule, to dominate
3. to usurp power or rights from another
4. to claim ownership, sovereignty, or authorship[10]

Furthermore, new sources in classical Greek literature demonstrate that *authentien* is often used to describe religious activity that was characterized by promiscuity and reversal of gender roles, sex and death mingled together in cultic practice, murder, and women claiming a monopoly on religious power (as among the Amazons). In addition they found several older dictionaries in which *authentien* is defined "to represent oneself as the author, originator, or source of something."[11] This definition is particularly interesting in light of the fact that in the ancient world of Asia minor, many viewed women as the ultimate source of life. These meanings put a whole new spin on 1 Timothy 2:12 as we consider how a more careful translation might clarify Paul's meaning.

Again, we ask ourselves, why would Paul, a scholarly writer, use such a rare word that carried with it such unpleasant connotations? If he meant to bar women from all legitimate authority, he could have used any of the other words that are much more straightforward in their meaning.

Grammatical structure. The grammatical structure of verse 12 is worthy of note. It contains three infinitives: to teach, *authentein*, and to be. The Kroegars suggest that the separation of "to teach" from the other infinitives (apparent in any Greek New Testament or interlinear) may indicate that one or more of these two infinitives deal with the content of a woman's teaching. They point out that Paul never uses the infinitive "to teach" without accompanying clarification as to the content of the teaching. In Pauline writing, the infinitive "to teach" is always accompanied by another verb that serves to sharpen its focus. For instance, in 1 Timothy 1:3-4 Paul says "instruct certain people not to teach any different doctrine nor occupy themselves with myths and endless genealogies." And in 1 Timothy he speaks of one who "teaches another doctrine and does not agree with the wholesome words of Christ." The verb "to teach" *(didaskein)* linked as it is to the verb *authentein* by the negative *oude* (meaning "nor") gives us the possibility that *authentein* serves to explain what *kind* of teaching is prohibited to women. An alternate translation would then be: "I do not permit a woman to teach nor represent herself as originator (or source) of man but she is to be peaceable."[12]

Putting It All Together

Since we understand from other Scriptures (such as 1 Corinthians 11:5) that women did pray and prophesy in church, Paul would be contradicting himself if he were saying that women could not teach or be in positions of authority "from now until forever. Amen." Additional information about historical context, meanings of key words, and grammatical structure helps us to understand that he was addressing the content of their teaching in direct response to the heresy that swirled around this fledgling church. He was also addressing the manner in which any new believers should learn—quietly and in submission to the authority of the Scripture.

This in itself was the start of something new. As we noted earlier, ordinarily Jewish women were not taught the Scripture. But now Paul is saying that women who were new to the faith should be encouraged to learn quietly[13] until they were ready to participate fully in the life of the church, as mature women such as Phoebe (Romans 16:1-2) and Priscilla (Acts 18:24-26) were already participating.

Translation is a complex process that all Bible scholars struggle with. When we bring the inspired Word of God over into another language, we face the difficulty of word equivilancy and cultural considerations. There is often a range of English words to choose from when translating particlular Greek words into English. The final word choice is left to the discretion of the translators. Additionally, in Greek sentence structure, the words are not in the order to which we are accustomed. This requires that the translator (again, at his discretion) arrange the words in an order that makes sense to the English reader. This is a process that is subjective, at best, and yet the order of words can have a significant impact on meaning. It is difficult for a translator to maintain objectivity; there is always the temptation to translate a passage to be consistent with the way one already sees life. When we consider that most translators have been men who have come out of societies that did not properly value women and some of their gifts, it is not so difficult to see how some of the more obscure words and passages could be translated with a bias.

Understanding the subjective elements of the translation process should, at the very least, make us cautious about developing an elaborate system of rules for gender relations based on words that have a range of possible meanings and passages that seem to be at odds with other Scriptures. Indeed, it should lead to a desire to explore any new evidence—such as the continuing discoveries made by linguists and translators—and trusting the Holy Spirit to lead us into truth.

Coming Out on the Other Side

It all sounds so clear now, so factual and convincing. But this whole process was never as "linear" as it sounds. Even as I journeyed theologically and intellectually, there was always an emotional side to the journey. Perhaps the fact that I was a preacher's kid and experienced my church almost as extended family made it extra difficult for me to ask the questions I needed to ask, to claim my beliefs and then live them out. Although many things were becoming clear, I was also aware that I had a lot to lose—respect (in my circles, people who believed in equality for women were considered to be liberal or worse!), ministry opportunity, and even relationships that didn't have the flexibility to accommodate my newfound freedom.

The awareness of what I had to lose caused me to hesitate, and the place in which I hesitated was a very dark valley indeed. It was full of the anger and fragmentation that comes when we do not live out of our core beliefs. I couldn't pray. I couldn't worship. All I could do was shout my questions and wrestle with the Scriptures and God himself.

And there was grief. Grief over a world that should have been and could have been, but wasn't—a world where a young woman could pour out her love for God in service with no thought to gender. Grief over the time I had spent, in the Psalmist's words, "as a beast before Thee," stewing rather than serving. Grief over my own mistakes and the mistakes of others as I went through this process of growth. And most of all, grief over the fact that I first came to know God through his church, and the church, at times, has terribly distorted the depiction of God's heart toward women.

Then, one spring afternoon in 1993, seven years after I had begun my search in earnest, the Holy Spirit spoke to me deep in my soul. The Spirit said, "I have spent years teaching you and leading you into truth. Now let that truth lead you out of this valley. It is time to stand for what you believe and never look back." If it had been any more clear it would have been audible.

So I left the valley to stand on the truth that the Holy Spirit had spoken to my heart: the truth that *women and men are equally sinful and yet equally redeemed for full participation in every facet of life, love, and service.* As painful as the process had been, how glad I was that I had taken the time to wrestle with God over these issues. For like Jacob who had wrestled with God's angel (Genesis 32:24), I walked away with the blessing of knowing where I stand in the presence God and people. Like Jacob, I have a painful place that is still sensitive, reminding me of the wrestling that I have done. But I wouldn't trade this part of my journey for anything because it has become a necessary part of growing in my love for God and continuing to serve him wholeheartedly. After all, it's hard to worship a God whom you do not feel free to serve.

Just How Important Is All This?

I must admit that I have very little patience for those who say, "This just isn't a major issue! We've got to get on to more important things." For those who want to know God more deeply and grow in relationship with him, what could be more important than knowing how God views us and whether or not we are free to serve him in the way that he calls us? Whether we realize it or not, the way we answer these questions affects all areas of life: self-esteem, emotions, relationships with husband, children, and parents, worship and service to God, and our view of ourselves at work and in society. It doesn't get any more foundational than that!

But I also believe that "this too shall pass." My parents just returned from a trip to Florida where they viewed pictures of ships on which slaves were brought to the United States from Africa. They described how the slaves were transported with their arms and legs tied, forced to lie flat on the deck like cords of wood. Of course, to those of us living in the 20th century this is a horrifying image, and I was reminded of how far we have come. Even though we still have a long way to go in rooting out racism, it is hard to imagine a time when such open brutality was accepted.

Similarly, I believe that there will come a day when women will enjoy their full rights as "sons" of God. And in that day, it will be hard to remember a time when anyone was barred from ministry or other life callings, simply because they were women.

Jesus said, "You will know the truth and the truth will set you free." History shows us that freedom never comes without a fight. But it does come.

FOR DISCUSSION

1. All of us begin collecting impressions of what it means to be male or female long before we learn how to evaluate their truthfulness. As a child, what were some of the impressions—both positive and negative—that you collected about what it means to be female? What were you taught about how God viewed you as a woman? What thoughts and feelings did you have about these impressions?

2. Now that you are an adult, do you agree or disagree with what you learned as a child about God's view of women and our place in his plan? Explain.

3. If a woman who was searching for the truth about God expressed her impression that "Christianity is male religion, written by men, for men, with a male God," how would you respond? How would you demonstrate your beliefs from your own experience of God and your understanding of the Scriptures?

4. Was there ever a time when you wanted to serve God in a particular way but others discouraged you because of your gender? How did you respond at the time? How would you respond now?

For Further Study
Kroeger, Richard and Catherine Clark. *I Suffer Not A Woman*. Grand Rapids, Mich.: Baker Book House, 1992.
Martin, Faith. *Call Me Blessed*. Grand Rapids, Mich.: Eerdmans, 1988.

Tucker, Ruth. *Women in the Maze*. Downers Grove, Ill.: InterVarsity Press, 1992.

Tucker, Ruth and Walter Leifeld. *Daughters of the Church*. Grand Rapids, Mich.: Zondervan, 1987.

Van Leeuwen, Mary Stewart. *Gender and Grace*. Downers Grove, Ill.: InterVarsity Press, 1990.

Notes

1. Linda Tschirhart Sanford and Mary Ellen Donovan, *Women and Self-Esteem* (New York: Penguin Books, 1984), p. 173.

2. You can read about these women in 1 Samuel 25, Judges 4–5, 2 Kings 22:14-20, Book of Esther, and Acts 18:24-26 respectively.

3. R. Ruth Barton, *Women Like Us: Wisdom for Today's Issues* (Wheaton, Ill.: Shaw Publishers, 1989).

4. Faith Martin, *Call Me Blessed* (Grand Rapids, Mich.: Eerdmans, 1988), p. 123.

5. Ruth A. Tucker, *Women in the Maze* (Downer's Grove, Ill.: InterVarsity, 1992), pp. 37-38.

6. L. E. Maxwell as quoted in Richard Clark and Catherine Clark Kroeger, *I Suffer Not Woman* (Grand Rapids, Mich.: Baker, 1992), p. 33.

7. Kroeger and Kroeger, *I Suffer Not a Woman*, p. 60.

8. W. E. Vine, Merrill F. Unger, William White, Jr., eds., *Vine's Expository Dictionary of Biblical Words* (Nashville: Thomas Nelson Publishers, 1985), p. 503.

9. *Huperoche,* meaning "preeminence, superiority, excellency"; *exousia* meaning "the right to exercise power"; *epitage* meaning "command, authority." From Vine's *Expository Dictionary of Biblical Words*.

10. Kroeger and Kroeger, *I Suffer Not a Woman*, p. 84.

11. Ibid., p. 102.

12. Ibid., p. 103.

13. The Kroegers note that the phrase "silence and submission" is a Near Eastern formula implying willingness to heed and obey instruction—in this case that instruction contained in the Word of God. Indeed, the rabbinic scholar himself was required to learn in silence as this was how one gained knowledge of God (*I Suffer Not a Woman*, pp. 75-76).

5

Games People Play

In a restaurant let your mate or date do the ordering. You may know more about vintage wine than the wine steward but if you are smart you'll let your man do the choosing and be ecstatic over his selection even if it tastes like shampoo.

Arlene Dahl

Do not lie to one another, seeing that you have stripped off the old self with its practices and have clothed yourselves with the new self, which is being renewed in knowledge according to the image of its creator.

Colossians 3:9-10, NRSVB

Bible stories can be surprising in their similarities to modern life. Take the example of Rebekah. She and her husband Isaac had twin sons, Esau and Jacob. Isaac preferred Esau because he was a hunter, and Rebekah favored Jacob perhaps because he stayed closer to home. This favoritism brought out the worst in everyone—especially Rebekah. She was determined that her favorite, Jacob, would get the blessing that rightfully belonged to Esau.[1] The Lord had already promised that this would be so (Genesis 25:23), but Rebekah, rather than waiting for God to fulfill his purposes, decided to help things along.

When Isaac was old, nearly blind, and ready to bestow his blessing on Esau, Rebekah sent Jacob to his father masquerading as Esau so that he would receive his brother's blessing. Jacob carried off the whole charade with precision. Shortly after Isaac had finished blessing Jacob, Esau returned from the fields ready to receive his blessing, and Isaac realized that there was something dreadfully wrong. He began to tremble violently (27:33) as his mind pieced together what had happened and he realized that he had irreversibly blessed the wrong son.

When Esau heard what had happened "he cried out with an exceedingly great and bitter cry, and said to his father, 'Bless me, even me also, O my father!' " But it was too late. Isaac had to give Esau the devastating news that his brother had come deceitfully and taken away his blessing. With gut-wrenching emotion Esau pleaded with his father to bless him with at least one blessing. Isaac did bless him but it was nothing like the blessing Esau should have received (27:39-40) and it did nothing to heal the wounds that Rebekah's and Jacob's manipulation had inflicted. Esau was so full of rage against Jacob that he purposed to kill him after Isaac's death. In order to protect Jacob, Rebekah sent him away until Esau's fury died down.

In a time and culture where women really had little power, Rebekah may have felt that this was the only way she could have influence; however, her manipulation cost her dearly. She lost her opportunity to trust God and see him come through with his best. She forfeited her own integrity. She failed to be an influence for good in the lives of those she loved. And she jeopardized every relationship that was important to her. As far as we know, when she sent Jacob away to escape Esau's murderous rage, it was the last time she saw her favored son.[2] And, in a turn of poetic justice, Jacob was deceived years later when his father-in-law-to-be gave him the wrong daughter as a bride (Genesis 29:15-30), which set off rivalry between sisters that embittered their home for decades.

Just Pretending?

Why is it that we often feel we have to resort to subtlety, indirectness, or even deceit to get what we want? As one woman shares, our schooling in the fine art of manipulation and pretending often begins at home:

In my family it was "unladylike" to say out loud what you wanted. I was admonished time and again that if someone wanted to give me something—candy, take me somewhere, read me a story, whatever—they would offer it of their own accord or just know that I wanted it. I got very good at hinting, pouting, and whining to get people to offer what I wanted without saying it straight out. Today as an adult, I've [been told] so many times, "Why can't you just say what you mean?[3]

We also receive strong messages from our culture encouraging us to pretend to be something we are not. Sometimes our efforts to "fit in" have disturbing results, as in the case of Linda, the forty-something woman who told me, "My husband has always been a quiet man and I've always been outgoing and involved. I enjoy being in the center of things, but I've learned to be quiet so that he can be the leader and my children can see that he is the head of our home."

I could hear the wistfulness in her voice as she talked about her accomplishments involving leadership and communication during her high school and young adult years. She wanted me to understand that those strengths were just as much a part of her as was this newly chosen "quietness." Although she intended for her comments and behavior to be respectful of her husband, it really communicated the opposite. I couldn't help thinking, *You mean the only way your husband can be a leader is for you to withhold your strength?* It just didn't seem honest. Did her husband know of the self-confessed sadness that surfaced every now and then when she remembered lost opportunites for personal development? He was a loving husband; how would he feel if he ever realized that the price of his development was his wife's atrophy?

As distressing as Linda's comments were, I could relate to her need to minimize her own strengths. I had done the same thing for years—in my own way. It was in a leadership class taught by the pastor of our church that I first began to realize what I was doing. All participants took the PERFORMAX (DISC) personality test in order to understand our leadership style better. We learned that according to this particular test, there are four personality types—D (dominant, type-A personality), I (influencing), S (steady), and C (compliant)—of which each of us has one as our primary type and another that is secondary.

The results of my test were unmistakable: I definitely had the high D, type-A personality. This wasn't exactly news to me; I was aware that my gifts and personality traits clustered around leadership. However, I had spent years trying to tone down that part of my personality. After all, what Christian woman wants to be called dominant when compliance and submissiveness are so much more highly valued in women? It took me a week to get over my embarrassment now that everyone knew my dreadful secret. My only comfort was the knowledge that most people in the class had guessed that I was a high I (influencing, inspirational) which seemed to me to be a lot more acceptable in a woman. I congratulated myself on the fact that I had done a pretty good job of hiding myself.

Psychologist Harriet Goldhor Lerner describes our socialization this way: "Pretending reflects deep prohibitions, real and imagined, against a more direct and forthright assertion of self. Pretending stems naturally from the false and constricted definitions of self that women often absorb without question. 'Pretending' is so closely associated with 'femininity' that it is, quite simply, what the culture teaches women to do."[4]

As an example of this, she quotes Arlene Dahl's book *Always Ask A Man:*

> The successful female never lets her competence compete with her femininity. Never upstage a man. Don't top his jokes even if you have to bite your tongue to keep from doing it. Never launch loudly into your own opinions on the subject . . . Instead draw out his ideas to which you can gracefully add your footnotes from time to time.[5]

By today's standards, this book (written in 1965) seems extreme. But before we dismiss it as a relic of bygone days, we need to realize that we have been influenced by it. If we are between thirty and forty years old, this was probably the thinking our mothers were imbibing as they modeled womanhood for us. Or if we are a little older, perhaps we were the ones reading these kinds of pronouncements and believing them for a while. If we weren't reading it from Arlene Dahl and similar authors, we may have picked it up in the Christian versions that followed closely on their heels. Versions that packed the double wallop of conventional feminine wisdom plus theological backing.

Take, for instance, these instructions from a popular book written for women on the subject of marriage. From Ephesians 5 ("For the husband is the head of the wife just as Christ is the head of the church.") the author teaches

If you have . . . assumed the role of leadership in your home, you can begin to ease out of it by gradually transferring to your husband the responsibilities he will most easily accept. . . . he will very likely enjoy the ego-boosting experience of taking charge and having you and the children follow his advice or decisions.[6]

From 1 Peter 3:7 ("Husbands . . . pay honor to the woman as the weaker sex") she extrapolates that a man is to be our "umbrella of protection" from hard tasks (moving furniture, building fences, doing carpentry) as well as from physical and sexual attacks, concluding that "when you try to develop the ability to protect yourself, you endanger your femininity."[7]

Her application continues with the explanation that

When you assume responsibilities that belong to your husband, you often encounter situations that subject you to undue emotional pressure. . . . You may mishandle situations because you are so upset, and . . . end up behaving like a shrew. This is often the case when you must deal with offensive salesmen, belligerent creditors, irritable neighbors, or even your own inconsiderate teenagers.

Your husband is to serve as a protective agent between you and such pressures. . . . [S]imply say, "I'll speak to my husband about it." It's his problem, not yours. Isn't that comforting?[8]

All that from one verse! Where does this leave single women? Furthermore, what impact does it have on a woman to believe that she can't handle stressful situations without turning into a shrew? With this kind of teaching, is it any wonder that we don't know how to offer our God-given strength to others or how to tell someone else what we need or want, that we resort to manipulation rather than the fresh wind of truth-telling?

God's Alternative to Playing Games

Authentic relationships provide some of the greatest joys and deepest feelings of fulfillment that we can experience in this life. "We yearn for relationships where we can be completely honest, open and vulnerable. Where we can share failures as well as successes, shortcomings as well as strengths. Where we can reveal doubts and fears. Where we can find empathy and confidentiality."[9]

Sometimes, in our desire to cultivate such relationships, we opt for peace at any price because it seems less risky. Somehow it even seems more "Christian" to hide the truth about ourselves, to deny feelings, and to overlook offenses in an effort to avoid rocking the boat. However, when we skirt the truth and play games, the depth that we long for in our relationships will never develop.

From the Scriptures we learn that the key to deep and meaningful relationships is truth-telling. It is only as we speak the truth in love that we grow up in relation to others, that we become knit together with them, and that each person offers their unique strength to the process of working together (Ephesians 4:15). But unfortunately, game-playing comes more naturally to us as human beings than truth-telling. Why? Because telling the truth is scary, especially in relationships in which truth has not been the pattern. We might think:

If I told my boss that I don't appreciate his suggestive comments, I could get passed over for a promotion.

If I told my parents that it still bothers me that they were too busy for me, they would get mad and deny it.

If I told my friend that some of her comments hurt me, she would just think I am overly sensitive.

If I admitted to my small group that I was really struggling, they wouldn't think I was very spiritual.

If I told my husband that I would like to pursue some of my own interests, he would panic.

If I admitted how disturbed I am over the fact that we don't have any women elders at church, everyone would think I'm a feminist.

Yes, truth-telling can be frightening, but the alternative is much worse. When we cannot bring ourselves to tell the truth in our relationships, they will stay at a surface level at best; it is even more likely that they will deteriorate and die. Misunderstandings arise but are never resolved. Feelings beg to be shared but are left to fester inside. Offenses occur but nobody talks about them. Our true personalities are hidden and never invited to flourish in the warmth of acceptance. Avoidance patterns set in. Hurt and misunderstanding lead to detachment, distrust, and bitterness. And love begins to die.

A realistic look at the results of game-playing motivates us to take courage in hand and cultivate greater levels of truth in our relationships.

Truth in the Inward Being

Truth-telling begins with telling *ourselves* the truth. Psalm 51:6 reminds us that God desires truth in the inward being—truth about our beliefs and doubts, truth about what is happening in our relationships, truth about how we feel, what bothers us, and how we need to change. It also includes telling God the truth, for as we are learning to speak truthfully with God, we begin being more honest with ourselves. The experience of talking to Someone who loves us unconditionally, coupled with the deep work of the Holy Spirit (his job, after all, is to lead us into truth) causes things to become clearer and leads us to greater honesty with ourselves.

It is fascinating to observe the healing powers of truth-telling in the life of David. In Psalm 73, for example, he is consumed by jealousy toward wicked people whose lives seem to be going so well while he, a man who is trying to live a godly life, seems to have one problem after another. He rages on and on for fourteen verses, laying it all out before God. Finally, in the quiet that usually follows a true catharsis, God showed him a bigger picture, a picture that included a long-range perspective ("Then I perceived their end . . . how they are destroyed in a moment"), self-knowledge ("I was like a beast toward you"), and heightened spiritual awareness ("There is nothing on earth that I desire other than you. My flesh and my heart may fail, but God is the strength of my heart") (NRSVB). No wonder David concluded that "for me it is good to be near God" for it was in his most honest moments that God was able to teach him wisdom "in my secret heart" (Psalm 51:6). And so it is with us.

Telling Our True Stories

Sometimes the hardest truth to tell ourselves and others is the truth about our experiences as women. So much of our literature, history, political context, and religious beliefs have been written and developed from a male perspective that we struggle to find a voice of our own—to talk about life the way we see it. We listen to male translators telling us "what the Bible really says," male pastors and authors telling us how we should feel about being mothers, male doctors telling us how to be sexually fulfilled, and male psychologists telling us what it means to be "healthy." We accept the roles assigned to us and believe it when we are told there must be something wrong with us if we're not satisfied with them. But every so often we wonder: *Why doesn't this fit for me? Why is mothering such a struggle for me? Why do I do I feel "less* than" in my family, church, or my work? Why am I uncomfortable going to a man for pastoral care? Why does fitting into the role carved out for me seem like shoving a square peg into a round hole? And why don't we hear the stories about all the brave, strong things women have done for God and humankind? Why are their struggles and triumphs saved for the women's coffee hour?

When questions like these surface for ourselves or for others, it seems much safer to silence them with thoughts or words like, Don't be ridiculous. This is what's best for us—everybody says so! But where is "truth in the inward being" if we don't give ourselves and others the freedom to ask our truest questions, to raise a hand (however timidly) and say, "Maybe that works for you, but my experience, my story, is very different."

It is hard to tell the truth when all the voices around us seem to be saying something different. I know because I've tried it. The hardest truth I ever told myself or God or my husband or my fellow Christians was how much it was hurting me to be a woman among many evangelical Christians. From my pre-teen years onward, I knew that there was something terribly wrong with the way many church people viewed women—and it was tearing my soul apart. But the truth I was trying to tell about myself and my questions was labeled "rebellion" almost as soon as it was uttered, so I quickly retrieved it and stuffed it down for a little while longer.

It took me years to come right out and say that I just didn't believe all that I had been taught about "a woman's place" in marriage and in the church, that I saw something different when I read the Scriptures. But how does a woman go about exploring the reality of her experiences when everyone around her says she is wrong and "shouldn't feel that way"? Or when other women insist that their lives are completely fulfilling and the whole system is working for them?

At the time I believed that other women really were as satisfied as they said they were, but now I know that there were those who also struggled. Some kept a stiff upper lip in public and cried their bitter tears alone. Some tried to tell their stories to "the powers that be" but found that they were never really heard.

(Ever since the Anita Hill/Clarence Thomas hearings, I understand that phenomenon much better.) Others melted away quietly from Christian fellowships, not always sure of the forces at work against them but knowing they would die inside if they stayed. The few brave souls who refused to be silenced had been so completely excised that I was only aware of them to the extent that they had been labeled liberal and dangerous. Understandably, I felt very much alone in my turmoil—as though I were the strange one.

It wasn't until I was grown and well established in ministry that women began to tell me their true stories. A fifty-ish woman who had taught with passion "wives submit to your husbands in all things" cried on my couch about a husband who made major life decisions without even consulting her. A single woman told me about having ministry opportunities withheld because she didn't have a man to team with. Several gifted women communicators told me about their rage and tears over being silenced in the church but asked me not to quote them because they feared the consequences of such honesty. A middle-aged woman admitted that her whole identity had been wrapped up in her children and now that they were gone, she was struggling desperately to keep depression at bay. A new Christian cornered me after a church service and asked in hushed tones, "Could you tell me why we don't have any women pastors or elders? I mean, I love our pastors but I could never go to one of them if I needed to talk about a problem." A young married woman told me her story of a husband who hit her when he got mad and a counselor who said, "You must be doing something to make him do that." And well into my married life, my own mother began to realize that wifely submission—as it had been taught in her generation— was an inadequate foundation for healthy relationships.

Why hadn't I heard these true stories when I needed them most? When I needed to know that my questions were legitimate and my unfolding story wasn't so unusual after all? Who was benefitting from this conspiracy of silence? And where is wholeness and integrity when you believe something and uphold it on an intellectual level but on an experiential level, you know it doesn't work?

It is very difficult to challenge what has already been accepted in society as the whole truth. Carol Gilligan, in her book, *In a Different Voice*, demonstrates the impact of this problem in the field of psychology. She notes that psychological theory has been developed largely from the study of males so that women never seem to fit existing models of human growth. Rather than recognizing the imbalance in the studies, experts have assumed that the problem was with women's development.

Harriet Goldhor Lerner puts it this way, "Once something is defined as unfeminine or gender inappropriate, the old rules cannot easily be challenged. When women differ from the theories, the exceptions only prove rather than probe the rule, and it is the woman—not the theories—who are brought into question. Women are still trying to fit into the predominant theories of the day rather than the other way around."[10] This at least partially explains why it can be frightening to present a different view than what is normally accepted; there is always the very distinct possiblity that someone will say, "The problem is not with the way things are; the problem is you."

Additionally, "females in our culture are reinforced in their avoidance of their own power. Not openly expressing dissent (or a different view of reality) is applauded as being cooperative, and not risking hurting others is seen as being self-sacrificial . . . For men, being seen as outspoken is not felt as pejoratively, as it is for women."[11]

So you see, there are very real reasons that we find it so hard to speak the truth about our experiences and questions. Yet truth, integrity, and wholeness call to us just like fresh air calls to us on a spring day. Integrity or wholeness is a strong theme in the Bible. William Backus points out that integrity as it is used in verses such as Proverbs 20:7 ("The righteous walk in integrity"(NRSVB) means manifesting in life and words the truth a person knows in her heart. When she knows the truth about what is in her heart and then allows that truth to surface, she has integrity.

The word *integrity* comes from the Latin *integer* meaning a whole number, not a fraction. The concept behind integrity is wholeness. When a person is the same without and within, when what others know about her is the same as what she knows about herself, she has integrity. When someone knows the truth about herself and and tries to hide it from others, she lacks integrity.[12] (feminine pronouns mine)

When we lack a true understanding of ourselves and are afraid to show others who we really are, we end up "faking it" much of the time, which leads to the kinds of manipulation already discussed in this chapter.

When we do work up the courage to be honest with ourselves and with others, there is the possibility that it will lead to a "crisis of faith" or, as Bill Hybels calls it, "the tunnel of chaos" in our relationship with God, with others, and within ourselves. It certainly did for me. At times my own truth-telling took the form of angry shouting, lots of crying, unbelievable sadness, frenzied studying (because I just had to know), and admitting (much more than I wanted to) that I just *didn't* know. It tested my relationships to their limit. But God was deeper than the abyss I thought I was falling into, faith was stronger than my fears, and I did come out on the other side. When I first went into the tunnel of chaos ("where hurts are unburied, hostilities revealed, and tough questions asked"[13]), I wasn't sure there would be anything on the other side.

But I found that, even though it sometimes feels like I have more questions than answers, the air is clearer on the other side of the tunnel (life is pretty hazy when we're not telling the truth) and the world is bigger, so big that at times I can't get my arms around it (truth is, after all, bigger than any of us). And I am more alive—spiritually, intellectually, emotionally, relationally—than I have ever been. That's what telling the truth does to you in the inward being.

Telling Each Other the Truth

Telling ourselves and each other the truth—about who we are, how we feel, what we know, what we're questioning, what is working and what is tearing us apart in relationships and life— well, it takes raw courage at times. And it takes courage plus diligence and discipline to bring that kind of honesty into our everyday communications.

Psychologist William Backus points out that

> our customs of speech frequently skirt the truth! We say, "I'd love to have you come," when we don't want the other person to come at all. We say, "Your wishes are all that matter to me," and then get angry when the other person tells us honestly what he wants. We hide what we really want and then act cross when others fail to discern our heart's desires. We fear honest refusals so we agree to do things we dislike. We explain to others why we simply must do something when the truth is we want to do it and there is no must to it. We manipulate others with expressions intended to arouse guilt before God, when our real motive is to control their behaviour.
>
> Is it any wonder our relationships often hang by a thread? Or that our attempts at communication don't work? Is it any wonder nobody really knows us? Or that we can't be as close to other human beings as we can to our dogs and cats? The truth can set relationships free, as it can set the individual free . . . Not harsh truth, but truth spoken in love.[14]

A good place to begin the journey toward greater truth in our relationships is to police ourselves for accuracy in our everyday communications. We can learn to let go of manipulative and less-than-honest communication patterns in favor of a more honest, straightforward approach. For instance:

- Instead of indirect communication such as dropping hints and "shoulding" ("You should stop watching so much T.V.") we can choose a more direct approach: "I am really concerned about how much time the T.V. is on in our home: it seems to keep us from spending time talking, reading, etc. Would you be willing to discuss setting some limits on the television?"

- Instead of "guilting" ("After all I do for you, the least you could do is . . . ") we can be honest about our feelings of being unappreciated ("Sometimes I feel like I do so much for you but then when I need help, you're too busy. You probably don't mean it that way, but that's the way I'm feeling right now").

- Instead of withholding ourselves by administering the silent treatment, pouting, or making ourselves unavailable sexually, we can talk about what is going on in the relationship ("I don't like it when you criticize me in public as you did today. It makes it very difficult for me to open up to you").

- Instead of intimidating, exaggerating, or issuing ultimatums ("If you do that again, I'm quitting!") we can say something that is more honest and realistic ("I am not willing to be verbally abused just to keep my job. If you do not stop, I will need to speak to our supervisor").

- Instead of secretly enlisting the help of others in pushing our agenda ("I just can't get through to my husband on this. Do you think you could talk to him about . . . ?") we can say directly to him, "Since we seem to be stuck on this issue, would you be willing for the two of us to get help from a counselor?"

- Instead of telling those little white lies ("Sure, it will be no problem to take care of your kids this afternoon" when you know it could just put you over the edge) we can tell the truth: "I wish I could help you out, but I don't think I'd better take that on this afternoon."

- Instead of faking sexual enjoyment we could say, "I'm really committed to having a great sex life with you and that's why I need to tell you that this just isn't working for me. Could we try something else?"

At first these new communication patterns may feel as uncomfortable as a new pair of shoes but the more we walk in them, the more comfortable they will become. Intimacy, trust, and kinship will grow because when we feel hurt, rather than withdrawing and losing closeness, we will talk about it, gain insight, and establish new patterns that protect love. When we say, "Yes, I would love to!" others won't have to ask "Are you sure?" because they will know they can trust what we say. And when, in the process of speaking truthfully, we get glimpses of the true selves that are often hiding behind facades we will experience connection with fellow human beings that is unspeakably fulfilling.

When the Truth Is Hard to Hear

Of course, the other side of our being "direct and forthright" is that we welcome others to be just as honest with us. We need to demonstrate that authenticity and growth in our relationships are more important than the personal comfort that can only be maintained through denial and defensiveness. We need to accept honest refusals when they are given. And we need to listen and receive others in the manner in which we want to be listened to and received.

This lesson was probably never more poignantly learned than the day I deeply offended some of the women in my church with comments I made during a Sunday service. Speaking on the topic of "heroes" I made the point that heroes are often people we look up to because they have succeeded in areas in which we would like to succeed. To illustrate my point, I mentioned a Christian author whose teaching on womanhood and marriage I had respected until she had gotten a divorce. I mentioned that I no longer looked up to her in the way that I used to.

One women who had gone through a divorce was so angry that she couldn't wait until the service was over to speak with me. She left her seat to request in whispered tones that we step into the hallway to talk. Then, her voice trembling with emotion, she said, "Do you have any idea what it was like to sit there with my children and listen to what you said today? I have worked so hard to regain my dignity after my divorce, to create a stable life for my children and to find my place here in this church. Then to have you get up there and say that you didn't think you had anything to learn from someone like me! I had hoped that you could respect me and maybe learn something from my mistakes. And those of us who have gone through a divorce—well, we would like to be married again someday—and we would like to be able to learn from those of you who are still married about how to make a marriage work."

There was more, but I think you get the idea. It was a painful experience, but—praise God!—the first thing that happened (after I told myself to calm down and just listen) was that I saw myself in this dear woman.

I saw that her pain (of being viewed as "less than" in the church) was very similar to the pain I had experienced in the church all these years. The fact that I had been honest about the pain in my life made me much more sensitive to hers. I too had been an outsider—a woman in a male-dominated system. Here she was, another outsider (a divorced woman in a system that valued women who had managed to stay married) trying to tell her story to one of those insiders (a married woman who happened to be in charge of the Women's Ministry). It was a story I needed to hear.

Of course I would have liked to defend myself, as anyone would, but there was no adequate defense. My comments had been thoughtless and insensitive; the fact that I hadn't meant them to be was completely beside the point. I needed to listen to her pain, to hear myself through her ears as she sat in the auditorium that day, and to tell her how sorry I was. I needed to tell her that yes, there was a lot I could learn from her and the struggles she had been through. In fact, I was already learning.

I shed tears that day. Some were tears of disappointment in myself for making such a hurtful mistake, some were tears for the women who came to church that day hoping for a word that would minister grace to their souls but instead received a barb. But there were also tears of gratefulness that this friend (and friend she was) didn't let me walk out the door ignorant of the pain I had caused, doomed to inflict it again at some other time and place.

I was honored that, rather than letting our relationship go the way of churning anger that would eventually cool into a numb distance, she struggled with the truth of her experience and then offered it to me. In that moment, I knew that even though the externals of our lives were so different, we were sisters who had many similarities. I knew that here was a friendship full of integrity—that when the truth needed to be told, this relationship could handle it. And I knew that the experience of hearing and being heard—of having affect and being affected—was very rich for both of us that day, richer than any word I could have spoken from any podium.

A Richer Life Experience

The struggle toward truth-telling is at the center of our deepest longing for intimacy with others. It is not that we have to tell everything, or tell it all at once, or even know beforehand all we need to tell. But an honorable relationship is one in which we are trying all the time to extend the possibilities of truth—and life—between us.[15] The point is not merely to get what we want (although that may very well happen). The goal of truth-telling is greater personal integrity and wholeness, life-giving intimacy with others, and the richness that comes when we accept the differences in experience that many people bring to our society, as well as to the body of Christ.

There is a power that comes from saying what we believe and believing what we say. This is the strength we have to offer our world. When we give that up, we become fragmented at our very core. It is painful and exhausting for a woman to begin to uncover the truth of her own experiences in a culture that has given more importance to what men think, feel, and say. But the relationships, the Christian communities, and the social/political structures worth having require that we engage in this difficult yet rewarding process. As people of integrity, we cannot settle for anything less.

FOR DISCUSSION

1. Can you think of a situation in which you felt that the only way to get what you wanted was to be manipulative? What was the result of your manipulation?

2. "Men who stand up for themselves are [seen as] competent and assertive; women who do the same are obnoxious and aggressive."[16] Do you agree or disagree with this statement? How comfortable do you feel about your strength at home, at church, at work?

3. Identify a relationship in which you need to do more truth-telling either in your every day communication patterns, regarding your life-experiences, or regarding issues that affect your relationship. What fears do you have about taking this step? What steps are you willing to take to achieve authenticity in this relationship?

4. Is there a true question, a lingering doubt, something you know about yourself (but have been hesitant to look at) that you need to explore in order to achieve more "truth in the inward being"? Who or what could help you with this exploration? Are you willing to pursue truth in this area?

For Further Study

Backus, William. *Telling Each Other the Truth*. Minneapolis: Bethany House. 1985.

Backus, William & Chapian, Marie. *Telling Yourself the Truth*. Minneapolis: Bethany House. 1980.

Hybels, Bill. *Honest to God?* Grand Rapids, Mich.: Zondervan. 1990.

Lerner, Harriet Goldhor. *The Dance of Deception*. New York: Harper-Collins, 1993.

Schaeff, Anne Wilson. *Women's Reality*. San Francisco: Harper & Row, 1981, 1985.

Notes

1. In Bible times, the blessing was like an oral will that was legally binding and could not be revoked. Each child usually received a blessing, but the oldest son got a special one that included prosperity, headship over his family, and divine judgment on those who opposed him. In the case of Esau, his father's blessing would also include the privilege of having God's promise to Abraham ("I will make you the father of a multitude of nations." Genesis 17:4-5) fulfilled through him.

2. It was assumed that Rebekah died during Jacob's long absence and was buried in the cave of Machpelah near Hebron (Genesis 49:31). Herbert Lockyer, *All the Women of the Bible* (Grand Rapids, Mich.: Zondervan), p. 140.

3. Linda Tschirhart Sanford and Mary Ellen Donovan, *Women and Self-Esteem* (New York: Penguin Books, 1984), p. 44.

4. Harriet Goldhor Lerner, *The Dance of Deception* (New York: Harper-Collins, 1993), p. 14.

5. Ibid., p. 49

6. Darien Cooper, *You Can Be the Wife of a Happy Husband* (Wheaton, Ill.: Victor Books, 1980), p. 77.

7. Ibid., p. 70.

8. Ibid., p. 74.

9. Bill Hybels, *Honest to God?* (Grand Rapids, Mich.: Zondervan, 1990), p. 51.

10. Lerner, *The Dance of Deception*, p. 56.

11. Carolyn Stahl Bohler, *When You Need to Take a Stand* (Louisville, Kent.: Westminster/John Knox Press, 1990), p. 63.

12. William Backus, *Telling Each Other the Truth* (Minneapolis: Bethany House, 1985), p. 26.

13. Hybels, *Honest to God?* p. 56.

14. Backus, *Telling Each Other the Truth*, pp. 16-17.

15. Lerner, *The Dance of Deception*, p. 218.

16. Anne Wilson Schaeff, *Women's Reality* (San Francisco: Harper & Row, 1981), p. 74.

6

The "Never-Enough" World

The trouble with being in the rat-race, is that even if you win you're still a rat.

Lily Tomlin

When my husband and I were first married and living in a small apartment, I thought that if we could just buy a house I would be satisfied. We had married right out of college and started our family shortly thereafter so the dream of owning a home seemed far off indeed. But miracles do still find their way into modern life: some acquaintances, who needed to sell a home they owned quickly, offered to help us with the downpayment. Consequently, we became proud homeowners much sooner than we had expected. Even though it was a modest, three-bedroom ranch in need of decorating and repair, it felt so good to have space! To walk out our front door into a grassy yard rather than a dank hallway seemed like heaven on earth. For the privilege of owning a home I could live with peeling paint, yellow and green wallpaper, and an outdated kitchen.

Or could I?

It didn't take long for me to realize that I'm not that easily satisfied. I was fine as long as the first flush of purchasing excitement lasted. But pretty soon, desire began to overtake me again. If we could just replace the shag carpeting, get rid of the avocado appliances, remodel the kitchen . . . then I'd be satisfied.

Well, here it is ten years later, we've done all those things (and more!) and I've made a startling realization: It doesn't matter how much we buy, there is always plenty more I want. The pull of things in my life is so deep and so strong that, at times, I have despaired of ever being free of it. I am very much a part of the "never-enough" world and chances are, so are you.

Exposing Culture's Hidden Messages

Do you ever wonder why, even though you understand the dangers of debt, you spend money that you don't have? Or why, when you are lonely or depressed, it seems to help to go shopping? Why, before the paint is even dry on one remodeling project, you are plotting the next one? Why you feel so much more credible when you're wearing full make-up and a business suit than when you're wearing a jogging suit and the face God gave you? Or why your husband feels that he can never satisfy your material wants? I wonder about myself sometimes, especially when my daughter comments (with perceptivity beyond her years), "Daddy works so Mommy can buy the things she wants."

There are reasons that, with all that we have in life, it seems there are so many more things things we just can't live without. In the never-enough world, the twin gospels of materialism and consumerism are preached nearly every time we open a magazine, turn on the television, or talk to a neighbor. Materialism[1] lulls us into believing that the physical, material world is the most "real" while consumerism, the dominant economic theory in America, entices us with the idea that the accumulation of more and better things is a worthy goal for our lives. Mix in a little religious flavoring and you get the idea that material things provide the answers to life's basic questions. **What am I worth?** The most expensive hair color. **What is success?** Being able to buy my husband dinner with my own credit card. **How do I find peace of mind?** Buy more insurance. **How do I show someone how much I love them?** Send them "the very best" greeting card. **And what do I do when the going gets tough?** Go shopping, of course.

Materialism and consumerism dovetail in their promises that if we can just achieve a higher income level, get our dream house, wear the right clothes, and enjoy the right kinds of leisure activities we will be satisfied. But these two outlooks often produce families that are unable to get off the treadmill because they are deeply in debt . . . parents who have no time for each other or their children . . . families with nicer things than their parents had at that age but little time to enjoy them . . . men and women who know how to dress for success but are full of inner doubts and questions.

Alongside our many acquisitions exists a profound sense of dissatisfaction that is never quelled for very long.

Always Consuming, Never Satisfied

Vance Packard, in *The Hidden Persuaders*, documents that, as Americans, we are programmed to "consume, consume, consume, whether we need or even desire the products almost forced upon us."[2]

He describes the situation after World War II in which American manufacturers were able to produce many more goods than people were consuming. The question that goods producers then began to explore was, "How can we stimulate the American people to buy more?" They tackled this question by engaging sociologists and psychologists to teach them how to stimulate consumer buying by creating wants in people that they didn't realize existed. These trainers, who called themselves "motivation researchers," taught merchandisers to probe people's subsurface desires, needs, and drives in order to find their points of vulnerability. What the merchandisers identified were the very deepest human longings: our longings for love, our dreams of fitting in and "being somebody," our desire for power, and our need for emotional security. "Once these points of vulnerability were isolated, the psychological hooks were fashioned and baited and placed deep in the merchandising sea for unwary customers."[3]

The way they began to "hook" us was to offer considerably more than the actual item involved. Consider the psychological hooks in a remarkable piece of marketing that came to our house a few weeks ago. It arrived in a beautiful 8½" by 11" envelope gilded in silver. Inside was a letter from a marketing vice-president inviting us to test drive any one of the luxury cars pictured in the enclosed brochure (which, by the way, was so exquisitely done that I felt privileged to receive one!).

On the cover of this mini-catalogue was a single quote: "The automobile we choose to drive represents our station in life . . . the level we have achieved in our profession or business." (That sure piqued my interest: I wanted to know what it said about us that we were driving a red mini-van with wood grain on the side and an eight-year-old Celebrity that has no radio and tends to rust.)

I quickly opened to the first page, which pictured the front bumper of a Lincoln. "Finally, a luxury car you deserve" it told me. (What happens if I can't afford what I am told I deserve?) On the succeeding pages it pictured several top-of-the-line Lincolns along with pictures of sophisticated couples in tuxedos and evening dresses. (Read: If you buy this car you will be all dressed up with some place to go.) The ad copy proclaimed that these cars offer "luxuries you may not have thought of" (how will I live without the luxuries I haven't even thought of?), the opportunity to drive a car that is "always seen as the one driven by those who know luxury" (I certainly want people to be aware that I know luxury when I see it!), the promise of always being "at ease because you drive with the priceless luxury of peace of mind" (So that's where you get peace of mind!) All this plus the assurance that environmental concerns were taken into consideration (Oh good, I can also be politically correct!).

If I actually believed all this—that I deserved this car, that it is symbolic of a successful life, that it would give me peace of mind—the fact that we can't buy it would be pretty depressing. Obviously, these manfacturers are selling much more than a car; they are "selling to our hidden needs" quite unashamedly.

It is important for us to realize that a lack of contentment is now a part of our American cultural fabric. Manufacturers depend on the consumer (you and me) to be dissatisfied so that we will buy more and thus stimulate the economy. As one ad executive proclaims, "What makes this country great is the creation of wants and desires, the creation of dissatisfaction with the old and outmoded."[4] So, if you are dissatisfied, it is a sure sign that you were born in the U.S.A.!

However, there is hope; we are not doomed to being eaten alive by insatiable desire. The more we understand the messages of consumerism and materialism the more we are able to spot their lies and free ourselves from their tyranny. Rather than being manipulated by these messages on a subconscious level, we will be able to "decode them by trying to cut through the layers of alibis, half-truth and image to get to the facts beneath."[5] It is only then that we are in a position to make real choices.

Great Expectations

To make matters worse, those of us who are Baby Boomers have a propensity toward materialism just because of when we were born. Landon Jones, researcher on the baby boom phenomenon, observes: "For most of human history, people had thought that life was hard, brutal and tragic. The baby boom's early affluence [in the post-war years of the 50s and 60s] developed within it what some have called 'the psychology of entitlement.' What other generations had thought privileges, the baby boomers thought were rights."[6]

In the words of author Mike Bellah, we are a generation of overexpecters—

those who think we deserve something we really do not. We baby boomers were raised to believe we deserved a college education—for us and for our children—whether we could afford it or not. We deserved a secure retirement. We deserved the best medical care. We deserved a nice home in the suburbs.

We deserved not just the pursuit of happiness. We deserved to be happy.[7]

How many of us see ourselves in that description? I've grown to expect that the "starter home" in which we live now is just that—a stepping stone along the way to something bigger. But recently I've had to ask myself, "Who says?" There are people all over the world and right here in our own inner cities who live with their extended families in small apartments. They never "expect" even to own a home let alone the Brady Bunch type on which I and so many of my fellow baby boomers have our hearts set. Today in my suburb, homes like that cost between $200,000-$300,000. Who says life owes that to me?

One Woman's Story

Although there are unique factors influencing us today, our struggles with attachment to things is not really new. The Bible tells us of a woman who was so attached to her things that it spelled major disaster for her and her family. We do not know the name of this woman but we know that she was married to Lot, the nephew of Abraham. When Abraham received his call from God to leave his homeland and go "to the land that I will show you," Lot accompanied him because his own father had died. Once in the land of Canaan they found that, because of the size of their herds, the land could not sustain them both. They decided to separate.

Abraham, even though he was the elder of the two men, graciously offered to give Lot first pick of the land, stating that he would then go in the opposite direction. Lot, evaluating the land purely for it's materialistic value ("he saw that the plain of Jordan was well watered everywhere like the garden of the Lord") chose the best land for himself. What he failed to take into consideration was that it was bordered by the notoriously sinful cities of Sodom and Gommorrah. Little did he realize the impact that living close to Sodom would eventually have on his family and his life. He thought that what he could see—the well-watered plain of Jordan—was all that was real in this situation. He didn't realize that the story would not end with him merely pitching his tent close to Sodom (Genesis 13:12). Indeed, it wouldn't be long before he moved right into Sodom (Genesis 14:12), married a woman from there, and became embroiled in it's wars, sexual perversion, and violence.

The Bible tells us that Lot was a righteous man whose soul was vexed by the filthy lives of the Sodomites. But he was a soul divided. Even though he was deeply disturbed by what was going on around him, "He liked the good life of Sodom's society. He preferred making money off its citizens to staying in the hills where there would be no filthy living but also no 'good life.'"[8] But there was a terrible price to pay for this indulgence, for rather than acting as an influence for good, Lot lost his own moral moorings.

The moment of truth came, as it always does, when the evil and sin of Sodom and Gomorrah became so great that God decided to destroy them. As a favor to Abraham, God sent two angels to remove Lot and his family before the whole place went up in flames. When the two men arrived at the city gates where Lot sat as an elder, he invited them to stay in his home for the night.

During the night, the Sodomite men became inflamed with homosexual desire for the handsome strangers they had seen come into town earlier in the evening. Every last man in the city, young and old, surrounded Lot's house, demanding that he surrender his guests. In an effort to placate them, Lot offered to bring his virgin daughters to the Sodomite men so they could "do to them as you please" (Genesis 19:8, NRSVB). This was the level to which this "righteous man" had sunk. The men of the city took Lot's offer as an expression of judgment on their sexual practices and became enraged to the point of violence. The angels then had to use supernatural force to draw Lot back into the house and cause blindness among the men of the city in order to ensure their safety for the night.

One would think that an incident like this would be enough to convince any God-fearing man that this was not a suitable place to live and bring up a family. But amazingly enough, the next morning when the angels informed Lot that "we are about to destroy this place, because the outcry against its people has become great before the Lord," Lot lingered. When he tried to rouse his family to leave by describing the impending doom, they just laughed in his face. They were so attached to their life in Sodom—their home, their luxuries, their pleasures—that they didn't care about what it was doing to them on any other level. They didn't realize that their moral standards, their personal integrity, and their spiritual vitality had been draining away day by day. Now that their very existence was being threatened, they couldn't comprehend that either.

Finally ("the Lord being merciful to him"), the angels grabbed Lot, his wife, and their two daughters by the hand and physically forced them to leave. In no uncertain terms they warned, "Flee for your life; do not look back or stop anywhere in the Plain; flee to the hills, or else you will be consumed" (Genesis 19:17, NRSVB). As they hurried to safety, Sodom and Gomorrah and the entire plain in which these cities were located were consumed by fire and sulfur. But Lot's wife, trailing behind, looked back and was overtaken by sulpherous vapors. Encrusted with salt, she died there on the plain, captured in the pose that symbolized her attachment to the wealth, society, and sin that had been her whole life.

We are not left to wonder about what was in the heart of Lot's wife that day. Christ himself interprets this story for us. When teaching his disciples about the coming of the kingdom of God, he warns them about being so caught up in the material world that they are out of touch with spiritual realities. As an example he mentions the people living in Lot's day, specifically Lot's wife:

> Just as it was in the days of Lot: they were eating and drinking, buying and selling, planting and building [in other words, completely caught up in the material world], but on the day that Lot left Sodom, it rained fire and sulfur from heaven and destroyed all of them—it will be like that on the day that the Son of Man is revealed. On that day, anyone on the housetop

who has belongings in the house must not come down to take them away; and likewise anyone in the field must not turn back. Remember Lot's wife. (Luke 17:28-32, NRSVB)

Christ is instructing the disciples to remember Lot's wife as an example of one whose attachment to material things had anesthetized her to spiritual realities. She had lived for physical realities for so long that she was unaware of the decay in her soul. Even when she came face to face with impending doom, she was unable to disentangle herself from the hold that the material world had on her heart. Her treasures were in Sodom and with them, her loyalty and affection. So she looked back and it spelled her destruction.

It would be tempting to distance ourselves from this woman with protests like "I don't know her. I don't understand her. I would never . . . " But we do know her; she is our sister and we share with her the same tendency to be deeply enamored with the things that we can see and physically know. Our doom may not be as sudden or dramatic as hers but we are in just as much danger.

Beware of the Dangers

"Credit ruined my marriage, my self-image, and our family's future," a more contemporary woman shares. "It was a dreadful spiral that almost led to the loss of our home."

She first applied for credit to pay off her overspending on Christmas presents. She was amazed at how easy it was to obtain credit and how accommodating the company was in hiding the loan from her husband:

Not only did I get it (cash in hand the following day!) but they also agreed to use my office address rather than my home address, so the deception began. From time to time they offered me further funds which I was too weak to refuse and I had, by that time, also contracted with various stores for credit card debts as well. Soon it was completely out of control and I had to borrow further just to meet monthly payments.

The worse the problem became, the harder it was to tell her husband the truth; it was only when she was close to a mental breakdown that the truth came out. In her desperation, she turned to her church where the pastor and treasurer took charge of the finances. Although they were able to negotiate a workable repayment schedule with her creditors, she still has at least ten years of repayment ahead of her. However, the worst part was the damage this situation caused to her relationship with her husband. In her own words, "The most awful thing to deal with is the lack of trust and forgiveness toward me by my husband, but who can blame him? Debt turned me from an honest trustworthy person into a deceitful liar . . . Whatever I hear about people's shortcomings these days my reaction is 'there but for the grace of God go I.' It's so easy to fall into the debt trap."[9]

This woman's story speaks to some of the most obvious pitfalls in a materialistic society: debt and the accompanying rat-race, loss of integrity, and fractured relationships. Our human desires for more and nicer things coupled with our existence in a society that encourages us to "buy now, pay later" is a highly combustible combination. She's right; there but for the grace of God go many of us, some of whom are already teetering right on the edge of financial disaster.

But there are other dangers lurking beneath the shimmering surface of the material sea. They are harder to spot, to be sure, but they are no less real. In the affluent community in which I live, most people are able to have the best of everything for themselves and their children. We are all very busy running our children to the best swimming lessons, piano lessons, and sports events, while somehow trying to fit in a few things for ourselves—a full- or part-time job, fitness classes, P.T.A. responsibilities, church fellowship, shopping, and so on. Although there is nothing inherently wrong with these things, I've been noticing that when I get too caught up in this constant offering of activities and purchases, my soul becomes numb. The stillness in which the voice of God can be heard never comes. The truth that is born of quietness and expectant waiting is lost in the din of a frantic world.

The opportunity to spend my life for a cause that is greater than myself is forfeited when I rush for those things that will give me instant but short-lived gratification. It's a vicious cycle: The more I give myself over to the material world, the emptier I feel inside. The emptier I feel, the more I am attracted to those things that will distract me from those feelings. The more distracted I am from the emptiness I'm feeling, the less opportunity there is to fill it with what is truly satisfying.

Recognizing the Source of Our Discontent

As much as I am influenced by the tide of cultural messages, I am learning that the source of my discontent goes far deeper than that.

You see, we are created to be in relationship with God and others. Just as our individual hereditary characteristics are imbedded in our chromosomes, so our need and ability for relationship is imbedded in the DNA of our souls. When sin, rebellion, or lack of attention causes rifts in our most important relationships, the emptiness of soul that results can be very painful. We may try to fill our emptiness by acquiring more things. But there will never be enough material things to satisfy the longings of the human soul. That is why Hebrews 13:5 draws such a strong connection between freedom from materialism and our relationship with God: "Keep your lives free from the love of money and be content with what you have; for [or because] he has said 'I will never leave you or forsake you' " (NRSVB).

The questions that materialism claims to answer are important questions indeed, but the answers can only be satisfied in a personal relationship with God that is growing deeper every day. **What am I worth?** I am worth so much that God sent his Son to experience the pain of sin and then take my penalty. **What is success?** Truly knowing God and accomplishing his purposes for my life. **How do I find peace of mind?** In knowing that God will never leave me. **How do I show someone I love them?** By giving myself sacrificially as Christ did. **And what do I do when the going gets tough?** I place my confidence in a loving God who has promised to help. The more consistent I am in pursuing the relationships for which I was created, the less obsessed I am with money and things.

Asking the Right Questions

Oftentimes, the questions we are willing to ask ourselves are just as important as the answers we think we know. In fact, I have found that the process of asking questions is the answer to my struggle with cultural influences, great expectations, and emptiness of soul. There is much to be learned from asking questions like:

- What do I expect out of life, and where do those expectations come from?
- What is success, and do I tend to measure it by outward trappings?
- How much of myself am I giving to my loved ones, and how much am I relying on expensive gifts to communicate love?
- What is happening inside me and in my relationships right before I go on an unnecessary shopping spree?
- What happens for me when I do let things get quiet? Is it peaceful, or is there unresolved pain that surfaces?
- What is the real source of emptiness or drivenness that I feel?

In the noisiness of our lives, it is hard to quiet ourselves and wait for the answers to questions as important as these.

Over the years I have experienced a growing awareness that I work and spend compulsively. Even when I've known that more commitments and more spending are not good for me, I just haven't been able to say no. It's been frightening to face the fact that there are areas in my life that are out of control. But this realization has become the motivation I have needed to quiet myself and ask the questions I have needed to ask. In the quietness I have found a Baby Boomer (me!) who has allowed the affluence of her community to shape her expectations and feed her dissatisfaction—a woman unsure of her worth when she is not achieving. A Christian who knows how to do all the Christian "stuff" but has a lot to learn about being still and experiencing the presence of God as completely satisfying. A wife who finds it much easier to buy things for her husband than to offer unconditional love, acceptance, and physical affection. And a mother who has let her children slip into the same frantic pace to which she was so prone, rather than building a life for them in which the material world is balanced with relationships, participation in the work of family life, and quiet time for reading, reflection and cultivating spiritual awareness.

These are the places I have needed to start in stemming the tide of materialism in my own life. As I have worked on issues of self-worth, experienced the deeply satisfying results of giving more of myself to Chris, worked with him to restructure our family life to include more of what matters most, spent more time quietly in God's presence (not doing, just being), the pull of the material world has begun to lessen.

Real Answers

In some ways, it would be easier if someone would just come along and tell us exactly how much is enough so that we could fall into line. But answers that fit into simple categories of right and wrong or 1-2-3 solutions are not real answers. Neither are answers that hold up someone else's lifestyle for us to copy. These rob us of the opportunity to stop our own material madness long enough to experience the empty places in our soul— the insecurity that is masked by all those "dress for success" clothes, the disappointment of an unfulfilling marriage that is numbed by constant activity, or the depression that is kept at bay by the "rush" we get when we go shopping. It is only when we have quieted ourselves long enough to listen to what is happening within us that real answers begin to emerge.

Real answers offer insights about ourselves, the material world, and the spiritual world that free us to choose a lifestyle consistent with our core values rather than cultural norms. Real answers help us to keep our perspective in a world where desire is out of control. Real answers take us deeper into the relationships for which we were created. And it is only then that we find satisfaction.

Keeping Things in Perspective

I would be unrealistic if I did not admit how much I enjoy the things money buys. Our home with its grassy lawn and good neighbors has been a wonderful place to raise our family and host our friends. My newly remodeled kitchen is saving me untold time and frustration so that I am free to devote more time to people and activities that really interest me. And life would certainly be more difficult without adequate, regular income. I enjoy these gifts without guilt because "God richly provides us with everything for our enjoyment" (1 Tim. 6:17, NRSVB).

But a balanced perspective reminds me that money does have its limitations. It can buy clothes but not confidence, cosmetics but not true beauty, an exotic vacation but not the ability to relax and sleep. Money provides alarm systems but not peace of mind, a shopping trip but not a friend to go with you, a *Better Homes and Gardens* house but not a mom who has time and energy left to play games or read stories. It buys expensive gifts but not love.

A balanced perspective also keeps me from being consumed by my desires and warns me about sacrificing what really matters in life for things that never quite satisfy. The material world offers a lot to women today—jobs, titles, sophisticated clothes, beautiful houses. It's tempting to try to grab for it all at once. But there is great potential for regret in this area, potential for getting to the end of our lives and realizing "I put so much pressure on my husband (or myself) to make more money or go into more debt, that the rat-race damaged our relationship." Or, "We got our dream house and car, but I had to go to work to pay for it all. I missed being home with my kids during the times they needed me most."

Contrary to the messages of materialism, it isn't the woman who dies with the most toys who wins. It is the one who has loved her family well and knows the joy of having that love returned. It is the woman who has spent her life for a purpose that is greater than herself. And it is the person who has known God and looks forward to an eternity with him.

FOR DISCUSSION

1. If you had to leave your home as suddenly as Lot's wife did for physical or moral reasons, what would be the hardest thing for you to leave behind?

2. Describe an incident during the past week or two in which a T.V. commercial, magazine ad, or salesman "sold to your hidden needs." Did you succumb to the sales pitch? Why or why not?

3. To which of the dangers of materialism are you most vulnerable?

4. Which of the questions raised in this chapter interests you the most on a personal level? Do you have enough quiet in your life to explore the answers?

For Further Study

Bellah, Mike. *Baby Boom Believers*. Wheaton, Ill.: Tyndale House Publishers, 1988.

Jones, Landon Y. *Great Expectations: America and the Baby Boom Generation*. New York: Coward, McCann & Geoghegan, 1980.

Packard, Vance. *The Hidden Persuaders*. New York: Simon & Schuster, 1957.

Starkey, Mike. *Born to Shop*. E. Sussex, Great Britain: Monarch, 1989.

Notes

1. Materialism is the theory that physical well-being and worldly possessions constitute the greatest good and highest value in life.

2. Vance Packard, *The Hidden Persuaders* (New York: Simon & Schuster, 1957), p. 14.

3. Ibid., p. 30.

4. Ibid., p. 16.

5. Mike Starkey, *Born to Shop* (E. Sussex, Great Britain: Monarch, 1989), p. 35.

6. Landon Y. Jones, "The Baby Boomers," *Money* (March 1983), p. 300.

7. Mike Bellah, *Baby Boom Believers* (Wheaton, Ill.: Tyndale House, 1988), p. 22.

8. Walvoord & Zuck, *The Bible Knowledge Commentary* (Wheaton, Ill.: Victor Books, 1985), p. 60.

9. Starkey, pp. 106-107.

7

A Marriage That Works

When I look at it [my wedding dress], it hurts that all that care is taken to preserve a dress when so little care was taken to preserve a family, but I guess it's easier to store a dress than to make a marriage work.

Patti Roberts

I have always been puzzled by the bachelor/bachelorette parties traditionally given for brides and grooms on the eve of their weddings. Somehow the idea of commemorating one's last night of freedom by watching raunchy movies and joking about the marriage trap seems completely contradictory to the joyful expectation with which most of us approach our wedding day.

Undoubtedly, many of society's images of married life—the nagging wife who lives in curlers and a bathrobe, the couch-potato husband whose most effective communication is yelling for his beer, unruly kids, bills that never end, perfunctory sex—do perpetuate the idea that marriage is a trap. But in actuality most of us get married because we have a great deal of hope that our marriage will be one of the exceptions—one of the few that really work. Deep down, we do not believe that marriage is a trap; we believe it to be a source of great joy and fulfillment. Otherwise, we probably wouldn't get ourselves into it!

Sometimes—when a marriage isn't working—it *is* experienced as a trap. This happens when conflicts are left unresolved, faulty communication patterns become entrenched, pain and hurt are "stuffed down" instead of dealt with, and fitting into traditional roles is more important than understanding individuals. When we feel trapped we have a tendency to feel desperate. And desperation can tempt us to ease the pain of a marriage that isn't working by getting involved in an affair, physically leaving the marriage, or shutting down emotionally. However, in a marriage that is working there is great freedom to love and be loved, to express ourselves sexually, and to experience the fulfillment that comes through an authentic, committed relationship.

So what does "a marriage that works" look like?

A Marriage Big Enough for Both of Us

Unfortunately, the emphasis in our culture on "roles" in marriage has hindered many couples' growth together. Rather than freeing individuals to function as a team according to their gifts, personality, and strengths, predetermined male/female roles create boxes so small that real people cannot fit into them!

Listen in on Diane's story of a marriage in which there is a lot of room for her husband and very little room for anyone else:

I became a submissive wife [as a means of] survival. It meant learning to live and survive in peace and getting as much my way as I could, without causing a lot of commotion. I would have to calculate: Clifford will only let me have my way on so many things within the next week, so I'd better decide what those things are going to be. I gave up some things for myself—personhood things—so the girls could have more . . . I had stamina enough to fight for what the girls needed, but not enough left over to get what I needed. It meant a lot of manipulation and very little confrontation . . . I know it wasn't healthy for me. After several years of this I began having all sorts of physical symptoms, and I think they're related to the stress that this submission caused. But I don't see any other way I could have done it. Clifford is just too strong of a person for me.[1]

Clearly Diane's marriage isn't working at some very deep levels and both husband and wife are extremely vulnerable.

Diane is vulnerable to emotional and physical breakdown, to falling for the first man who comes along and treats her kindly, to getting to the point someday where she says, "I've had it up to here and I'm leaving!" Clifford is also vulnerable to the boredom that comes from living with a woman who has lost herself and her vitality because she has given most of it away for so long.

James Olthuis describes the dangers inherent in this kind of one-way marriage:

> Although at times it may seem easier to let one partner take over, a husband and wife can jeopardize their entire relationship by establishing a male-dominated marriage. When a woman virtually surrenders her personality to her husband, she has less to give to the relationship as the years pass. Outwardly she may seem rather content, but inwardly she grows more and more dependent until she is only an adjunct. Often powerful feelings of hostility well up inside her, against herself for succumbing and against her husband (and God) for demanding such subservience. She feels her marriage is a "trap" with four walls and a husband as keeper.
>
> The situation becomes more complicated when the husband continues to grow through outside contacts while the wife languishes at home. He may have begun to grow away from her when he promised to keep his office problems out of the home. Unfortunately, after years of living separate lives, he may begin to feel that his wife no longer has the understanding to be his confidante and equal. Despite her dutiful obedience and continual adoration, he begins to see her as an embarrassment. Sometimes, feeling guilty, he pampers her even more (just the wrong thing if he wants her to grow up); at other times he suddenly drops her for "no apparent reason," using her childish behavior (accentuated by his pampering) to justify an affair.[2]

Diane isn't doing herself, her husband, or her children any favors by maintaining the status quo of a marriage that isn't working. In fact, by working so hard to fit into a dysfunctional family system she is actually helping to perpetuate it and pass it on to future generations. She needs to consider whether God is calling her to lead the way into "the tunnel of chaos" in order to move toward a marriage that is really working rather than one that just looks good from the outside.

We don't want to ignore the kind of dysfunction that goes the other way—wives who become dominant while husbands become more and more distant from their partners as well as their children. Most of us have known families in which the husband spends most of his time out in the garage or basement puttering, or sitting at a bar with people who give him a sense of importance and belonging, or glued to the television in numbed silence. Meanwhile the wife runs the household, brings up the children, decides the social agenda, and frequently verbalizes what she sees to be her husband's weaknesses. Men aren't the only ones with strong personalities that, when left unchecked, crush the life out of their relationships. Certainly the male-dominated marriage is the more common one, but imbalance in either direction is unhealthy and not the plan God ever had for marriage.

Invariably, the subject of submission comes up whenever I speak or teach about men and women in marriage. The fact is, I do believe in submission, but not the kind that only goes one way. Scriptural instruction on headship and submission is always given in the context of mutual submission among believers who are bearing with one another, forgiving each other, loving each other, telling each other the truth, and teaching and admonishing each other with thankful hearts in the name of Christ. This is a far cry from the "submission for the sake of survival" that has Diane tiptoeing around a man who does a lot of taking and very little giving.

The biblical concept of headship is modeled on the example of Christ and the church—not the hierarchy of corporate America with its presidents and vice-presidents. The way we learn about headship is by observing Christ's relationship with the church. According to Ephesians 5:22-33, Christ's role as "head" of the church involves being her savior (giver of life), her lover (to the point of laying down his life), and her nurturer (caring for her as he would care for his body). Contrary to popular interpretations, headship has nothing to do with demanding obedience, being the one who makes final decisions, or being the one who pursues his calling while the wife tries desparately to be supportive and fit in. Rather, the word "head" is virtually synonymous with "beginning" or "origin."[3] In the context of Christ, the church, and marriage, headship has to do with being the one who initiates and leads the way in loving. The woman responds (as the church does) to this kind of love with a heartfelt desire to please her husband.

Dr. Gilbert Bilezekian states in his careful word study:

> the concept of headship in the New Testament refers to the function of Christ as the fountainhead of life and growth and to His servant role of provider and sustainer . . . Because Christ is the wellspring of the church's life and provides it with existence and sustenance, in return the church serves Him in loving dependency and in recognition of Him as the source of its life. Because man as the fountainhead of the woman's existence was originally used to supply her with her very life, and because he continues to love her sacrificially as his own body in marriage, in return a Christian wife binds herself to her husband in a similar relationship of servant submission that expresses their oneness. The imposition of authority structure upon this exquisite balance of reciprocity would paganize the marriage relationship and make the Christ/church paradigm irrelevant to it.[4]

Now that sounds like a marriage that works! Two individuals love and give to each other in such a way that both souls are nourished. A husband commits himself to love, nurture, and see that his wife has what she needs to be all that she is meant to be—to the point of laying down his own comfort, indeed his very life. The wife gives to her husband out of the fullness that comes from being truly loved and nurtured into full personhood.

Their balance and unity speak volumes to a world burdened with trying to find love in relationships fraught with domination, manipulation, power struggles, and selfishness.

"But," I hear you saying, "What about those times when you and your husband just can't agree? In that case, shouldn't the husband be the one to make the decison?" There is nothing in the Scriptures to support this idea. Rather, the Scriptures speak of unity as the goal for relationships among Christians, married or otherwise: "Be of the same mind, having the same love, being in full accord and of one mind. Do nothing from selfishness or empty conceit, but in humility regard others as better than yourselves. Let each of you look not only to your own interests, but to the interests of others" (Philippians 2:3-5, NRSVB). This is the norm for Christian marriage.

How many decisions come along in life that are truly worth sacrificing the powerful unity that we have discussed so briefly here? How many are so important that we cannot wait for each other and listen and work lovingly to achieve the one mind spoken of in Philippians 2:3-5? My husband and I haven't come up against a decision yet that was worth such a sacrifice.

The rush to designate the husband as the one who makes the final decisions is rooted in simple fear: fear that unity and consensus is not possible. Fear that if we don't give more power to one or the other, we'll never be able to make decisions. Fear that if you don't keep women in some sort of authority structure, they will lead their men and their families down the path to destruction. *While some of these fears may be understandable, they are woefully inadequate as a foundation for marital relations. They totally discount the efficacy of the Holy Spirit's work in creating unity among us.* They discount the power of Christlike love and mutual submission.

Faith, on the other hand, holds out for God's ideal of agreement and oneness before moving ahead. Faith says, "I believe that unity is God's will for us and he can bring our hearts and minds together."

Certainly, there are times when one spouse may say to the other, "You know what? I think this decision affects you more than it does me, so let's go your way on this one." But that is a concession voluntarily given, not forced upon another on the basis of gender or anything else. There is a world of difference between a marriage in which deference is freely given and one in which it is understood that the husband always holds the trump card in the nitty-gritty of decision-making. There is a great difference between a marriage where issues are worked out in a reasonable way and one in which the husband is outwardly "head of the house," while his wife pulls all the strings through deception and manipulation.

Stuart Briscoe, whose marriage has been working for many years, offers this bit of advice for couples who are feeling pulled in two different directions:

> Sometimes the reticence of one partner can be alleviated with better information. And sometimes the spouse who is charging ahead is neglecting to consider issues of real concern. Clearly they have got to talk about it. Assuming they've each got that willing spirit, these problems can be worked out. But one spouse should never push the other into something. They should go slowly, working together. They say the Atlantic convoys of World War II used to go at the speed of the slowest ship. That's the way to go.[5]

A Marriage Flexible Enough to Accommodate Growth and Change

When Chris married me he thought he was getting a traditional gal whose main goals in life were to be a good wife and mother. He thought that because that's what I told him! At the time (I was barely 21 years old) I guess it was true. Can you imagine his surprise (and mine, too!) at finding out that even though I valued marriage and bringing up children, I needed more in my life? I found that I experienced a great deal of fulfillment in work that involved leadership and communication. In fact, the Lord began leading me into ministry at the same time he was giving us babies; our relationship had to stretch in order to accommodate these changes.

There is no way either of us could have ever envisioned the life that we have today—a life that is an odd combination of the traditional dad-works-while-mom-stays-home-with-the-kids (to accomodate our continuing commitment to our kids being parented by their own parents) and the dual-career juggle in which Chris flexes his schedule in order to cover the home front so that I can be involved in ministry.

Little did we know that we would be stretching our schedule, our finances, and bursting out of stereotypes in order for me to go to seminary in preparation for my long-range dream of church-related, full-time ministry. Fortunately, all the changes didn't have to happen overnight; it's been a step-by-step process over years of time. We would be the first to admit that it's not always easy to stretch; it requires an awful lot of giving and taking. But we are working into a marriage configuration that fits for both of us—who we are now and who we are becoming. And it's anything but stifling!

Facing Problems and Getting Help

Somehow, as a young girl preparing for marriage I didn't realize that marriage would be so hard and that we would need more than love and a commitment to Christ to make it work. Either no one was saying it or I just wasn't listening—probably a combination of both.

Now I know that most married couples (the honest ones anyway!) will sometimes encounter in their married life: anger so deep that it cannot be fully dealt with "before the sun goes down," depression that cannot be lifted by one more sermon or book on victorious Christian living, sexual difficulties that are not alleviated by simplistic teaching about sex as God's beautiful gift, or a crisis that threatens to overwhelm them. I know this because Chris and I have experienced these kinds of difficulties. They were difficulties that brought us to the point of saying, "Look, we have a problem. We have tried everything we know to try and it's just not working. We need help."

It's a little traumatic at first—a real blow to the pride—to admit that you need help and then to seek it actively. Then there is the challenge of finding someone who has the expertise, experience, and perhaps professional training to be of real help and placing yourself in the position of being guided and helped. But the beauty of having a helper for times of stress in marriage is that the helper can become a kind of "safety net" as we move toward greater levels of intimacy in the relationship. Rather than being afraid of new awareness and new issues that need to be dealt with in the marriage ("If I told my husband that I really don't like sex, he would be devastated." "If I told my wife about my struggle with pornography, she would never forgive me." "My husband would be revolted if I told him about my eating disorder." "How can I tell my wife it really bothers me that she has gained so much weight?"), we can put our issues out there knowing that there is someone to help if we get stuck or the problems become bigger than we know how to handle.

We all have unresolved issues that keep us from experiencing the fullness in life we have always envisioned for ourselves. Much of the work of maturing and healing the hurts of the past can only be done in meaningful connection with another person over time. Dysfunctional thinking patterns, poor communication skills, and character weaknesses don't change overnight or in isolation. The beauty of a marriage that works is that these areas are viewed matter-of-factly rather than as disasters that cannot be coped with. We are then freed to grow in the context of commitment and love.

Yes, pride does die hard. That's why some people wait until it hurts so badly they can't stand it or until some kind of crisis forces the issue. But in marriages that are working well, admitting problems honestly and getting help is seen as a strength and not a shortcoming. "With those who receive counsel is wisdom" (Proverbs 13:10, NASB). The sooner the better.

Learning to Let God Be Our Source

I used to be egocentric enough to think that somehow I could take away all of my husband's pain, that my answers would solve his problems, that I could fill up his empty places. And I expected that he would do the same for me. It was pretty draining because, in reality, only God can do those things.

Psychologist Jeff Van Vonderen observes in *Families Where Grace Is in Place* that much of the tiredness and "trapped-ness" that married people feel is a result of having the wrong job description. Many of us enter into marriage thinking that it is our job to meet each other's deepest needs. Inevitably, we both fail to live up to these expectations and so we try to fix each other. The problem with fixing is that it just doesn't work and pretty soon everyone ends up feeling like a failure; the "fix-ee" because he/she hasn't lived up to his/her spouse's expectation and the "fixer" because he/she hasn't been able to effect change.

Eventually we must face the truth that no human being is capable of "filling up" another human being no matter how much fixing we do. And we can't really change anyone but ourselves. I realize now that my "job" as a married woman is to keep learning to let God meet my needs and change my destructive behaviors. As I mature in my ability to deal with anger, communicate truthfully with love and respect, break annoying habits, and conquer my own selfishness, I find that I have much more to offer Chris. As I see more clearly what I can't do for him (fixing and filling), I am freed to offer what I am best equipped to offer: My presence on the journey, a listening ear, any tools or insights I have gained along the way, and my support and participation in wrestling with life's great questions.

Does this mean that we are not concerned about each other's needs? On the contrary, in a marriage that works both the husband's and the wife's needs are very important. However, even as we express our deep care for one another, we are realistic about what one human being can do for another. We can love one another wholeheartedly, *but that love cannot be expected to fully ease the pain of a mother or a father who could not love.* One human being can be a source of deep joy to another *but cannot singlehandedly stave off depression*. Being a husband or a wife can be a part of our identity for the time that God gives us to be together, *but it cannot give ultimate meaning to our lives*. We can cultivate our sexual relationship, *but we cannot accept responsibility for the other's choice to go outside the marriage for sexual fulfillment when the going gets tough*. We can ease each other's pain with our presence, *but we must each take responsibility for whatever work needs to be done in our own lives—be it forgiveness, righting past wrongs, grieving loss, or wrestling with God*. There are parts of the journey that we each must take alone, and God is the only one who can go with us.

For those of us who are used to fixing and controlling, the idea of letting go of those responsibilites can be frightening. We may fear that our spouse or our marriage will never change unless we're right in the middle of things pushing, manipulating, or giving advice! But faith can free us: faith in God's power to change people, faith in each other's capacity to change, and faith in the whole process of being changed by marriage.

Freedom Worth Fighting For

Sometimes when we experience the normal stresses and strains of becoming truly intimate with another person, we begin to believe that marriage *is* a trap. We begin to believe that if we could only get out of the marriage or try a new partner we would be free. The truth is that even if we did get out of the marriage, we would still have to live with ourselves and those things in ourselves that keep us from joy, intimacy, and effectiveness. In most cases true freedom is still to be found in a marriage where we continue to grow and change, even through difficulty.

Fighting for this kind of a relationship is not for the faint-hearted. It is for hearty souls with courage enough to explore new frontiers and conquer the enemies of intimacy. It is for those who know deep in their hearts that where there is no risk there is no reward. And it is for all of us who know what it is to push past our own limits of courage and strength, because a marriage that really works is worth whatever it takes.

FOR DISCUSSION

1. Do you feel that your marriage is dominated by one spouse or the other, or is it big enough for both of you? Explain.

2. In what areas have you had to stretch or are you now stretching in order to accommodate growth and change? How do you feel this is going?

3. How do you feel about the way you and your spouse make decisions? What happens when you just can't agree?

4. How easy or difficult is it for you and your spouse to discuss problems in your marraige? Do you have someone to whom you can go for help when you need it?

5. On a scale of one to ten (ten being the highest) how do you feel your marriage is working? How do you think your spouse would rate it? (Go ahead and ask!) What changes would be meaningful to one or both of you?

For Further Study

Bilezikian, Gilbert. *Beyond Sex Roles*. Grand Rapids, Mich.: Baker Book House, 1985.

Gundry, Patricia. *Heirs Together: Mutual Submission In Marriage*. Grand Rapids, Mich.: Zondervan, 1980.

Kindig, Eileen Silva. *Goodbye Prince Charming: The Journey back from Disenchantment*. Colorado Springs: Pinon Press, 1993.

Olthuis, James. *I Pledge You My Troth*. San Francisco: Harper & Row, 1975.

Van Vonderen, Jeff. *Families Where Grace Is in Place*. Minneapolis: Bethany House, 1992.

Notes

1. Alice Slaikeu Lawhead, *The Lie of the Good Life* (Portland, Oreg.: Multnomah Press, 1989), pp. 70-71.

2. James H. Olthuis, *I Pledge You My Troth* (San Francisco: Harper & Row, 1975), pp. 36-37.

3. Girard Kittel, editor, *Theological Dictionary of the New Testament*, Vol. 3 (Grand Rapids, Mich.: Eerdman's, 1965), pp. 673-82.

4. Gilbert Bilezikian, *Beyond Sex Roles* (Grand Rapids, Mich.: Baker Book House, 1985), p. 161.

5. Annette LaPlaca, "Teamwork," *Marriage Partnership* (Fall, 1993), p. 87.

8

Fighting for Your Marriage

If the grass is greener on the other side of the fence, then try watering the grass on your own side.

Cheryl Biehl

Oh no," I groaned. "Here we go again!" Chris was on the phone telling me that his boss wanted to take his department out for dinner on Friday night.

Nice gesture.

The clincher? As usual, spouses were not included.

To make matters worse, the restaurant his boss had chosen happened to be one of our favorites. It was the perfect spot for a romantic dinner complete with candlelight, curtained booths, and strolling musicians. I couldn't imagine either of us going there without the other.

I experienced a number of emotions in the moments of silence that followed Chris's announcement. The strongest was total outrage as I realized again that the people in his place of business really did not care about protecting or supporting the marriages of those in their employment. To them it was perfectly natural for men and women to socialize without spouses after hours in very intimate settings. But in my opinion, they were just asking for trouble. A glance at the divorce rate among those in the business community convinced me all the more that there is danger in passively following what some have come to view as acceptable business practice.

This threat to long-lasting marriage that Chris and I are sensing in our own small corner of the business world is far more than personal paranoia; it is part of a larger societal trend. A cover article in *Fortune* magazine confirms that whereas there used to be some pressure to stay married, at least for the sake of appearances, today we are being pressured in the opposite direction. In one article Helen Singer Kaplan, second wife of the founder and chairman of Toys 'R' Us, notes: "The change has been radical. There's no longer a prejudice against divorce and remarriage—almost the reverse. In some cases the man with the old, nice matronly wife is looked down on. He's seen as not keeping up appearances. Why can't he do better for himself?"[1]

George Barna, in his book *The Frog in the Kettle*, takes this trend a step further and predicts that by the year 2000, "Americans will generally believe that a life spent with the same partner is both unusual and unnecessary. . . . People will begin to consciously acknowledge that they are likely to have several spouses over the course of their lifetime and will choose partners who will best satisfy their needs during the different periods of their lives."[2]

For those of us who are committed and looking forward to being married to our spouse "till death do us part," these observations are not very encouraging. In fact, they are frightening.

A Battle Worth Fighting

It has been said that you have to choose your battles carefully. Whereas some issues are not worth doing battle over, others call for all-out war. The battle for our marriages, in a society that does very little to promote faithful commitment to one spouse, is such an issue.

For Chris and me, fighting this particular battle is a team effort involving "strategy-planning sessions" and a series of common-sense pro-marriage choices. Ultimately, faithfulness in marriage comes down to trust—in each other and in the God who gives us the strength to be faithful. But we also realize that we are involved in a battle characterized by subtle dangers and fine lines that many do not recognize. Rather than follow society's trends, we have chosen to think through our own strategies and standards for protecting "what God has joined together."

We work at keeping our marriage fulfilling and fun.

There is probably nothing a man enjoys more than being with an attractive woman who enjoys him and respects him. We, as wives, can be that attractive woman to our husbands. We have the opportunity to build them up and meet their legitimate needs for companionship and sex based on our unique understanding of them. And while we may, at times, feel threatened by the reality of attractive men and women in our respective work-places, a marriage characterized by growing intimacy and trust, coupled with the playfulness of a good sex life, is a combination that anyone would be foolish to jeopardize by even considering extramarital involvement.

Chris and I are at the stage in our lives when it is often difficult to find the time, energy, and money that a growing relationship requires. Children, careers, ministry, schooling, home mainte-nance and improvement, and extended family threaten to absorb these limited resources. As a young mother with varied interests, it is a constant temptation for me to use up so much of my time and energy on these other things that I have very little left for Chris, much to his disappointment. It takes constant vigilance to monitor my use of these resources. I've learned the hard way that a woman can *say* her husband is a priority, but her use of time and energy may not demonstrate such a commitment.

I remember one Sunday (these things always seem to happen on Sundays right before church!) when my husband hit rock bottom with me, convinced that I didn't love him and didn't care about his needs because I had not been spending much of my time and energy in his direction. To him, the future looked bleak as he contemplated another forty years of not being a priority and living with unmet needs. I was totally discouraged because that very week I was preparing to speak at a retreat about living our lives and spending our time according to God's purposes. Here I was failing to live purposefully in such a key area. This crisis in our marriage necessitated immediate change.

For starters, we set a new goal of getting to bed by 9:30 so we would have time for being together while I still had some energy left. Our normal bedtime of 11:00 usually found me pretty well spent. Also, Chris's birthday was the same week as this retreat, and he was expecting (and rightly so!) that I would be so engrossed in my preparations that I wouldn't have time to celebrate. I had a choice to make: I could either let the retreat consume me or I could conserve some of my resources for Chris. As I faced the reality of our present struggle, I determined not to allow the retreat to overshadow his birthday and keep me from making it special. I took time to shop for presents and cards, and on the day of his birthday I studied early in the morning and then put it away for the day so I could serve him breakfast in bed and have celebrations with both of our families. He had a wonderful day—much to his surprise.

Practically speaking, my investment in keeping my marriage fulfilling and fun means listening with interest and asking questions about the details of Chris's day. It means shopping for clothes and lingerie he would find sexy and attractive. It means remembering to be playful with each other even though the realities of dishes, diapers, and bills sometimes make us feel like we have forgotten how to play. It means planning a few surprises here and there—like an envelope with the key to a hotel room inviting him for a "one-night stand"! It means having "dates" as often as possible because we both need it.

Not all dates and surprises have to involve major time and expense. More often one of us will surprise the other in the middle of the day with an invitation to lunch. Or later in the evening, we'll go out for a walk or a cup of coffee at a nearby restaurant. It's amazing how such simple occasions energize our marriage and help us get "in tune" with each other. Another discipline that has really helped is getting our children to bed at a decent hour. Early in our marriage, some friends shared that they made it a priority to get their four children (who were older than ours) in bed by 7:30 or 8:00 so that they had some time for themselves and for each other. As we have followed this simple advice, we have become convinced that we would have lost some sanity without it! An early bedtime for the children assures us that on most days there will be some time for regrouping.

We also work at developing mutual interests. "Creeping separateness"—the tendency to be so engrossed in our own activities and interests that we have less and less in common with our spouse—can be a marriage killer. When we are dissatisfied with the level of sharing in our marriage, it is easier to become attracted to someone who seems to be more of a kindred spirit. Consequently, Chris and I have made it a priority to read and discuss books together, be involved in ministry together (we have worked with youth, led small groups, practiced hospitality, and ushered at church together), and to pursue friendships with other couples whom we both enjoy. I know several women who have taken up golf just so they could play with their husbands—especially as they approach retirement—and I respect their effort to cultivate a mutual interest.

It does take work and planning to keep a marriage fun and fulfilling but the benefits are significant. When we have a good thing going at home, we are much less likely to be looking around for other people to meet our needs for companionship and intimacy.

We are committed to mental fidelity.

Proverbs 6:20-25 shows us that the best way to keep our actions in line is to keep our thoughts in line. The instruction found here (written to a young man but easily applied to us as women) is to keep proper teaching and wisdom at the forefront of our minds continually and refuse to entertain sinful desires so that we can avoid sexual sin. When we fail to monitor our thoughts, it is easy to drift into dangerous territory.

One woman became aware that, over time, her boss's assessment of her had become more important to her than her husband's view of her. Eventually, she realized she was developing an inappropriate emotional attachment to her boss and purposefully set about changing her thought patterns.

Ruth Senter, in *The Seasons of Friendship*, tells of a time when her friendship with a grad school classmate drifted from a working relationship into a mutual attraction. First she noticed that the days she would see him in class took on special significance and she felt at loose ends when he was gone. She also sensed that she wasn't as open to God as usual and was reluctant to tell her husband about this friend's phone calls. Fortunately, she saw red flags while the battle was still taking place in her mind and she made the difficult choice to withdraw from the friendship rather than take any more risks.

Most of us, at some time or other, will be attracted to someone who is not our spouse. This itself is not surprising, nor is it sinful; we are sexual and emotional beings who have the ability to form attachments to other people, especially those with whom we work closely or see frequently. This is the way we were created. However, extramarital attractions can "give birth" to sin depending upon how we respond with our thoughts and actions.

I look at it this way: sexual attraction is energy—emotional, mental, and physical. When that energy becomes available to me, I can choose how I am going to direct it. I can use it to think about, fantasize about, and involve myself with that other person or I can redirect that energy toward my husband and my marriage. I can refuse inappropriate thoughts about someone else and try to figure out why I am vulnerable to them at this time. Maybe there is something missing in my marriage. Or maybe some old insecurities and conflicts of my own are making appearances again. Once I understand where the weakness lies, I can work on shoring up those areas. Sexual energy can be directed toward creativity and enthusiasm in my relationship with my husband, something that is always appreciated!

James 1:13-14 tells us that sin begins when we are tempted by our own desires and that desire conceives and gives birth to sin. It makes good sense, then, to weed out any of those things that could contribute to the process: impure thoughts about friends and coworkers, "innocent" flirtations, suggestive or pornographic literature, and entertainment that portrays infidelity and sexual immorality as attractive options. We are responsible to know ourselves, to know our vulnerable areas, and to know when we are crossing the fine lines and drifting into danger zones. So much of the battle for our marriages will be won or lost in the realms of the mind.

We refuse to take unnecessary risks.

Society encourages us to play the odds by continually putting ourselves in situations that invite failure and sin. But Proverbs 6 and 7 say that we can guard against sexual sin by steering away from tempting situations. The naive young man in these chapters didn't realize he was playing with fire and that if he scooped fire into his lap he could expect to get burned. He made the big mistake of simply being in the vacinity of the adultress (7:8-9) and he got caught. That's why, where sexual temptation is concerned, Scripture counsels us to run the other way (2 Timothy 2:22). God knows us better than we know ourselves.

Chris and I have chosen to reduce the odds of temptation by evaluating each business, ministry, and social opportunity to be sure that it supports our marriage. Our first major evaluation came while we were still engaged. Chris's job of examining banks required a lot of travel, often with other women. This meant that they would travel together, work together all day, eat dinner together, and then stay in the same hotel—all in a town where neither of them knew anyone else. As young and inexperienced as we were, we recognized this as a situation that involved risk, more risk than we were willing to take. So Chris asked that he not be scheduled to travel alone with other women. His boss was able to accommodate him for awhile, but soon it became impossible. So Chris pursued another job opening and the Lord opened the way for a change.

Not every situation necessitates something as drastic as a job change. But sometimes it does mean bowing out of after-hours business functions where spouses are not included, or suggesting alternatives that are more beneficial to our marriage. For instance, in the situation mentioned at the beginning of this chapter, Chris suggested that spouses be included in the dinner plans, offering to pay for my dinner if cost was the issue. We were pleased that his boss agreed. Our experience that night confirmed the importance of spouses being together in such situations. Once people started drinking, the atmosphere became less than professional and we were glad we were together.

We are alert to subtle dangers to our marriage and respond accordingtly.

In Proverbs 5 the writer takes great pains to describe the problem of sexual temptation so that the reader can understand the dangers and then translate that knowledge into wise behavior. Verse 23 points out that we can die for lack of such instruction!

Staying informed of societal trends helps us understand the dangers. For instance, the *Fortune* article alerted me to ways a woman can weaken her own marriage, leaving her husband vulnerable to societal pressures and advances from women who have no conscience about pursuing illicit relationships. The men who were interviewed for this article indicated that while the first wife was "cold and unresponsive," the second wife was "supportive and sexy." The first wife was seen as unable to adjust to her husband's changing interests and unsupportive of the demands of his professional life, often becoming his self-appointed critic and conscience. In short, "she didn't keep up."[3]

Of course none of these reasons are acceptable excuses for a man to leave "the wife of his youth." However, it does make me aware of the need to pay attention to these areas of our life together. I need to keep up my appearance so that my husband can be proud to have me as his companion at business functions and enjoy looking at me from across the table. I need to be sensitive to his needs for love and sexual fulfillment. And I need to encourage him and build him up rather than tear him down.

Certainly there are areas of need in a woman's life to which her husband should be attentive and thus lessen the power that outside temptations have on her. A woman who feels valued and respected by her husband, who knows that her opinions, gifts, and concerns are important to him, who receives reassurance of his love, commitment, and attraction to her, has little need to look elsewhere for support or intimacy. Yes, we do need to hear "I love you" regularly! And we need to feel that our partner continues to have our best interests in mind. Men also need to realize that women are quite vulnerable today, due to the pressures of a changing society.

> When you live life in a dog-tired, gotta-meet-everybody-else's-needs state, you lose a sense of who you are and what you're about in life. That makes you depressed and vulnerable to whoever comes along and tells you great things about yourself. . . . Women use affairs as an escape hatch. It happens a lot, especially when a woman's life is stressful, trying to work, take care of the kids, be the good wife, whatever. They freak out and want no responsibility at all, which is what an affair is.[4]

Again, self-awareness is key. It may be one of the most important things a woman can do for her marriage to be assertive enough to say, "Hey, I'm running on empty too much of the time—we need to make some adjustments." When a couple is serious about protecting their marriage, they assimilate this kind of information and brainstorm ways to prevent the tiredness and emptiness (in the individual and in the marriage) that leaves a woman today open to making a choice she will later regret.

We Keep Talking

"Recently the possibility of having an affair with a married man—a Christian—presented itself," Anita says.

> Although many things were strong in my marriage, there was not a real cherishing of each other. After so many years of marriage and so many children, maybe we were taking each other for granted. And here comes someone who opens my

doors, and treats me with respect, and understands a lot about me. I could have done two things: I could have kept my temptation secret or I could have shared the whole thing with Chuck. I chose to tell my husband. And things really changed for us. We started spending more time together, we spent hours in the bedroom, talking; we started behaving differently toward one another. . . . We came out with an appreciation for our relationship we hadn't had before. We realized that to lose what we had would be totally devastating. We would be destroyed.[5]

Even if we have a marriage that is working (basically) and we are exercising wisdom in protecting it, most likely there will still be times when one or the other of us is attracted to someone else. As difficult as it is to talk about and hear about this reality, these are times when it is most important to keep talking—to keep telling the truth in love. Issues we leave unacknowledged and unspoken have more power over us than those we have brought to light. Denying that one's partner or oneself is vulnerable to outside attractions is just that—denial. While we may wish to spare each other from information that is painful, such secrecy can actually weaken the marriage, because we are are hiding something important about ourselves.

Says Peggy Vaughn, "Only honesty can create the ground-work for monogamy. Attractions kept secret from a partner are far more likely to be acted upon."[6] But an honest look at sexuality requires courage and a common commitment to increasing intimacy. The one doing the telling must communicate that he/she is doing so out of a commitment to honesty and a desire to protect the marriage. The one listening must work hard to share his/her honest response without trying to punish, control, or withdraw. Both should have the freedom to ask each other about outside attractions and to remind each other that honesty, faithfulness, and true intimacy are among their highest shared values.

Some people feel that talking to their partner is not always the best *first* step, in cases where the attraction with another person has developed outside any perceptible problems in the marriage.

If there is nothing for the spouse to correct or work on, he or she could be left feeling helpless and worried. At such times—when the attraction is in the beginning stages—some people choose to make themselves accountable to a close friend, pastor, or counselor, while redirecting their desires. They find that a third party can help them deal with the problem without their spouse ever knowing or being hurt by it. Some people prefer not to know, while others want to know everything. These are matters you and your husband should talk about before a problem ever comes up. You can assure one another that you will keep each other informed, no matter what. Or you can give your promise to handle situations of attraction with the help of someone both of you know and trust.

Some couples may decide that it is best for their marriage if they maintain close, same-sex friendships in which they can confide the details of such struggles. This can be a healthy choice as long as it is made together and with the understanding that it is not meant to take the place of open sharing within the marriage. A woman who had several affairs during a particularly vulnerable time in her life shared (in a seminar she was giving with her husband) that the road back to fidelity in her marriage was paved with such honesty and accountability. After a period of separation, she reunited with her husband based on a renewed commitment to faithfulness. However, because of old patterns, she was still drawn to other men. Realizing her vulnerability, she committed herself to talking with a friend about these attractions as she became aware of them. She found that once she talked about these feelings, they were not such a big deal after all.

When we keep talking honestly about our sexuality we provide significant protection for our marriages.

Brothers and Sisters in Christ

Yes, there is good reason to be cautious in a society where affairs are commonplace, divorce is no longer frowned upon, and accusations of sexual harassment fly. But are relationships ruled by fear and mistrust all we can hope for in the body of Christ? Or is it possible, in our reaction to societal trends, that we have gone overboard?

Karen Mains confronts this tendency in a powerful chapter from her book *Friends and Strangers:*

> Men and women are starving for healing between the sexes, which is why they keep seeking it in inappropriate and ultimately destructive sexual liasons. Unfortunately, Christians have not forged a Christlike peace; we have become compulsively protective, reactionary. Women must be kept in their places. Men and women must not become too friendly. If you are married, fidelity requires you to keep yourself so much unto your spouse that only superficial relationships with other women are allowed. ("And no wonder we are rigid," some might object, "when so many of our leaders fall prey to infidelity, promiscuity, and sexual addiction." "And no wonder so many of them fall prey when we are so unnatural," I reply.)[7]

Scripture, on the other hand, instructs Christian men and women to treat one another as we would treat beloved family members (1 Timothy 5:1-2). All the way through the New Testament Christian men and women are referred to as brothers and sisters in Christ. I wonder what it would look like, what it would feel like if we were really behaving toward one another as brothers and sisters? In trying to envision this, invariably I think of my own biological brothers.

I have two wonderful brothers. Both are younger than I am (one by five years and one by eight) and now that we have negotiated the transition from a big sister/little brother relationship to acknowledging each other as peers, I am realizing how important they are to me. They have both chosen a path that involves ministry and seminary training, which gives us much in common. My youngest brother and I are similar in personality so we butt heads quite a bit; you should hear our theological "discussions"! The other is quieter so that you almost have to coax him to speak; but when he does, there is wisdom and insight that still takes me by surprise. Both are honest and brave and communicate their love for me in different ways.

Recently, after our families spent Christmas together, I found myself powerfully aware of the richness that is mine for having these two men in my life; I was unspeakably grateful for the closeness we share. At the same time I realized with sadness that if it wasn't for them, I probably wouldn't have any close relationships with men other than my husband. Because of paranoia in the Christian community about what happens when men and women get too close, we have almost completely given up on the idea that Christian men and women can be friends and contribute significantly to each other's lives. More often than not we opt for the cloister and safety of same-sex groupings. Because my brothers live so far away, this lack of close male friends feels like a significant loss to me and engenders a profound loneliness within. Because I have three daughters and no sons, I also wonder *Where will my daughters get what I have gotten from having these two men—so different from my husband—as my intimate brothers? Will they have men with whom they can argue theology, share struggles, gain the male perspective, and experience intimacy that is not sexual?* Already I grieve over the possibility that they might miss out on such life-enhancing relationships.

I agree with the conclusion Karen Mains has reached after ten years of wrestling with this issue.

> There is a better way a few of us with strength enough, with wisdom enough, must forge. In fact, I would like to state boldly that some of my best friends are Christian men. Some have been in small groups with me, some I have met in travels, some are professional colleagues, some hold me accountable for my own spiritual growth, some are older, some are younger, some are my age. Not one of these friendships has been sexualized in any way (by that I mean no fondling, no flirting, no stolen caresses, no dishonest appointments). Yet we are free to touch, to embrace in passing, to give a peck on the cheek, to share human feelings and struggles. In short, we are discovering what it means to be part of Christ's new order,

brothers and sisters in a spiritual family, a confederacy of holiness.[8]

Somehow this description sounds much closer to what God intended for his family than the elaborate sets of rules for male-female relationships I've read about. Chris and I have tried to live by those rules—I've even written about them! But we have found that building hedges around our marriage that are too high only serves to keep our fears growing strong and our relationships with spiritual brothers and sisters withering away. Somehow there has to be a balance between the wisdom it takes to protect a marriage and the maturity it takes to love our brothers and sisters with all purity. Holy cross-gender friendships are not for everyone, as Karen Mains admits, and they are not to be entered into ill-advisedly. Their success depends upon the health of individual marriages, self-awareness (especially regarding our sexuality), courage, honesty, and a commitment to Christlike love.

The challenge is to walk the narrow road between the extremes of self-protective fear on one hand and a false sense of safety on the other. Fear will not do because it is exactly the opposite of the faith by which we are to walk. A false sense of safety is equally inadequate because none of us will be safe until we are Home. Somewhere between the two lies the way of protecting our marriages and partaking of the brother/sister relationships that Christ came to create among us. I am convinced that those who search will find it.

Developing Your Own Marriage Protection Plan

Perhaps the suggestions offered in this chapter would be impractical in your situation or would need to be reworked to fit your lifestyle; they are merely ideas that have worked for us. However, these are perilous times for marriages and it is impossible to over-emphasize the importance of coming up with your own marriage protection plan. If your husband is willing to consider these ideas and work with you to come up with some guidelines to which you can both commit yourselves—great! Even the process of working through these issues will reaffirm your commitment to do whatever it takes to preserve your marriage over the long haul. If he is not willing, you can make commitments to yourself and to God to guard the areas over which you have control.

We have all seen tragic examples of godly men and women who have fallen into sexual sin, wreaking havoc on personal lives and public ministry. We simply cannot afford to go along passively with societal trends that threaten our marriages. Instead, we must shore up our defenses on the home front, keep ourselves mentally faithful, refuse to take unnecessary risks, and boldly uphold a different standard. These choices will not only result in the preservation of our marriages but will have a transforming effect on those around us as well.

FOR DISCUSSION

1. What threats to long-lasting marriage are you aware of in your corner of the world?

2. In what areas do you think your marriage might be vulnerable to attack at this time? How do you think you could shore up your defenses in these areas?

3. Are you and your spouse able to speak honestly with one another about outside attractions? Why or why not?

4. What commitments do you need to make in order to strengthen and protect your marriage?

For Further Study

Conway, Jim and Sally. *Traits of a Lasting Marriage*. Downers Grove, Ill.: InterVarsity Press, 1990.

Jenkins, Jerry. *Loving Your Marriage Enough to Protect It*. Chicago: Moody, 1992.

Mains, Karen. *Friends and Strangers* (Chapter 19). Dallas, Tex.: Word, 1990.

Notes

1. Julie Connelly, "The CEO's Second Wife," *Fortune* (August 28, 1989), p. 53.

2. George Barna, *The Frog in the Kettle* (Ventura, Calif.: Regal Books, 1990), p. 72.

3. Connelly, p. 55.

4. Deborah Diamond, "The Affair: Is Betrayal Therapeutic or Merely Common?" *Chicago Tribune* (Womanews section) (November 28, 1993), p. 11.

5. Alice Slaikeu Lawhead, *The Lie of the Good Life* (Portland, Oreg.: Multnomah Press, 1989), pp. 126-27.

6. As quoted in *The Dance of Deception* by Harriet Goldhor Lerner (New York: HarperCollins Publishers, 1993), pp. 164-65.

7. Karen Mains, *Friends and Strangers* (Dallas, Tex.: Word, 1990), p. 127.

8. Ibid., p. 128.

9

The Sexual Journey

I praise you, for I am fearfully and wonderfully made.
Wonderful are your works; that I know very well.

Psalm 139:14, NRSVB

On the eve of my wedding, a friend shared with me a great truth of human sexuality. She said, "You know, Ruth, before marriage the temptation is to have sex. After marriage, the temptation is not to."

Of course, in my virgin state—having waited what seemed like an eternity for the opportunity to express my sexuality more fully—I scoffed at this little bit of marriage wisdom. Certainly Chris and I would be the exception to that rule. Certainly we would be those who would achieve perfect sexual harmony that would last well into our golden years. After all, I planned to be Chris's sexy little wife for all of my days!

Well, education is wasted on the young, as the saying goes, and I was slow to realize the truth of this bit of education. For the first year or so everything went fine: we were typical newlyweds who could hardly wait to get home from work or church to enjoy this wonderful new way of being together. However, with the arrival of our first child (coincidence?) sexual expression got a little more complex and I remembered my friend's wise words. They didn't offer any particular solution, but it did help to have been forewarned and to know that our experience was not unusual after all.

My friend's words encapsulized the dilemma in which many a woman finds herself. If she is a Christian or has spent time in and around the Christian community, she has been taught that sex is "God's wonderful gift" to be shared with her one-and-only in the context of marriage. So she spends the first part of her life slightly uncomfortable with her sexuality, waiting for it to find it's fullest expression in marriage. But then she gets married and finds, to her chagrin, that it does not always fulfill the expectation.

A survey by popular columnist Ann Landers illustrates the point. In 1989 she asked her readers to respond to this question: Has your sex life gone downhill after marriage? If so, why? She obviously hit a raw nerve for she received an overwhelming 141,210 responses—52 percent from males and 48 from females—and the verdict was clear: 82 percent said that sex after marriage was less exciting, using adjectives such as boring, dull, monotonous, and routine.[1]

While Ann Landers' survey can hardly be considered "scientific" research, the results are telling and, I believe, representative of the reality in which many married people live. After some futile attempts to understand the forces that are at work, a woman may be tempted to dismiss the possibility of great sex as a cruel hoax. But sex will not be dismissed that easily.

One can hardly pick up a book or magazine, watch television or a movie, go to the mall or to the beach without encountering something that is intended to arouse us sexually. And unless we are completely unaware of it, our sexuality continues to call to us with inexpressible longing for more meaningful expression, for deeper connection with another human being. Each of us, married and single, is created by God with a sexual dimension; we have the potential to unite—body and soul—with another human being. That is the way God made us.

Beginnings

The sexual journey begins long before we think of ourselves as being sexually awakened. It begins with all the early verbal and non-verbal messages that we received about our physical bodies generally and our sexuality more specifically.

No one was born thinking sex is bad, or thinking sex is the greatest thing in the world either. Our attitudes toward sex, positive and negative alike, all were learned later from our culture . . . the earliest messages we got about sex, however, reached us when we were most impressionable, and they may stay with us well into adulthood—even when we wish they wouldn't. Unfortunately, those early messages were more likely than not negative ones.[2]

For many, feelings of shame, embarrassment, or confusion regarding their sexuality go way back to messages they received about sex from their family of origin, the church, society, early sexual experiences, and early experiences in marriage. For some, sex was a taboo subject that made everyone uncomfortable, leaving children feeling ashamed of their natural curiosity about their bodies and their discoveries about the sources of sexual pleasure. Others received verbal teaching that sex was good within marriage but received so many warnings about not falling into "sexual sin" that the whole thing seemed frightening and impossible to control. At the same time, they may have been observing a mother who pulled away from her husband whenever he tried to be physically affectionate or a father who grew distant from his daughters as they began to mature physically. Thus our *experiences* with sexual issues spoke louder than any verbal messages we were receiving.

Still others received overtly negative messages about sex being bad, sinful, suspect, or a duty to be endured. Many a woman shares Jody's experience of trying to disregard what her mother has told her her whole life: "My mother told me that sex is something we do to please our husbands and good women don't enjoy it. She never affirmed my sexuality, and my Dad died when I was fifteen, so I grew up believing no man would find me attractive. It took a lot of years to unlearn what she taught me and find out sex could be joyful."[3]

In addition to the verbal and non-verbal messages we receive early on, certain kinds of experiences will shape us sexually as well. Early introduction into sexual activity by a family member, sexually arousing play with a member of the same sex, and sexual abuse are all experiences that influence who we become in terms of sexual knowledge and response. Child sexual abuse, in particular, is much more prevalent than many of us realize. It has been only recently that we have begun to lift the shroud of silence that has obscured this painful issue. More and more victims of this abuse of power are finally beginning to speak about their suffering and to grapple with the long-range effect it has had on their lives.

> There is increasing evidence that child sexual abuse can be a severely traumatizing and emotionally damaging experience with long-term negative consequences for the victim. Clinical contact with adult survivors of child sexual abuses often reveals memories of a joyless youth filled with pain. Survivors speak of their loss of childhood innocence, the contamination and interruption of normal sexual development, and a profound sense of betrayal at the hands of a beloved family or trusted friend . . . . Many victims have difficulty forming intimate adult relationships, particularly with men. When relationships with men are established, they are frequently devoid of emotional and sexual fulfillment. Sexual abuse is not uncommon in the histories of women who seek treatment for sexual difficulties.[4]

Although there are no simple or painless solutions to this problem, an abuse survivor owes it to herself and to those she loves to deal with this painful part of her past.[5]

We may not all have experiences in our past that are as devastating as sexual abuse, but each of us does carry with us early messages about sex, as well as experiences that have shaped our attitudes about sex. Once we have taken an honest look at those early messages, we are able to decide, as adults, whether or not we agree with them. And once we have looked honestly (and more objectively, with our own growth and the passing of time) at the experiences that have shaped us, they no longer have so much power over the way we think and act. This kind of search for the truth can give us insight into the ways that certain early experiences might be affecting our present sexual functioning. *As we look at ourselves and our development honestly, we have the opportunity to embrace what is good and true, and move beyond what is no longer helpful.* In so doing, we can also be more purposeful about what we communicate to the next generation about their sexuality.

The Sexual and the Spiritual: Are They Connected?

For many who have grown up in and around the church, the relationship between sexuality and spirituality has been an uneasy one. Part of our religious heritage (at least for Protestant Christians and Catholics) has been "the sexless image of spirituality." In its most extreme form, true spirituality has been viewed as sexless, celibacy as the ultimate commitment to God, and bodily mortification and pain as conducive to spiritual purification. Origen, one of the church fathers, spoke of two distinct creations, the spiritual and the material, one higher and one lower. Acting on his beliefs, he actually castrated himself "for the kingdom of God." Similarly, Jerome said "Blessed is the man who dashes his genitals against the stone."[6] Women as the object of men's sexual yearnings became particularly suspect, especially in their sexuality. St. Thomas Aquinas stated, "God foresaw that woman would be an occasion of sin to man. Therefore he should not have made woman"(Summa theologica, 1267-1273).

Fortunately, the church has begun to offer some clearer thinking on sexuality, recognizing that it was created "good" and continues to be good. Particularly during the last couple of decades we have witnessed a shift away from overtly negative views that are driven by fear and thinly veiled disgust. Yet despite what, in many churches, amounts to a few statements about "God's wonderful gift of sex," discussion of topics related to sexuality are conspicuous in their absence. One notable exception is the annual "sex talk" for young people during which time a pastor or youth worker gives instruction about sexual abstinence. Although abstinance is an important subject, it fails to address many other issues of sexuality. Despite some progress, many are still exceedingly uncomfortable with open discussion of sexual topics. Recently a woman wrote to a Christian magazine with this comment: "I feel the topics covered in your [sexual issues] column have absolutely no place in a magazine for Christians. Questions about sexuality should be handled only in private conversation or counseling."[7]

This woman probably doesn't realize that her discomfort with matter-of-fact discussions of sexuality in a Christian magazine or in the church is due in part to a view that has remained strong in the church—that, rather than whole people, created by God, we are divided into body and spirit, with the spirit being superior. This dualistic outlook causes us to avoid whole areas of life that are an important part of God's plan. Says one writer, "churches shy away from dealing vigorously with sexuality because it seems incidental or inappropriate to 'the life in the spirit.' "[8] And yet, it is obvious that we desperately need to "deal vigorously" with sexual issues within the context of the Christian community. The Christian church suffers just as much as the rest of society from problems related to sexuality—teenage pregnancy, sexual abuse, troubled marriages—and it is time for the church to deal with sexuality openly, positively, and systematically, just as it would any other part of the Christian experience. Only by doing this can we learn to integrate the sexual and spiritual parts of our lives into the healthy combination God intended.

The Need to Think Spiritually About Sex

We've all heard the saying that the biggest sex organ is the brain. It's true! What we think and feel about sex probably has a greater affect on our sexual functioning than anything else. The problem is that many women think on an intellectual, rational level that sex is good but they still feel uncomfortable with it. Exposing some of the early, faulty messages we received about sex will help with these uncomfortable feelings. It is also crucial that, as Christians, we gain a more accurate understanding of what God thinks about sex.

The foundation for embracing our sexuality more whole-heartedly can be found in the creation story where we are told that "the man and his wife were naked and not ashamed." The fact that their sexual parts were exposed was as comfortable for them as the fact that they had bare feet! There was none of the shame and discomfort that is so prevalent today. For Adam and Eve in their sinless state, sexuality was a wonderful reflection of God's image, as were other aspects of their created being. *Any discomfort they would later develop with their bodies and with their sexuality was a direct result of their sin and the subsequent shame it introduced* ("I was afraid because I was naked; so I hid myself" Genesis 3:10).

Somehow many of us have developed the idea that it is "more spiritual" to minimize our bodies and sexuality. But in fact, it is clear from this record of the earliest days of human existence that the opposite is true: the sexual side of ourselves cannot be separated from the spiritual—together they make up who we are. To try to divide ourselves leads to confusion, rather than spiritual health. From the creation story we understand that maleness and femaleness and the dynamics between the two are a work of God that he pronounced very good. The very existence of the woman's clitoris is evidence that sex was given to us for our enjoyment. Unlike any other body part, the sole purpose of the clitoris is sexual pleasure.

Furthermore, Adam and Eve's comfort level with being naked is a beautiful picture for us of the openness and intimacy that is possible in marriage. The powerful experience of uniting one's body with another's is the physical manifestation of the "one-fleshness" that God intended for the man and woman who come together in mutuality and commitment. *God* is the one who connects these sexual, relational, and spiritual realities.

Paul illuminates this truth further when he speaks of the one-flesh relationship as an effective picture of the relationship between Christ and the church. Yes, it is full of mystery, but as we grow more comfortable with our sexuality, we will be more able to understand what it means to be intimate and open with God in the spiritual sense. These areas of our lives are meant to reflect and complement each other.

Once we understand that sex is "some of the best stuff God did" we need not feel embarrassed about getting all the information we can about this wonderful aspect of life. There is so much we need to know.

The Need for Reliable Information

"I was very naive sexually when I got married," says Nicolette. "I wanted sex to be something wonderful, and it turned out to be a crock. It didn't stop hurting until after our first child was born. It sure wasn't fulfilling. I was on the pill . . . I had no knowledge that being on the pill is like being semi-pregnant, in terms of hormones, and that being pregnant often brings a decrease in sexual interest. Nobody told me. I thought it was all me. I thought something was wrong with me.

"I was a pretty reserved person. . . . I *was* orgasmic once I got to the proper stage, but I was never aroused before the encounter, and that seemed like it would be so much fun! My hope was that I would be as interested in sex as Dave was, that our appetites would be the same. . . . All the time, I'd be thinking I've got to get better, I've got to get better. But there was no better to get; I was really stuck."[9]

Nicolette's comments reflect a deplorable lack of information, which is a predictable result of our discomfort with speaking plainly about sexual matters. Somehow moral people have developed an assumption that if we do what is right and save ourselves for marriage, then everything will just fall into place when the time comes. While this may be true for some, most of us could benefit from as much information as is available. There are all sorts of information that would have been helpful to

Nicolette and her husband as they prepared for marriage and as they adjusted to each other sexually after marriage—information about the mechanics of sex, the effects of birth control on sexual functioning, a more accurate understanding of female orgasmic response, help with communicating about sex, and much more. Unfortunately, Nicolette had absorbed faulty information that had shaped her unrealistic expectations.

Nicolette and others like her are then faced with a dilemma—do without information or go outside the Christian community to get it. Many Christians who are conscientious enough to want the best for their relationships end up going to secular sources for help. This is not to say that such sources are automatically inferior; many of them give excellent information—and they don't shy away from "embarrassing" details. But many Christians would prefer to get advice and help from within the faith community. Outside sources of information say little in terms of how sexuality affects other areas of life (social, spiritual, and family), and some include descriptions of sexual activities (such as group sex, pornography) that do not fit the Christian's world view.

Men Want It; Women Don't (And Other Sexual Stereotypes)

A stereotype is a conventional, formulaic, and usually over-simplified conception of a person based on his or her sex, race, religion, ethnic background, etc. Stereotyping on the basis of sex is so prevalent in our society that it is the relational air we breathe. Much of what we would like to call gender roles are no more than stereotypes, behaviors that we as a society have dubbed "normal" and "appropriate" over the years so that they have become widely accepted as the norm for human functioning. Some of the prevailing notions about men maintain that they are aggressive (or at least assertive), logical, unemotional, independent, dominant, competitive, objective, athletic, active, and above all, competent. Conversely, women are frequently viewed as passive, non-assertive, illogical, emotional, dependent, subordinate, warm, and nurturing.

What is so striking about the above lists is that we all know so many women and men who just do not fit them. That is the problem with stereotypes: they are simplistic and they fail to take individuality into account, making life more difficult than it needs to be for the person who does not fit the stereotypes. Furthermore, acceptance of such narrow gender role expectations can have a profoundly negative effect on our sexual functioning.

"Women are less interested in sex than men are."

One long-standing, slow-to-die assumption in many societies is the mistaken idea that women are inherently less sexually inclined than men. A related gender assumption is that "normal women" do not enjoy sex as much as men do. Such gender stereotypes may result in women being subjected to years of negative socialization during which they are taught to suppress or deny their sexual feelings.[10]

This was the case with Jody, the woman we heard from at the beginning of this chapter. She had learned from her mother that sex was for men to enjoy—not women. This made it very hard for her to express interest in sex or actively seek her own pleasure, even after marriage. It made it hard for her to admit that she had any sexual needs or desires at all.

For the woman who is interested in sex and easily aroused, this stereotype can cause emotional ambivalence about her sexuality. She may have a hard time accepting her responsiveness as part of herself and is then prevented from relaxing and enjoying sex as it is meant to be enjoyed. She may even begin to use her energies to block or hide her normal response rather than risk feeling like she is more interested or responsive than a "virtuous" Christian woman ought to be.

Clifford and Joyce Penner, respected Christian authors in this area, describe the problem very well:

The natural noises and behaviors typical of the sexual response cause in some women an inhibiting embarrassment that must be corrected. . . . As we—men and women—get aroused, we respond. Our heartbeat increases, we breathe faster and louder, we may experience muscular contractions, our bodies may feel like moving in thrusting or pushing motions, and we may have the urge to make gasping noises. Women who have difficulty allowing themselves to experience arousal or release are often unable to let themselves exhibit any or all of these behaviors. They are embarrassed and uncomfortable, and as with any other discomfort, they tend to avoid that which causes these negative feelings. Thus they will hold back their natural sexual responses.[11]

If a woman continues to cut herself off from her sexual feelings in this way it will become a vicious cycle; as she distances herself from her sexual feelings, she will experience less pleasure, and when she experiences less pleasure, she will lose interest. Buying into the "men want it, women don't" stereotype (consciously or unconsciously) can inhibit a woman from fully experiencing the sexual nature God has given her.

"Men are the initiators and women are the responders."

Unfortunately, this stereotype encourages women to be passive and allow themselves to be "acted upon" rather than actively seeking pleasure during lovemaking. The problem with accepting this stereotype is that being active and initiating at least some of the time is a key to enjoying the sexual experience fully. Indeed, the Scriptures make it very clear that sexual pleasure and release is a need for women as well as men and is equally important for both: "The husband should give to his wife her conjugal rights, and likewise the wife her to husband. For the wife does not have authority over her own body, but the husband does; likewise the husband does not have authority over his own body but the wife does. Do not deprive one another except by agreement . . . " (1 Corinthians 7:3-5).

Again, the Penners' comments highlight the importance of rejecting stereotypes that cast men as aggressors and women as passive receivers:

> Women who experience little arousal or are still preorgasmic . . . must take responsibility for and control of what you need. Your partner cannot give you arousal or release. He can participate in your having it, but only you can allow it to happen as you free yourself to experience it. This may seem obvious, and yet it is one of the most difficult mental shifts to make, because for so long the subtle teaching has been that it is the man's responsibility to bring the woman sexual pleasure.[12]

Another natural result of our belief that men are to be competent leaders and women are to be not-so-competent followers is that men are then expected to be "sexperts," which places an unnecessary burden upon them. Rejecting this stereotype is helpful for men because sometimes they tire of being so responsible for the success of the sexual relationship. As one man says, "Sometimes sex is more like work than fun. I have to make all the decisions—when and where we are going to have sex and what we are going to do together. It's my responsibility to make sure it works out good for both of us. This can put a lot of pressure on me and it gets real tiring always having to run the show. It would be nice to have someone else call the shots for a change."[13] Indeed! When two adults are involved in a sexual relationship it is much more healthy and fulfilling if the responsibility for acquiring information and planning the fun is shared by both the woman and the man.

"Men cannot control their sexual expression, so it is up to the women to control them."

This idea is particularly damaging to women. One of the strongest messages I received as I was growing up was that men are out of control when it came to sex and it was my responsibility as a young lady to conduct myself in such a way that I didn't cause men to lust or to exceed the limits that I would set. Men, I was told, would "take as much as they could get," so it was my responsibility to control their rampant lust by making sure they did not coerce me into unacceptable activities. Consequently, if a man did show signs of interest or (gasp!) lust or began behaving inappropriately, it was somehow my responsibility: I must not have been sitting properly, wasn't dressed discreetly enough, shouldn't have been so friendly, or *something*.

The natural result of this stereotypical view was that rather than feeling comfortable with my sexuality and viewing it as a dynamic that is a natural part of life, I experienced an uncomfortable mixture of shame and pleasure as it began to awaken. Because of my ambivalence, increasingly I distanced myself from my own sexual feelings and minimized any sexual feelings that others might have toward me.

This concern with control is not uncommon for adolescent girls during their dating years and it can be effective in helping them not give in to compromise. The problem is that, while there are some helpful elements to this stereotype (that's why stereotypes are so easy to fall into), sexuality is not a light switch that we can turn on and off at will. Therefore, it is not surprising that a woman who spends a great deal of time and energy regulating sexual intimacy to preserve her "honor" may have difficulty experiencing sexual feelings when it becomes appropriate for her to "let go" of those controlling behaviors in marriage.

For the sake of healthy sexual development we must reject the idea that men cannot control their urges and therefore women are responsible for them. To the contrary, men are just as capable of and responsible for controlling their sexual urges as we all are responsible to control our urges to spend money, eat, and indulge in angry tirades. Yes, they have strong sexual desires and are stimulated by what they see perhaps more than women are. Women do well to be sensitive to this. But we must not confuse sensitivity with responsibility. Young girls need to be encouraged to embrace their developing sexual interest and sensations as a part of becoming all that God created them to be, as cause for the celebration of growth and life that it is. When a young man experiences sexual desire for her she will then perceive it as evidence that everything is functioning as God intended, *not that she has done something wrong.* In the context of how exciting and right it all is, we have the perfect opportunity to discuss the benefits of saving the fullest expression of our sexuality for the commitment and intimacy of marriage. Then when the time comes, the sexual switch need not be turned on from having been completely off. Rather, the part of our sexual journey that includes marriage will be more like turning a dimmer switch from low to medium to high—a much more gentle transition.

"Men are unemotional and strong, and women are nurturing and supportive."

There is perhaps no stereotype more damaging to intimate relationships than this one. A man who accepts this view will find it difficult to express common human experiences of vulnerability, deep feelings, and doubts or to be tender, loving, and nurturing. He will have a tendency to approach sex as a purely physical act rather than the culmination of emotional, spiritual, and physical sharing and openness. This results in a limited kind of experience for both the man and the woman.

In addition, if a woman feels she is the only one sharing on an emotional level she will eventually grow tired of her nurturing role and shut down completely.

We must recognize these generalizations for what they are— partial truths based largely on socialization and personality types rather than anything that is inherently male or female. For instance, my husband is more emotional in some ways than I am, and he is highly sensitive to whether or not we are "connected" both physically and relationally. Although he has been aggressive in his professional life, we have observed that I have a strong independent, competitive streak that is very different in its intensity from his personality. For me, being nurturing and supportive is not inherent to my being a woman. I have to struggle at times to cultivate that side of myself that will make me the wife and mother I want to be. Therefore this stereotype is not helpful to us and has, during those times when we have tried to fit into it, made it difficult for us to accept ourselves as God made us.

Even for those couples who do seem to fit the stereotype, it is harmful to believe that the tough-guy stereotype is "just the way men are" because it reinforces patterns that do not ultimately lead to intimacy. True intimacy is only possible in a relationship where both parties are capable of strength, emotion, vulnerability, and deeper sharing.

There are many other stereotypes functioning within our culture that limits of time and space do not permit me to address; however, be assured that the experience of having had a few exposed here will make it easier for you to spot others. I encourage you and the men in your life to watch out for these over-simplified generalizations and challenge them. Because if you don't, they could keep your relationships less satisfying than they can and should be—and greatly hinder the growth of a healthy sex life in your marriage.

Are All Orgasms Created Equal?

I think many of us can relate to the woman who said, "I finally had an orgasm, but my doctor told me it was the wrong kind." Misinformation about female orgasmic response has been prevalent in our culture and has caused some couples to be overly focused on the woman achieving the "right" kind of orgasm—one experienced simultaneously with her husband during intercourse.

Ann describes the problems this misinformation caused in her sex life:

My husband and I were both virgins when we got married. We were very excited about our newfound sexual freedom and enjoyed our physical relationship immensely. I did not experience orgasm right away but the closeness that we shared was so meaningful that I was not at all concerned. However, we were reading one of the few Christian sex books available at the time which stated that simultaneous orgasm through intercourse was our "right" and we should pursue it. It also made a big distinction between "vaginal" orgasms and "clitoral" orgasms—vaginal orgasm (through intercourse alone) being the kind that mature women experienced. Well, we bought into this idea hook, line, and sinker until it began to rob us of the joy and uninhibitedness we had experienced early in our marriage. John started feeling pressured to produce such an orgasm and I started feeling pressured to have one. The orgasms I was having regularly [through direct stimulation] suddenly seemed "less than." I felt like I wasn't a "real woman" yet.[14]

Let's put this myth to rest for good, shall we? It was advanced by Freud, a man who was convinced that every woman wished she had a penis and that that is exactly what the clitoris was—a stunted penis. This led him to conclude that erotic sensations, arousal, and orgasm resulting from direct stimulation of the clitoris were all expressions of "masculine" rather than "feminine" sexuality—and therefore undesirable. At adolescence a woman was supposed to transfer her erotic center from the clitoris to the vagina. If she was not able to do so at this time, psychotherapy was sometimes used to help her to attain "vaginal" orgasms. Unfortunately, this theory led many women to believe incorrectly that they were sexually maladjusted.[15]

Today we understand that Freud's theory is physiologically inaccurate. Masters and Johnson found that all orgasms women experience involve the same physical components, from muscular contraction to the rise in heart rate and blood pressure. The body's physiological response is the same regardless of what brings her to climax.

This is not to say that there isn't any difference on an emotional level. Many women find that they enjoy different ways of experiencing orgasm at different times; it is purely a matter of personal preference, rather than a "right" and "wrong" way of doing things.

For Anne, this understanding was very freeing. She admits that, "Sex became one big stress-point until we got more accurate information about the fact that most women need direct, clitoral stimulation . . . We read authors who encouraged us to relax and enjoy all the ways that we receive pleasure from being together. We're having a great time now that we're not so goal-oriented."

Masturbation: Wrong or Right?

There is probably no area of sexuality about which there are stronger taboos than the subject of female masturbation. Even though research indicates that anywhere from 60-80 percent of women masturbate to orgasm, broaching this as a topic of conversation with a friend usually results in nervous laughter or dead silence rather than any kind of meaningful dialogue. It is even more intimidating to consider including a discussion of this subject in a book one is writing! In this case, it seemed both inaccurate and unfair to discuss female sexuality without dealing with this issue.

Many of us have strongly negative feelings about masturbation, but we would be hard-pressed to figure out where those negative feelings come from. The reason for this, as Clifford and Joyce Penner observe, is that most of us received the messages before our first birthday that shaped our views.

It is inevitable that children will reach for their genitals in the process of discovering their own bodies. When they do, regardless of their age, they will discover that touching themselves genitally brings pleasure. Naturally, they will want to do it again. This is often the moment when the first messages about sexuality are communicated. If the child reaching down and touching the penis or clitoris causes the mother to move the child's hand away, this is a unique experience. There is nowhere else that the child is not allowed to touch himself. He can poke his fingers in his ears, his belly-button or his nose without a negative reaction . . . Pulling the hand away from the genitals, therefore, may be connected with instructions not to touch things that are dirty, bad, or dangerous.[16]

So, you see, our shame and fear about touching ourselves is formed very early in our development. And since the source of these feelings are most often events that happened before we were old enough to remember, it is very difficult to think clearly about this aspect of ourselves.

In addition, there have been strongly negative attitudes toward masturbation in the Judeo-Christian view that procreation is the only legitimate purpose for sexual activity. Because masturbation does not result in pregnancy, it has often been condemned. This, added to the sexual/spiritual split we discussed earlier, has made it easy for religious folks to look askance upon this particular way of enjoying one's own body.

The "evils" of masturbation received a great deal of publicity in the name of science during the 1800s and early 1900s due largely to the writings and teaching of several physicians who attributed such maladies as blindness, stupidity, consumption, insanity, and idiocy to this vile practice.[17]

In order to examine this issue objectively, we must first understand that the Scriptures do not address the subject of masturbation. The story of Onan (Genesis 38:8-10) has been cited at times as a relevant passage in this regard, but a careful reading of the story makes it quite clear that Onan's sin had nothing to do with masturbation. It had everything to do with the fact that he disobeyed God by refusing to do the duty of a brother-in-law.[18] Passages such as 1 Thessalonians 4:3-4, 1 Corinthians 6:9, and Romans 1:24 have also been thought to condemn masturbation but are now understood to be speaking about homosexuality or sex outside of marriage.

Negative and positive aspects

So are those who say masturbation is wrong completely off base? The most obvious negative about masturbation is its capability of controlling us. Any habit that causes us to reshape and reschedule the rest of our life has gained undue influence over us. There are many things in this life that are good but have the potential to become enslaving (food, shopping, exercise) or to be used selfishly (sex, money, power).

In their book, *The Gift of Sex*, Clifford and Joyce Penner offer three biblical guidelines by which we can evaluate whether or not masturbation has become a positive or negative activity in our lives. I have adapted them here.

Is it loving? If our behavior takes something away from our marriage partner, then it is not loving. However, if masturbation helps to alleviate pressure between two people who have differing degrees of sexual interest or helps a woman learn to be more responsive to her husband, then it could be viewed as a loving choice.

It is addictive? If a woman is masturbating excessively as a way of avoiding relationship issues or emotional needs, then this is not healthy. If a woman uses masturbation as a way of becoming more comfortable with her body and her sexuality, then this can be life-enhancing.

Is it lustful? There is the mistaken notion that you have to lust in order to enjoy self-pleasuring. However, many people report that when they masturbate they think only of their spouse or the physical sensations they are experiencing.

Medically speaking, we now know that there are no harmful physical/medical effects from masturbating. And there is actually ample evidence that the practice can be beneficial—especially for women. In fact, much of the time when couples go to therapy for sexual dysfunction, one of the first things they are instructed to do is to become more comfortable with their own bodies, before they can relate in the most open, healthy way to each other's bodies. This can be particularly difficult for women, who in many ways have been conditioned *not* to be sexual. Therefore women are precisely the people who can gain the most from learning about and accepting their own sexual responses.

One study found that married women who masturbate have greater marital and sexual satisfaction than women who did not. There are many reasons this might be the case.[19] Self-stimulation is also very helpful for the woman who has not yet learned to experience orgasm (anorgasmia).[20]

"Many women have never looked at themselves," reports Joanne Marrow, Ph.D., sex researcher and professor of psychology at California University in Sacramento. "They have no idea what their gynecologists see, what their lovers see. Men know more about the female anatomy than women do." Obviously, this puts a lot of pressure on our husbands to figure out how to please us—and it keeps us from taking any responsibility for finding out what we need to know in order to achieve greater sexual fulfillment. For the woman who is uncomfortable with her body or with her body's sexual response, the freedom to explore in privacy may make it easier for her to share this knowledge with a partner and be responsive to him.

Manual stimulation of oneself and of one's partner is one means of keeping a sex life vital during periods when intercourse is not possible. There will be times in a marriage when, due to stress, fatigue, medications, pregnancy or other hormonal changes, one or the other partner is unable to function sexually through intercourse. These are times when touch can do more than merely substitute for "regular" sex, by becoming a means of serving one another with love and tenderness.

What if I'm not married?

Unmarried adults have become used to suffering in silence when this subject comes up. There are basically two schools of thought on singleness and masturbation. One belief is that the single person must be celibate in every sense of the word, avoiding sexual stimulation or experience of any kind. The other view sees sexuality as too much a part of the whole person to be completely repressed and ignored.

Christian writers and counselors fall into both camps. Some view the physical release of sexual tension as a gift from God for women who are single, helping them to embrace their sexuality. Masturbation is seen in some ways as a deterrent to sexual sin; some women have found that when they are feeling comfortable with and in control of their own sexuality, they are less likely to act inappropriately in their male/female friendships or fall into sexual relationships out of desperation or the mere pressure of unmet sexual urges. At the same time, those who view masturbation as off limits maintain that there are non-sexual ways of channeling the sex drive, such as physical exercise, expression of creative gifts, and service to others.

Whichever view you take, if you are single it is most important that you think through the reasons for your decision to allow yourself this practice or prohibit it. We are in the most danger of being negatively influenced by our sexuality when we neglect to take an honest, well-reasoned look at it. This area, certainly as much as any other, should be explored in the context of prayer. God, who created us as sexual beings, will not turn away in embarrassment when we ask him for help and wisdom!

Sexual Satisfaction: What Some Women Have Learned

Although lack of sexual fulfillment in marriage is very widespread (82 percent of couples in Ann Landers column indicated problems, 50 percent in a more scientific study conducted by Masters and Johnson), there is a significant percentage of married couples who are having good sex. One woman from Dickinson, North Dakota, responded to Ann Landers this way: "Our sex life gets better all the time. Why? Because it is an honest expression of a love based on respect, courtesy, honesty, admiration, and mutual trust." There are also women who are single (never married) and single again due to divorce or death who are able to embrace their sexuality even though they may or may not have a partner. What might we learn from them?

Women who are enjoying their sex life know that great sex develops in a loving, committed relationship.

Even though Chris and I have been married for thirteen years, there are aspects of ourselves and new sexual experiences that we are just beginning to share. I know that it would be shattering to my own sexual journey if, after a time of connecting deeply on an emotional and physical level, there were any possiblity at all that he would walk away with a vague promise of "I'll call you sometime." For women in particular, love and sexual intimacy cannot grow in a garden of uncertainty.

The reality is that plenty of women are trying it the other way. Many single women are struggling to reconcile the reality of their sexual desires with the circumstances of their singleness in a society that throws sex in their face at every turn. Times of singleness—which will come to all of us at one time or another—are enormously difficult in this regard. But if the sexual revolution taught us anything, it taught us that there are very good reasons for God's ideal of saving sexual intimacy for those who commit themselves to each other in marriage. The words of this woman who tried it both ways are haunting in their description of our very real need for connection and also in the disillusionment that comes from trying to meet it in the wrong way:

> Sexuality mimics love. It compels tenderness and embraces, it forces the lovers to hug one another, to allay one another's pain through the revelations of sexuality, as when true love is exchanged. What follows such experiences? Disappointments, a bitter aftertaste, mutual accusations of bleak loneliness, feelings of exploitation and defilement. Neither of the two gave true love but only expected to receive it, therefore, neither received it.[21]

On the other hand, sex therapist Dr. David Schnarch proclaims, "The greatest sexual ecstasy comes, not with a Cosmo cover girl, but with your spouse." He describes the electrifying sexual connection that can be reached by two people in a close, intimate relationship. However, he goes on to say that the reason many married couples don't achieve it is "because they are scared to reach their sexual potential within the overwhelming intimacy of marriage." Intensely intimate marital sex is more threatening than people realize, and it only takes place as couples "work past their fears and the discomfort that comes from breaking barriers of intimacy together."[22] In others words, good marital sex only happens as we become "increasingly naked" in the presence of the other person and are not ashamed.

Women who are finding sexual fulfillment understand that the growth of a sexual relationship is not about technique but about two people learning how to be loving and intimate. They know it is a process complete with stops and starts, days when it seems like a lot is happening, and days when it seems like nothing is happening. They accept the fact that there are obstacles to overcome, heights of ecstasy to be scaled, and dry spells to wait through patiently. They understand that sexual freedom is not the freedom to have sex with anyone they want; it is the freedom to stay in the process of achieving true intimacy with another human being.

Women who are experiencing sexual satisfaction do not worry about "how things ought to be."

They are not agitating themselves with thoughts like: *We should make love more often. I should be experiencing multiple orgasms. We should be trying this new position or that new toy.* Even though they seek help when they need it, they enjoy their sex life as uniquely their own and not to be compared with national averages or the latest magazine article. They accept the changes that different seasons and circumstances bring—pregnancy and child-birth, infertility, stress, work that requires travel for either partner, differing sexual appetites at different times, menopause, "mid-life crisis," and aging. They do not view these as problems so much as opportunities to adjust, accept, or search for new ways of loving.

A woman who is enjoying herself sexually is also becoming increasingly "at home" in her body.

We live in a culture in which it is extremely difficult for a woman to feel good about her body. Anorexic actresses and models parade before us on television and in magazines while busty *Playboy* bunnies scream at us THIS IS WHAT A SEXUAL WOMAN LOOKS LIKE!

All of us, when we compare ourselves to these images, feel inadequate in some way. Many of us bring negative feelings and images with us from growing-up years when sexual organs and functions (such as menstruation) were considered dirty. It doesn't help that so much of the "street talk" and profanity we hear chooses sexuality as its main subject. And yet these bodies are our vehicle for enjoying sex and they are part of the gift that we give when we make love. But how can we give ourselves over to the sexual experience when we feel that our bodies are ugly, inadequate, or the reason men lust (as some churches teach)?

There are many different ways in which a woman can move toward accepting and enjoying the body God has given her. We can get to know our bodies, take stock and discover what we think is beautiful, and accept those things that aren't quite what we want them to be.

We can learn a simple appreciation of our bodies in the many ways they function: "I really enjoy the things I can do in my body. I enjoy letting go and experiencing orgasm, I love a good game of softball or volleyball, I'm amazed that my body has given birth and nursed children, or I'm so glad that I can comfort someone with a hug. Thank you, God, for this wonderful gift."

In addition, being physically fit or at least physically active is a wonderful way of getting in touch with and enjoying the physical you. I am more physically active in my thirties than I have been to this point. I have discovered that walking, biking, and participating in sports heightens my feelings of gratefulness to God for the gift of life in this body and keeps me more in touch with my physical, sexual self. Participating in these physical activities with Chris is another way of enjoying one another that contributes to our sexual attraction to each other.

All of us—married or single—can embrace the "sexy" or sensual side of ourselves quite apart from the presence of a man in our lives. One woman notices, "Swimming in warm water, dressing in silks, exercising until I feel "high"—all of those things are sexual feelings to me. Even if I'm not involved with someone else, I can still feel sexually alive."[23] Others are aware of their sexuality as an *energy,* and rather than being uncomfortable or ashamed of it, they channel it toward caring for those around them and making a difference in this world.

There are many ways of learning to be at home in our bodies and as we do so, we bring pleasure to the heart of God by enjoying the gift he has given.

Women who are experiencing sexual fulfillment in their lives know not to use sex as a weapon.

Because of the way relationships between men and women have traditionally been structured (the man being dominant and the woman being his supporter), it can be quite natural for a woman to see sex as her only weapon in a situation where she feels she has very little power.

In the workplace a woman may be sorely tempted to flirt with the boss just a little, feeling that this is the only way for her to get into his good graces. In marriage, it doesn't take long for a wife to figure out that withholding what her husband wants most puts her in a pretty powerful position; she may begin to see this as her only way of registering a complaint or displeasure. These tactics often get results, making it easy to fall into a pattern of using sex or withholding it—without even being aware of what we are doing. The resulting sexual difficulties then are not really about sex but are indicators of other problems in the relationship, for instance, and imbalance of power or the inability to resolve conflict.

Ann Birk, director of a sex therapy program in Boston, says that the major predictor of sexual dysfunction in women is chronic and underexpressed anger. When a woman is angry with her husband or boyfriend and that anger cannot vent itself, it can have a direct and crippling effect on sexuality. Repressed anger and loving abandon just aren't able to exist side by side in most cases. Birk recalls the case of one young woman who was very angry with her husband because he was rarely home. "She could not bring herself to confront him with her anger and developed a vaginal condition that prevented her from having intercourse. As soon as she was able to confront him, to say, 'I need you home more,' the condition vanished almost immediately and she was able to function sexually."[24]

I do not wish to make this process seem simpler than it is—it takes hard work to resolve these kinds of issues to the satisfaction of both parties in a relationship. However, many women have found that when they learn to deal more directly and effectively with anger and other relationship issues, they begin to flourish sexually.

Women who are experiencing sexual satisfaction also know that they have to conserve time and energy for it.

A newspaper article entitled "No Sex, Please, We're Tired Americans" highlights the fact that one of the biggest reasons married couples do not have sex is their pace of life. After the job, children, school functions, meals, care of the home . . . couples end up in bed very tired. And when you're not getting enough sleep in life, it's easy to let sex go by the way or to have it but not put too much into it.

It's simple: Good sex takes energy. The sexually vital woman knows this and makes a conscious effort not to use up her last bit of energy at night washing the floor, putting last-minute touches on a presentation, or talking on the phone to a friend. There certainly are "crunch times" when it is inevitable that we fall into bed exhausted or don't even make it to bed at the same time. But the woman who is enjoying a fulfilling sex life does not allow this to become a pattern. She lets the floor go, gets up a little earlier in the morning, and gracefully excuses herself from the lengthy phone conversation. She doesn't just see sex as being for her husband; she understands that she needs it, too. The warmth of being close, the release of tension, the reawakening of loving feelings that get lost in the rush of everyday tasks and schedules are elements of life that she cannot afford to lose touch with. And so, with at least some regularity, she saves part of herself for it.

The Joy of Sex

Psychiatrist M. Scott Peck tells the story of working for many months with a "rigid, frigid woman in her mid-thirties" who underwent a sudden and profound Christian conversion, and within three weeks of her conversion she became orgasmic for the first time in her life. Peck observed that the timing was not incidental and concluded that when this woman became able to give herself wholeheartedly to God, in very short order she became able to give herself wholeheartedly to a human partner. He quotes these words of a friend, "The sexual and spiritual parts of ourselves lie so close together that it is hardly possible to arouse one without the other."[25]

I am fascinated by Peck's story and his conclusion. One has to wonder what it says about our spirituality when those who know the Creator have trouble being sexual. And one has to wonder what we are missing out on sexually when we are unable connect every aspect of our physical, sexual, and emotional natures with the One who dreamed it all up. As I continue to contemplate the meaning of human sexuality, I am beginning to realize that there is a strength, a dignity, an abundance in the life of a woman who embraces God's gift of a physical body with it's amazing capacity for sexual pleasure and oneness. My delight in living in this body with breasts, womb, and vagina, my abandon in sharing my body with my husband, the sexual energy that keeps me seeking appropriate connection with others, the freedom I experience in becoming the unique individual God created me to be rather than squeezing myself into society's stereotypes—all of these are ways of bringing glory to the Giver of the gift. They are a powerful testimony to the fullness that comes when we live our lives in harmony with him.

FOR DISCUSSION

1. What were some of the early messages—positive and nega-tive—that you received about sex, and how do you think they affected your sexual development? What about early sexual experiences?

2. How comfortable are you with considering your sexuality in the context of spirituality? Is this a new concept for you?

3. What sexual stereotypes have you spotted that have affected your sexual functioning? Can you identify others that were not addressed in this chapter?

4. If you are married, do you feel that you have had adequate information about sexuality in preparation for marriage and during your marriage? What kind of information did you feel you were missing or what misinformation caused you trouble? Where would you have liked to have been able to get this information?

5. Describe your experiences of being a sexual person in a state of singleness. What was (or is) most difficult about it? What were (or are) some ways in which you were (or are) able to be comfortable with your sexuality even though you were (or are) not married?

6. What would you like to communicate to the next genera-tion—your children, grandchildren, nieces and nephews, teenagers in the church—about sexuality that was the same

or different from what you learned? Brainstorm practical ways in which this could be done.

For Further Study

Crooks, Robert and Karla Bauer. *Our Sexuality,* 5th ed. Redwood City, Calif.: The Benjamin-Cummings Publishing Co., 1993.

Hybels, Bill. *Tender Love: God's Gift of Sexual Intimacy.* Chicago: Moody Press, 1993.

Penner, Clifford and Joyce. *The Gift of Sex.* Waco, Tex.: Word Books, 1981.

Smith, Harold Ivan. *Singles Ask: Answers to Questions About Relationships and Sexual Issues.* Minneapolis, Minn.: Augsburg, 1988.

Wheat, Ed, M.D. and Gaye Wheat. *Intended for Pleasure: Sex Techniques and Sexual Fulfillment in Christian Marriage.* Grand Rapids, Mich.: Baker Book House/Revell, 1979.

Notes

1. Ann Landers, *Chicago Tribune* (January 22, 23, 1989).

2. Linda Tschirhart Sanford & Mary Ellen Donovan, *Women and Self-Esteem* (New York: Penguin Books, 1984), p. 389.

3. Marian Liautaud, "What's Amore?" *Marriage Partnership* (Summer 1991), p. 26.

4. Robert Crooks and Karla Bauer, *Our Sexuality* (Redwood City, Calif.: The Benjamin-Cummings Publishing Co., 1993), p. 656.

5. Karen, a survivor of child sexual abuse and rape has this to say: "Healing is painfully slow and difficult. Both therapists I have worked with have suggested a seven-to-ten-year recovery process. I have struggled to overcome guilt and shame, finally being able to admit I did not invite the experiences of childhood abuse or rape. I am still working on remembering parts of my story. I continue to express anger and rage, which are essential to my healing. I have learned to trust some people. And I still grieve for the losses, not only for me but for the rest of my family as I have struggled with healing. I can now cry in a limited fashion, and my self-concept and self-esteem are fairly restored.

"Incest and rape are not about sex. They are about power and control. It's about big people over little people, superior over subordinate. To heal requires that I gain a sense of control over my life. I've gained enough control to make the transition from victim to survivor. The healing process is long but I've surrendered to the fact that being in the process of healing is a respectable and legitimate place to be. I deserve to heal. My greatest victory is to break the promise [not to tell] and tell my story. I have been able to use the power of writing and speech to transform, to change anger, fear, shame and guilt into useful tools for cutting away lies and deception." James Newton Poling, *The Abuse of Power* (Nashville: Abingdon Press, 1991), p. 41.

6. As quoted in James Nelson, *Body Theology* (Louisville, Ken.: Westminster/John Knox Press, 1992), p. 37.

7. "Letters," *Marriage Partnership* (Summer 1994), p. 9.

8. James B. Nelson, *Body Theology,* p. 19.

9. As quoted in Alice Slaikeu Lawhead, *The Lie of the Good Life* (Portland, Oreg.: Multnomah Press, 1989), pp. 114-115.

10. Crooks and Bauer, *Our Sexuality,* p. 68.

11. Clifford and Joyce Penner, *The Gift of Sex* (Waco, Tex.: Word Books, 1981), p. 304.

12. Clifford and Joyce Penner, *The Gift of Sex,* p. 305.

13. Crooks and Bauer, *Our Sexuality,* pp. 79

14. Ann (not her real name) is a friend of the author.

15. Crooks and Bauer, *Our Sexuality,* pp. 171-172.

16. Penner, *The Gift of Sex,* p. 231.

17. Crooks and Bauer, *Our Sexuality,* p. 252.

18. It was the custom among the Israelites that if a man died without an heir, it was the duty of his living brother to provide an heir for him by having intercourse with the widow. When a son was born, he would be considered the son of the deceased brother rather than the biological father. When Onan was called upon to provide an heir for his dead brother, he withdrew in the middle of intercourse with the widow and "spilled his semen on the ground" so that he would not give offspring to his brother (Genesis 38:9). Onan's sin was his disobedience to the law of God.

19. Women can learn a lot about their own sexual responses—which kinds of touch feel good, which are irritating, which body movements and positions enhance sexual response—from self-pleasuring. Too often women leave knowledge about their sexual anatomy to their husbands or doctors because of their phobias about touching themselves. D. Hurlbert and K. Whittaker, "The role of masturbation in marital and sexual satisfaction: A comparative study of female masturbators and non-masturbators," *Journal of Sex Education & Therapy,* (1991) 17, pp. 272-282.

20. Therapy programs for anorgasmia are based on progressive self-awareness activities such as body exploration, self-examination of the genitals, self-stimulation to learn about pleasure and arousal, and self-stimulation to orgasm. Once a woman has experienced orgasm through

self-stimulation she progresses step-by-step toward experiencing orgasm with her husband by guiding him in stimulating her to orgasm. They can then incorporate what they have learned into their experiences with sexual intercourse. This process takes time and commitment but can greatly enhance a woman's ability to respond to her husband. Her willingness to take responsibility for learning about herself, for pursuing the pleasure of orgasm and sharing what she has learned with her husband is one of the keys to her sexual fulfillment.

21. Elizabeth Haich, as quoted in Gabrielle Brown, *The New Celibacy: Why More Men and Women Are Abstaining from Sex—And Enjoying It* (New York: McGraw-Hill Book Co., 1980), p. 212.

22. As quoted in Dana Kennedy, "The New Monogamy," *The Chicago Daily Herald,* (February 18, 1993), Section 8, p. 1.

23. Sanford and Donovan, *Women and Self-Esteem*, p. 401.

24. Caryl Rivers, Rosalind Barnett, and Grace Baruch, *Beyond Sugar and Spice* (New York: G.P. Putnam's Sons, 1979), p. 207.

25. M. Scott Peck, *Further Along the Road Less Travelled* (New York: Simon & Schuster, 1993), p. 225.

10

Children: Bane or Blessing?

Of course a mother gives up a lot for her child: blood, sleep, tears, not to mention time, money, and peace of mind. But a mother must not feel obliged to give up herself. Not unless she wants to raise a motherless child.

Lisa Cronin Wohl

I have a confession to make. Mothering has not been all that easy for me. Sometimes when I am at home scrubbing "tinkle" out of the carpet while my husband is making intelligent conversation at a business lunch I wonder, *Who says mothering is the most wonderful thing a woman can do? Who says women are better suited for this than men are?* (Personally, I think I am better suited for power lunches than for dealing with messy diapers, but my husband isn't jumping at the chance to switch places with me.) Then my cynical self pipes up and suggests that perhaps this was an idea the men came up with: If they could convince us that childrearing and housekeeping were "a woman's highest calling," we would stay home and do it so they wouldn't have to!

All kidding aside, it *is* difficult to admit how hard mothering has been for me. It's not the mechanics of it—the pregnancy, the birthing, knowing what to feed when, figuring out what to do when they're sick. No, it is the relentlessness of the demands, the never-ending nature of the needs to which I must attend, the interruptedness of life, the constant delayed gratification of my own desires, and the uncertainty about how my children will turn out after all the parental words of wisdom have been said and all the hard work has been done.

Is This Any Way to Begin?

I have thought long and hard about whether I should begin a chapter on children this way, vacillating between burying the negatives somewhere in the middle and leaving the chapter out all together. Still embroiled in the struggle, I wonder what I have to offer. I cannot point to three or four successfully raised children (my oldest is only eleven) and say, "If you want your kids to turn out like this, here's how you do it." So far things are going pretty well, but I realize that some of our greatest challenges still lie ahead. And I am not yet at the point where I can offer such long-range perspectives as "Enjoy it while you can; these years go by so fast." In my head I know this is true, but having already been at mothering for eleven years with fifteen more to go (barring anything unforseen), "fast" is not the first word that comes to mind.

When I mentioned to a friend the possibility of taking the cowardly route and leaving this chapter out of my book, she admonished me in no uncertain terms: "But that wouldn't be fair! I think a lot of women struggle with their role as mother. I know that for me, mothering is nothing like I thought it would be. I mean, I love my daughter, but I just live for nap-times. I always pictured myself spending hours reading to her, but I don't. She wants me to get down on the floor and play with her, but I've discovered that I just don't like to play. I'd much rather be working on the house or reading a magazine. My self-concept has really suffered because I haven't lost the weight I put on during pregnancy. I hardly ever have reason to get dressed up, and nobody listens to me as though I have anything intelligent to say (like they did when I was working). So you see, you can't leave this subject out of your book; at least you need to share your struggle!"

It is a lot harder to start with a realistic picture of the way things are rather than a glowing picture of the way things ought to be. Why? That many women find mothering to be more difficult than they had imagined is yet another truth of female experience that has been effectively censored in many circles.

Thanks to the media and ever-present childcare experts, women are constantly bombarded with ideal images of the perfect mother and are constantly admonished to live up to an endless set of unrealistic expectations. A good mother is supposed to be totally devoted to her children; she is not allowed to get tired or bored by childcare and housework. Nor is she supposed to feel anything but love for her children. A woman who feels—as most mothers do—moments of boredom, anger, frustration, resentment, and other "negative" emotions toward her children is taught not that she is a normal mother but that she is a bad mother."[1]

In addition, our theology informs us that children are a gift from the Lord. Motherhood has been emphasised as a woman's highest calling in a more all-consuming way than fatherhood is for men. When our experience doesn't match our belief system, we're not quite sure what to do with ourselves. Our shelves overflow with how-to books and magazine articles written by earth-mother types who have an unlimited supply of ideas for planning day-trips, craft projects, holiday traditions, and morning devotionals, but these examples just overwhelm us further. I, for one, am in awe of these women but rarely encouraged by them.

A Struggle Within a Struggle

The struggle that women experience on an individual level takes place within a culture that is also grappling with the issue of "what to do with the children." A quick glance at recent magazine and newspaper headlines draws a powerful picture that requires little commentary:

The Daily Herald (Chicago area)—"Are We Forgetting the Kids?"

Christianity Today—"After School Orphans"

Newsweek— "A Mother's Choice" (to leave kids in day-care)

Moody Monthly—"Who's Minding America's Children?"

Fortune—"Executive Guilt: Who's Taking Care of the Children?"

The Chicago Tribune—"Forever Theirs: The Dark Side of the Job From Which You Cannot Resign" (this one was accompanied by a large drawing of a mother gagged and bound to a chair, held captive by a child with a gun. A real encouragement!)

As women we have been told that we can have it all—a good marriage, children, a successful career, material possessions, and other personal achievements—and that children don't have to interfere with any of these pursuits. At best, children are viewed as an option that we can fit in at our convenience or decide against altogether; at worst, they are seen as a nuisance or an interruption.

As a country, our financial investments speak volumes about our values. We spend nearly $300 billion annually on military weapons while failing to provide the relatively nominal sums needed to care for poor expectant mothers and their children. While we expend all sorts of effort to protect whales, elephants, bald eagles, condors, Panda bears, minks, etc., over one million unborn children are killed every year primarily because they would be an inconvenience.

In an article in *Time* magazine entitled "Shameful Bequests to the next Generation" the author describes our legacy to the young—bad schools, poor health care, deadly addictions, crushing debts—and utter indifference:

Mothers and fathers worry about the toxic residue left from too much television, too many ghastly movies, too many violent videos, too little discipline. They wonder how to raise children who are strong and imaginative and loving. They worry about the possibility that their children will grow wild and distant and angry. Perhaps they fear most that they will get the children they deserve.

"Children who go unheeded," warns Harvard psychiatrist Robert Coles, "are children who are going to turn on the world that has neglected them." And that anger will come when today's children are old enough to realize how relentlessly their needs have been ignored.[2]

Is it any wonder, then, that "guilt and uncertainty make childrearing the No. 1 topic of conversation among young mothers today. Today's parents are raising children in ways that little resemble their own youth. The question that haunts them: Will the kids be all right?"[3]

Is This a Job for Supermom?

If we are at all aware, we understand that the chances of "the kids being all right" are slimmer than they have ever been. Dr. James Dobson notes in a recent newsletter, "It has become a daunting task to shield the younger generation from 'safe–sex' instruction in school, from profane and sacreligious language in the neighborhood, from immorality and violence on television, from homosexual and lesbian propaganda and from wickedness and evil of every stripe."[4]

After reading the litany of threats facing our children today—drive-by shootings, illegal drugs, sexual molesters and kidnappers, murderers and rapists taking children from their own bedrooms, degrading television programming (such as "Beavis and Butthead"), and commercials featuring dancing condoms—it is easy to feel overwhelmed by the responsibilities of parenting, the majority of which still falls to women in our society. The fact that our culture no longer supports morality and religious truth as it has in the past just adds to the gravity of the situation. As Christians we labor under the weighty realization that, to a certain extent, the future of our children depends on our ability to counter the culture in which they live and breathe.

The job of raising children today is not a job for supermom. It is a job for mothers and fathers who feel equally responsible for the physical, spiritual, and emotional well-being of their children. It is for mothers and fathers who realize that they cannot delegate their responsibilities as parents to anyone else—not to their spouse, not to the nanny or the day-care workers, not to the church, not to the school system.

I used to wonder why it bothered me so much to hear men preach Mother's Day sermons extolling the value of children and the high call of nurturing them. Now I realize that the emptiness I felt when listening to these messages had nothing to do with the truth of the message but was due to the fact that much of the time it was being presented by a person who walked out the door almost every day of his life to do something else—pursue a career, build a successful ministry, or just play basketball with the guys. I understand human nature enough to know that when a man thinks something is really important (such as clinching a big sale, making an important presentation to the board) he usually wants to do it himself. So I was receiving a very mixed message from the menfolk: The job of bringing up children is important but not so important that *we're* willing to do it. The message that parenting is of secondary importance was communicated, as so many important messages are, not by the loudness of their words but by the loudness of their actions.

There is no biological necessity for the pattern into which we have fallen, and this pattern of mothers as primary caretakers has not always existed. In Jewish culture for example, education of the children was the mother's responsibility for the first three years (probably until weaning), but after that religious education of the sons became the father's responsibility. During this time he also taught them the family trade. In addition, extended families lived together so that grandparents, aunts, uncles, and older children participated in caring for the younger ones. It was in this context that the most powerful instruction regarding childrearing was given to the entire congregation of Israel—men and women together: "Keep these words that I am commanding you today in your heart. Recite them to your children and talk about them when you are at home and when you are away, when you lie down and when you rise. Bind them as a sign on your hand, fix them as an emblem on your forehead, and write them on the doorposts of your house and on your gates" (Deut. 6:6-9, NRSVB). These verses presuppose involvement in the childrearing process by both parents in ways that, by today's standards, could seem almost radical.

What's Good for the Goose . . .

The most encouraging thing that has happened for me as a mother is that Chris and I have begun seeing ourselves more clearly and completely as a team in this challenge-of-a-lifetime called parenting. I have found that I do not need another book on how to be a better mother. I do not need a support group. What I have needed is my husband, the father of these children, to participate more fully with me in this great call of God upon our lives. I have needed to hear him say with words and with action, "You are not alone. These children are just as much my responsibility as they are yours. Yes, I have my own vocational calling and you have yours but together we have received the high call of parenting." I have needed to know and experience in relationship with him that raising children is not "women's work" but kingdom work that is worthy of the very best we both have to offer. And it has been in working together—rather than in listening to one more sermon or reading one more book—that my feelings of being overwhelmed and isolated and inadequate have begun to subside. For in this area more than any other I am sure that together we can do anything.

Of course, a greater sharing in the joys, frustrations, and hard work of parenting will benefit not only women but men and their children as well. Mary Stewart Van Leewuen describes the benefits to children at great length in a chapter on co-parenting in her book *Gender and Grace*. As one example she cites a study in which psychologist Michael Yogman found that men and women tend to play with their children in different ways: fathers were more likely to engage in physical play, tapping or patting younger infants and doing controlled rough-housing with older ones. Mothers made more sounds and played more verbal games with their children, particularly games involving imitation and taking turns. Yogman's conclusion (surprise! surprise!) is that "children need both kinds of play for social and intellectual development. The mother-infant dialogues encourage language development and turn-taking, while the father's more physically oriented games help develop spatial and motor skills."[5] Other studies indicate that, later on, a father's availability or absence also affects such things as academic achievement (in sons in particular) and career success (in girls in particular). Of course the benefits to the child's self-esteem are incalculable when there are two adults who are highly involved and available (as opposed to the "exclusive mothering and marginal fathering" that is so common).

Back to Basics—Together

Every couple who becomes aware that, yes, children need what both their fathers and their mothers have to give, embark on a very personal journey. The journey begins with a reaffirmation—together—of basic Scriptural teaching regarding children. Mother and father enter the process of organizing family life so that children are nurtured by meaningful relationships with both parents, income is generated to provide for the needs of the family, and the call of God upon the lives of individuals is answered and supported. And part of this parenting journey involves confronting the influence of our culture on our own attitudes and reaffirming our commitment to valuing our children the way God does.

We affirm that children (including the unborn) are human beings created and known by God.

Psalm 139 makes it clear that God knows and forms each child in the womb. Even before they are born God already has a plan for them. As he pointed out to Jeremiah: "Before I formed you in the womb I knew you, and before you were born I consecrated you; I appointed you to be a prophet to the nations." As Bible women knew so well, life does not begin merely because of human action—God is always involved in conception and birth. Eve said, "I have gotten a manchild with the help of the Lord" (Genesis 4:1), the Lord was the one who opened Leah's womb (Genesis 29:31), and Ruth 4:13 says "the Lord enabled her [Ruth] to conceive and she bore a son" (NASB). Because God is, in some mysterious way, involved in the giving of life we can be assured that every child is valuable and given by God for a purpose.

We also affirm God's view that children are a blessing.

It is not only that children in general are a blessing to the world but that the specific children God sends to my husband and me are given as his blessing for our lives. So it is with hearts that believe God that we are sensitized to the blessings that God is bringing through our children. Some of these blessings are fleeting in nature—the pleasure of soft baby cheeks perfect for nuzzling and pug noses perfect for kissing; the pride that fills our hearts as we watch a child—our child—run with strength and grace down a soccer field; the fullness that we feel as we don pajamas and cuddle under blankets to watch a movie together on a snowy night; the amazement of seeing strengths that are so different from our own surface in our child . . .

These are the moments of blessedness that come when we are least expecting them. They are the moments of joy that give us perspective when the stress and tedium of childrearing threaten to overwhelm us. Sometimes these moments are gone as quickly as they come, but we can hold them in our hearts as evidence that God sent these children to bless us in ways we couldn't imagine until we experienced them.

Other blessings are of the long-lasting sort, blessings we carry with us into eternity. The greatest of these is the blest-ness of knowing that you have influenced another soul to embrace Christ as Savior; this is the one treasure that you *can* "take with you." We have the opportunity to invest in the life of a child who will then go out into the world to make an impact for Christ, thus multiplying our own efforts at being light and salt in this world. And we can know that when we leave the scene we leave behind sons and daughters to whom we have passed the baton of faith.

In addition, the task of parenting requires the development of character qualities such as selflessness, unconditional love, humility, servanthood, faith, and perseverence that we might otherwise feel we could do without. Working on our character deficiencies as they surface in dealings with our children, and listening to their unedited evaluation of our Christianity as it is lived out before them, can provide us with wonderful growth, if we are willing! And of course there is the familial bond of love that, in most cases, is passed from generation to generation, making life very rich indeed. These are the blessings God intends for us when he gives us the gift of children. And in a culture like ours where it seems that children are "God's least wanted blessing," it is the eye of faith that knows how to see them and the believing heart that knows how to receive them.

We embrace the sovereignty of God in our lives.

In my mother's day, nearly every pregnancy was "unplanned" because there weren't as many options for controlling conception and birth. I don't really want to go back to those days, but I often wonder if we haven't gotten so good at "family planning" that we have lost sight of God's role in the whole thing! Perhaps we even feel that we are better family planners than he, believing at some deep level that if we left it up to him, he would probably give us more than we could handle. While I am not against conception control, I've seen enough infertility, as well as pregnancies occurring even when precautions were taken, to realize that we do not have ultimate control over the giving and taking of life on this earth. This is an awareness that infertile and fertile couples alike do well to to cultivate, for we must all work out our faith in God's will for us and take our *why?* questions to him.

We accept the responsibility to make informed choices.

This acceptance of our responsibilities balances our faith in the sovereignty of God. As I mentioned in an earlier chapter, there is nothing wrong with having choices. However, the fact that we have options today that we didn't have a generation ago places an even greater responsibility upon us.

I appreciate Bill Hybels' encouragement for newly married couples not to make the choice to have children unadvisedly. He mentions several important considerations that should inform such a decision. "First," he says, "newly married couples should devote themselves to solidifying their marriage before they even consider having children. Raising a healthy, well-adjusted, Christ-honoring child in today's world almost demands a strong marriage and family unit." He also recommends that couples consider whether either of them carries "the deep trauma of a painful or tragic past" that they have not yet worked through fully. They need to consider the implications of passing on their debilitations to another generation and make the investment in dealing with unresolved issues (i.e. substance abuse, sexual abuse, domestic violence, parents who were unable to give love, etc.) before bringing a child into such a complicated scene.

A couple may also decide, after listening to God and paying careful attention to what he is doing in their lives, to make "the legitimate choice" not to have children in order to participate in building Christ's kingdom by pursuing full-time careers in ministry or in the marketplace. It is unfortunate that, in some Christian circles, couples who choose not to have children are considered incomplete, selfish, or unfaithful to the whole idea of marriage. Yet, we can't ignore the "normal" families that have turned out to be quite unhealthy because someone didn't count the cost—either to the children or the parents—of adding family members to a life already consumed in ministry or career.

Speaking from his own pastoring experience, Hybels says, "I regularly talk with expectant married couples who are clearly annoyed that the baby is going to make the mother miss six weeks of work. 'Right during the busiest season of the year!' The father, of course, won't interrupt his climb up the ladder, so they face a dilemma. Who'll take care of the baby? Repeatedly I'm asked if I know a church member who can babysit from 7:00 A.M. to 6:00 P.M., five days a week, and sometimes on weekends . . . The mindset is fast becoming: We'll make them; you raise them."

The fact of the matter is that "it takes time and energy to raise children. Young couples hoping to find a system of child-rearing that doesn't inconvenience them or overload their already full schedules should rethink their decision. It may be they're missing the whole point of having children."[6]

Children: Are We Willing to Love Them?

The story of Hannah is a true parenting success story. Perhaps you remember the story of this woman (see 1 Samuel 1 and 2) who struggled with infertility and promised God that if he gave her a son she would then dedicate him to the Lord's service. The Lord answered her prayer and gave her a son whom she named Samuel. When Samuel was weaned, Hannah kept her promise and took Samuel to the temple in Shiloh to serve God with the priest Eli. Despite Eli's spiritual deadness and some pretty poor influences (Eli's unruly sons), Hannah's early training stood Samuel in good stead and he went on to become the greatest prophet, priest, and judge Israel ever knew.

Although the details of Samuel's upbringing are a bit unusual, the story of Hannah and her son reminds us that God can work in a variety of situations to produce children who will serve him faithfully throughout their lives. This is of particular comfort to single parents who labor under the added pressure of trying to fill the roles of mother and father while at the same time trying to generate all or most of the family income. When our situation seems impossible, Hannah's story reminds us that God can be trusted to bring our children through whatever the disadvantages of our situation happen to be. Hannah's story also underscores some basic elements of effective parenting and causes us to ask ourselves if we are willing to love our children in some very practical ways.

Love them enough to welcome them.

Believing that children are a blessing, Hannah prayed that God would give her this gift and welcomed her son when he was born. Her response mirrored Christ's welcoming attitude toward children in Matthew 19. Even though the disciples were anxious to shoo them away, Christ used them as an example of faith and said that when we welcome children we welcome him.

As women we have a unique opportunity to welcome the little ones by bearing them in our bodies. This is the first sacrifice we make and it *is* a sacrifice! In a body-worshipping culture such as ours—it is no small thing to realize that your breasts and stomach may never be the same! But that is only the beginning. Beyond that, we (both father and mother) choose to welcome children into our lives, making a place for them where emotional, spiritual, and physical needs are met. In so doing we show love to Christ himself.

Love them enough to make them a priority.

As would any woman who believed that her child was a wonderful gift, Hannah made Samuel a priority. In her case, this attitude was symbolized by the time she took to nurse and wean him. In Jewish culture weaning (which literally means "dealt fully with") was accomplished when the child was around three years old. It is interesting to note that until Hannah felt that she had dealt fully with her son she didn't even take the annual trip to Shiloh to worship at the temple. She knew that the time would come when it would be right for her to go and fulfill her promise. But until the Lord freed her to do that she made Samuel her priority.

Hannah was forced by her unusual circumstances to see her time with Samuel from a perspective appropriate to the reality we all face. The window of opportunity for training and loving and being with our children is very short indeed—maybe not as short as it was for Hannah and Samuel—but short nonetheless. In the early years especially, most children want to be with their parents more than anyone else and are wide open to our influence. I am glad that my children have been able to put these desires into words so that I have been forced to consider how important I am to them. They are too old to cry or throw temper tantrums but old enough to say with disappointment, "I don't like it when you're gone. I like it when you're here."

"But what's wrong with the babysitter?" I probe.

"Nothing. I just like it when you're here."

What a privilege! And how long do you think that will last? How long before they are embarrased to be seen with me and want to hang out with their friends rather than their family? What is worth giving up being with my kids when they want to be with me more than anyone else in the world? These are the questions that every mother must answer for herself.

Love them enough to discipline them.

The story of Samuel (1 Sam. 1–4) offers a poignant study in contrast. While Samuel ministered to the Lord and experienced his presence, Eli's sons grew up to be scoundrels. The Bible says that they had no regard for the Lord or for the duties of a priest to the people. They stole from the offerings people brought and seduced the women who served at the place of worship. Eli knew about his sons' sinful behavior but only offered a weak reprimand. Finally God intervened and said to Eli, "I chose your family out of all the families in Israel to perform the sacred duties of priests. I revealed myself in a special way to your ancestors. Why then have you honored your sons more than me by fattening yourselves on the choicest parts of every offering of my people Israel?"

To Samuel God communicated this message, "I am about to punish his [Eli's] house forever, for the iniquity that he knew, because his sons were blaspheming God, and he did not restrain them." And that is exactly what happened. It wasn't long before Hophni and Phineas were killed in battle. When Eli heard the news he fell from his seat, broke his neck and died. A tragic ending to tragic lives.

The point of this true story is that we don't do anyone any favors by refusing to discipline our children. In fact, we do our children, ourselves, and our society a great disservice when we allow them to be disrespectful, immoral, and undisciplined. We have the same problem today that Eli did, although perhaps for our own set of reasons. Leading pediatricians T. Berry Brazelton and Benjamin Spock (remember him?) worry about the disappearance of discipline, particularly when both parents work. "Parents don't want to spend the little time they have with their children reprimanding them," says Spock. "This encourages children to push limits and test parental authority."[7]

It's true! Children have an uncanny ability to play on the guilt feelings to which today's parents are so susceptible. I know that when I am stressed out because I have taken on too much in life and I am not sure if the kids are getting what they need, it is very easy to give in when they accuse Chris and me of being unfair in requiring them to pull their weight around the house, behave respectfully, or live without something they very much want. Then, in an effort to assuage my own guilt, I tend to spend the time when I am available over-compensating. However, when I am more consistently available for my children's legitimate needs, I am much more confident about insisting that they do the dishes, accept the fact that they cannot have another sleep-over, respond respectfully to the limits we have set in our home, or whatever. When I know they are getting what they really need from us—time, attention, limits, physical needs (not necessarily wants) met—then I am a lot less likely to give in to doubt when it comes time for strong discipline or saying no.

Limits set by loving parents are good for children because young people who do not know how to work, how to respect authority, and how to control themselves will not get very far in life. In fact, these qualities are becoming so rare that just by cultivating them, our children will distinguish themselves and be well on their way to success in work, marriage, family life, and spiritual service. We cannot expect them to have this long-range perspective while they are young; that's why we must keep it for them until they are old enough to realize how important it is.

Love them enough to impart our faith.

We do not know how many years Hannah was able to spend with Samuel before she took him to the temple. However, we do know that in whatever time she had, she trained him effectively and cultivated his spiritual life. Even though he was surrounded by poor influences at the temple, Samuel continued to serve the Lord faithfully. And even though Eli was ineffective as a father and as a spiritual leader ("the word of the Lord was rare in those days; visions were not widespread"), it was Samuel who began to hear and respond to God's voice. In fact, as Samuel grew up, "the Lord was with him and let none of his words fall to the ground . . . And all Israel knew that Samuel was a trustworthy prophet of the Lord . . . For the Lord revealed himself to Samuel at Shiloh and the word of Samuel came to all Israel."

Amazing! God had given up trying to communicate with the elderly priest Eli, but this young boy had a heart that was sensitized to the voice of God. So it was through this mere child that the horror of spiritual drought in the land of Israel was relieved. Where do you think Samuel's strong character and spiritual receptivity came from? My guess is that it was a combination of the heart God gave him and the training he received in his home.

When I read about Samuel, I am provided with such a vision for my parenting. To think that my children also have the potential to be those through whom God speaks and from whom a river of life can flow to those who thirst for a taste of God's presence. But I know that bringing up the kind of children who will know God and bless others doesn't happen by accident. It happens in homes where children are important, where limits are set, and where spiritual awareness is cultivated.

Another observation we can make from Deuteronomy 6:6-9 is that effective child training is a mixture of structured and spontaneous instruction. This verse presupposes that both parents are with their children enough to be able to teach them throughout the day as they walk together, talk together, and as they drop off to sleep and wake in the morning. These are the times and places when moments of openness develop. But today this kind of parent-child contact cannot be taken for granted. A grandmother who cares for her grandaughter while her daughter (the mother of this child) works illustrates the point. She describes the day her grandaughter came home after having had sex education class at school. She was full of questions like "Does it hurt?" and "Isn't there some other way?" but since her mother wasn't available, this little girl ended up asking these questions of her grandmother. The grandmother wrote to Ann Landers with this comment and question, "A mother should be here for moments like these. How can I make my daughter see what she's missing?"

Moments like these are the teaching opportunities to which Deuteronomy 6 is referring, quality times of talking and fielding questions made possible by the quantity of time that parents and children are together. These informal times of training and instilling values are just as important as more structured family prayers and Bible reading. Our decisions about priorities and use of time should always include consideration about being with our children during those crucial moments when their hearts are open and ready to receive truth.

Love them enough to let them go.

It was a beautiful, sunny day in March—the kind that makes you glad to be alive, glad you made it through another Chicago winter. It was the kind of day in which I felt compelled to walk rather than drive to pick up Charity, then six, from kindergarten. After we connected in front of the school, Charity took off and started walking a couple blocks ahead. I called her back and tried to convince her to walk and talk with me but she said, "Can we do that when we get home? I want to be a big girl." There was no malice. No impertinence. Just the honest expression of a little girl trying to grow up.

I said, "Sure." How could I refuse?

So we walked that way and I had the pleasure of watching her walk ahead of me—pony-tail bobbing, backpack carried proudly. And I was so pleased that she was my grown-up girl who had been able to put her heartfelt desire into words. Every block or so she would turn around and wave—just making sure I was there. And I would wave back, trying to communicate with every wave that I loved her and was proud of her and that it was okay that she wanted to walk alone.

I realized that day that this was a taste of things to come. It was a picture of the process parents and children begin at birth: the process of letting go, of allowing our children to gain their independence little by little. It is, after all, what we raise them for, and we must never forget it. For Hannah, the moment of letting go all the way came much sooner than it does for most of us. After weaning Samuel she took him back to the temple to dedicate him to the Lord's work just as she had promised. It is hard to imagine that she was unaware of Eli's lack of spiritual effectiveness or Hophni and Phineas' sinful behavior. Yet the time had come for her to trust that the training she had done and Samuel's own personal relationship with God would give him the moorings he needed. Certainly that is what we must trust when we face those moments of saying good-bye.

Fortunately, letting go comes gradually for most of us, one good-bye preparing us for the next. The first time we leave our baby with grandma prepares us for the church nursery. The first day of school prepares us for that first overnight. Dropping them off at the big Jr. High or High School prepares us for the day we drop them off at college. Teaching them to choose their dates wisely and then letting them go prepares us to let them go with the one they choose to marry. Dedicating our children to the Lord at birth, as Hannah did, helps prepare us for the day when he calls them into service that may take them far from us.

There is a balance to be achieved between letting children go in age-appropriate ways while providing the undergirding for their explorations. We mustn't hold them too tightly, yet always be there, in the background, waving at them with support and love, ready to come to their aid when they need us, protecting them from dangers that they are not quite ready to handle. And somewhere along the way, as we negotiate their transition into adulthood, we become more than parents and children. We become friends.

Radical Teamwork

I am convinced that women today struggle so greatly with their role as mothers chiefly because we have allowed the huge responsibility for the nurturing and rearing of children to fall primarily on them.

God's instruction for us to attend to our children is huge and multifaceted, but when men and women are committed to it together, it is much less overwhelming.

There's a multitude of ways by which nurturing children, generating income, and following God's call to minister to a lost world can be blended into a rich family life. It should not necessarily be assumed that the wife's ministry or career is the one that must come to a grinding halt. In some cases it is feasible for the husband, the wife, or both to slow down, adjust, and find ways to give and take in order to accommodate the arrival of children. One couple I know (both pastors now) have made a variety of arrangements throughout the life of their family. Steve finished his graduate work B.C. (before children), but Jamie had not finished hers when they had their first child. During the early months of his son's life, Steve worked part-time and helped out with child-care while Jamie finished her degree. Then for four years, Steve worked in his career of choice while Jamie stayed home with child number one and added another. At a previously arranged time they switched and Steve stayed at home for three years while Jamie got her career off the ground.

Today the children are well on their way to adulthood and both Jamie and Steve are settled into their respective pastorates. Steve looks back on the years he stayed home with his children as "the best years of my life" and says "I know that I did something that was right for my children, my wife, and even me." He concludes,

More and more fathers are investing themselves in parenting because they realize there is joy and satisfaction there that can be found nowhere else. And they realize that their children need them in ways that are important and unique . . . Who better than a father to mold healthy self-image through play and everyday activities like these (playing horsey on the living room floor)? Who better than a father to teach his children that they are important and worthwhile by investing his time and energy into them? Who better than a father to nurture body, mind, and spirit, showing that all of these are part of an integrated whole? Fathers who stay at home with their children have the same goal as everyone else—to bring up happy, well-adjusted children. But this modest goal is surely one of life's greatest challenges. When parenting is shared, however, the objective may be more easily attained.

Kari Torjesen Malcolm recalls growing up in China with her missionary parents:

Long before Mama and Papa were married they believed they were called to be messengers of the good news. They also wanted children, and so agreed to take turns caring for them. They had an egalitarian marriage, in which there was no "captain of the ship" to call the shots. Instead, decision-making, preaching and the care of children (including home schooling) were all a joint venture for husband and wife. They were conscientious about our physical and spiritual safety. They did not leave us alone with our Chinese playmates, or local adult visitors who might indoctrinate us with pagan superstitions. Their rule was that one of them was always at home . . .

but this arrangement took careful planning. Mama purposely had the clinic and some of the women's Bible studies in our home. But when she went out to visit from house to house in pagan homes, or to teach Bible classes, Papa was on duty at home. Of course when he travelled to villages and was gone for a week or more, Mama had to limit her local outreach.[8]

The story of Peter and Valborg Torjesen is a stirring example of how two individuals blended their lives and organized their family in such a way that four children were nurtured physically and spiritually, while both parents continued to answer the call of God to preach the good news of Jesus Christ.

Mary Stewart Van Leeuwen offers this challenging perspective for families today:

The root issue is not primarily . . . some historically fixed way of structuring family economic, domestic, and childrearing tasks. The root question is one of priorities. How can a given Christian family, with its particular constellation of talents, limitations, and needs, so structure itself that it contributes to the advancement of God's kingdom on earth? Perhaps the best environment for children is not one in which the mother stays home, but one in which the whole family, as part of the larger family of God, reaches out to meet the needs of others. Just how an individual family accomplishes this at various stages of family life is a matter of responsible Christian freedom. There is no one, "best" answer that fits every case.[9]

The Well-Balanced Perspective

It strikes me that one reason we get so discouraged with mothering is that we fail to keep it in perspective—the perspective that it is one part of a whole life lived for kingdom purposes. Mary Stewart Van Leeuwen observes that in recent days our "near-idolatry" of the traditional family has, in some ways, caused us to place kingdom priorities in a position of secondary importance. While it is true that some of this has been needed to right some of the wrongs of the past (parents who have been unavailable to their children because of over-commitment to career or ministry), once again balance is needed.

It is a grave mistake to invest mothering with all of our hopes and dreams for meaning in this life. For you see, while motherhood is a rich and deeply rewarding experience to which God calls most women, motherhood is only half a life work. One author notes that thirty-five is the age at which most women send their last child off to school, leaving many years for them to make other meaningful contributions to the kingdom of God here on earth. Many who have not kept their mothering in the perspective of the greater call of God on our lives, find themselves feeling useless after their children leave the nest, with very little sense of what they should do next. Many end up biding time in dead-end jobs that do not capitilize on their giftedness or give them a sense that they are contributing to a cause that really matters. The sense of how much of themselves they "gave up" to be mother can be overwhelming when they begin to realize it.

This does not have to be! Mothering may be a full-time job for ten to twenty years (depending on how many children we have and how they are spaced) but even those who have full-time jobs can find time to take a class, keep up a marketable skill, stimulate their thinking with quality reading and conversation, or serve on a committee that stretches them in an area where they need to be stretched. It is possible to plan for the future while enjoying and investing in the present.

The Bottom Line

I have experienced a wide range of thoughts and feelings about my role as mother. I, too, have thought the grass looks greener on the side of the fence where women carry briefcases (or at least get a few minutes to themselves!). I, too, have taken a long, hard look at the inequities women have experienced as a result of having all the homemaking and parenting responsibility placed on them. And I have had days when anger and frustration have threatened to overwhelm me. But in the midst of all that I realize that there is no other area in my life in which the ramifications of my choices are so far-reaching and the potential for regret so great.

It is all this and more that I carry into God's presence over and over again because I trust him. I know that he cares equally about me and about my children; he alone can give me perspective and help me put my life and the lives of my children together in a way that is best for all of us in the long run. You see, there is a middle road that women must walk, a road that runs between two harmful extremes—neglecting our children or neglecting ourselves. The only way to find the middle road and stay on it is to keep looking to God for guidance as each choice presents itself. I cling to his promise in Psalm 32: "I will instruct you in the way you should go; I will counsel you with my eye upon you." With his loving eyes upon me and my eyes on him I have gotten better at knowing, "Yes, this ministry will fit right now . . . no, this class would take to much of my energy . . . two evenings out this week, not three . . . No committee work now but maybe after this project is finished . . . Time to put my own reading away and read to the children . . . The kids have gotten what they need from me today, now I can give some time to other work . . . Oops, I overdid it today, I'll do some adjusting tomorrow . . . "

As I bring my wrestlings to God and open my heart to what he wants to teach me about being a mother, I notice that some concerns pale into insignificance while other concerns give birth to certainty. Most recently (in my research for this chapter) I have been shaken to the core by the realization that OUR CHILDREN ARE IN DANGER! And that danger is not just "out there" in the big, bad world. Our children are also in danger because as a generation they have suffered our neglect, our indifference, and our inability to do what it takes to keep our families together.

The March 1994 issue of *Parents* magazine cites recent studies showing that during unsupervised hours, latchkey children of all social and economic groups are twice as likely to abuse drugs, engage in sexual intercourse (one psychologist mentions that usually a girl has her first sexual experience in her or her boyfriend's empty house), join gangs, or contribute to the astonishing 48 percent increase in the juvenile violent-crime arrest rate in the last five years. In addition, these children may be extraordinarily isolated and lose out on valuable life-shaping experiences with friends and role models during the critical period of adolescent development.

Another study highlights the "negative long-term consequences of interparent conflict and divorce for preadolescents and adolescents." Of 170 children of divorced parents interviewed, one-fourth blamed themselves for the divorce and suffered low self-concepts; more than one-fourth harbored illusory hopes that "once my parents realize how much I want them to, they'll live together again"; and approximately one-third lived in fear of being abandoned by their parents.[10]

The message of these statistics is simple: Our children need us! Now I consider myself to be a liberated woman. But there is no way I can, nor would I want to "liberate" myself from the fact that I have children and they need me. I know all about gender inequity in the distribution of family responsibility. I know that parenting is hard and lacks the immediate rewards that other types of success offer. I know that mothers have been undervalued and disrespected. But as the emotion surrounding these issues subsides a certainty emerges: The answer is not for women or men to pull out and renege on their God-given responsibility.

The answer is for men and women together to fall on our faces before God and confess selfishness and upside-down values where they exist. To believe God when he says children are a blessing and to translate that belief into the obedience of making them a priority in our lives. To slow down our frantic rush for success, money, and power so that we can adequately supervise our children all the way through their teenage years. To share parenting responsibilities so that women and men alike can nurture other parts of themselves even as they nurture children. To daily cast ourselves upon God for wisdom and strength. To daily inquire of God, "What will it require of me to nurture the emotional, physical, and spiritual well-being of my children?"

It is in this area more than any other that our generation needs to trust and obey God on a very personal level. For it is in trusting and obeying that we will find our answer to the question CHILDREN: BANE OR BLESSING?

FOR DISCUSSION

1. Although the Scriptures tell us that children are a gift from the Lord (Psalm 127:3-5), in today's society they are often viewed as a nuisance or an interruption. Why do you think children seem to be "God's least-wanted blessing"?

2. How does an understanding of God's role in conception and birth affect your view of children? How can we communicate God's view of children to those around us?

3. Practically speaking, what does it mean to love our children? What factors keep us (men and women) from throwing ourselves wholeheartedly into parenting?

4. What are some of the things that only you can give to your child(ren)? What do you need to do to insure that your children receive these things from you?

For Further Study

Adeney, Miram. *A Time for Risking*. Portland, Oreg.: Multnomah Press, 1987

Malcolm, Kari Torjesen. *Women at the Crossroads*. Downers Grove, Ill.: InterVarsity Press, 1982.

Dacey, John S. and Alex J. Packer. *The Nurturing Parent*. New York: Simon & Schuster, 1992.

Van Leeuwen, Mary Stewart. *Gender and Grace*. Downers Grove, Ill.: InterVarsity Press, 1990.

Van Vonderan, Jeff. *Families Where Grace Is in Place*. Minneapolis, Minn.: Bethany House, 1992.

Yates, Susan Alexander. *And Then I Had Kids: Encouragement for Mothers of Young Children*. Dallas, Tex.: Word Publishing, 1988.

Notes

1. Linda Tschirhart and Mary Ellen Donovan, *Women and Self-Esteem* (New York: Penguin Books, 1984), p. 144.

2. Nancy Gibbs, "Shameful Bequests to the Next Generation," *Time* (October 8, 1990), p. 43.

3. Philip Elmer-Dewitt, "The Great Experiment," *Time* (Fall 1990, special issue), p. 72.

4. Dr. James Dobson, *Focus on the Family Newsletter* (February 1994), p. 3.

5. Mary Stewart Van Leeuwen, *Gender and Grace* (Downers Grove, Ill.: InterVarsity Press, 1990), p. 158.

6. Bill Hybels, *Honest to God?* (Grand Rapids, Mich.: Zondervan, 1990), pp. 85-88.

7. Philip Elmer-Dewitt, "The Great Experiement," *Time*, p. 75.

8. Kari Torjesen Malcolm, *We Signed Away Our Lives* (Downers Grove, Ill.: InterVarsity Press, 1990), p. 60.

9. Van Leeuwen, *Gender and Grace*, pp. 176-177.

10. Focus on the Family Bulletin (June 1988).

11

When Life Is Less than Perfect

Other people don't create your spirit, they only reveal it.

Dr. Henry Brandt

Even though my present lifestyle does not lend itself to wearing fine jewelry very often, I do enjoy window shopping in jewelry stores every now and then. When I do, I am always amazed at how the stones, especially the diamonds, are displayed in such a way that they are absolutely brilliant. Even the cheapest, most ordinary diamonds look beautiful under the bright lights when displayed against a background of black velvet.

It can be that way with people, too. Sometimes, against the backdrop of pain, tragedy, or difficulty, beauty shines forth that is accentuated by the darkness of the surrounding circumstances.[1]

Abigail was such a woman—a diamond whose beauty and worth shone against the backdrop of a difficult, heart-breaking marriage. Abigail was everything I would like to be—godly, intelligent, and beautiful. However, the most striking thing about her is not that she was all of these things but that she managed to achieve it in what, to me, would have been an intolerable situation. How did she do it?

Abigail's story is found in 1 Samuel 25. The writer describes her as "intelligent and beautiful in appearance" while her husband, Nabal, was "harsh and evil in his dealings" (25:3, NASB). As the story unfolds we see more evidence that Nabal was no knight in shining armor: he was impossible to reason with, he was selfish and rude, and he was an alcoholic who got abusive when he was drunk.

It is not hard to imagine the disappointment and loneliness Abigail lived with on a daily basis. Certainly she had the same hopes that we all do for tenderness, intimacy, companionship, and spiritual oneness in marriage. How she must have wished that her life was different and perhaps, at times, cried out to God to deliver her from the pain of such a hurtful, unhealthy relationship.

One day, the normal stress of living with a difficult man escalated into a true crisis. David, who was running from a jealous King Saul, happened to be hiding out in the desert of Paran, which bordered Nabal's property. During that time, David and the six hundred men who were with him provided protection for Nabal's shepherds while they were in the fields. In fact, one of Nabal's servants commented that David's men were "very good to us, and we were not insulted, nor did we miss anything as long as we went about with them.... They were a wall to us both by night and by day" (verses 15-16, NASB).

The crisis came during a festive day of sheepshearing when David politely requested some kind of payment for services rendered: "Let my young men find favor in your eyes.... Please give whatever you find at hand to your servants and to your son David" (verse 8). True to his character, Nabal responded with rudeness and ungratefulness, denying any knowledge at all of David or the protection his men had provided. This sent David into a murderous rage and he quickly organized four hundred of his men to kill all the males in Nabal's household (verses 21-22).

One of Nabal's servants understood the gravity of the situation but also understood that Nabal "is such a worthless man that no one can speak to him" (verse 17), so he went straight to Abigail and explained the situation. She obviously had the complete confidence of her household staff and with good reason. She immediately swung into action, initiating a plan that was characterized by insight, godly wisdom, courage, and diplomacy. She hurriedly gathered together the provisions that David's men needed and rode out with her servants to meet him. The Scriptures tell us that the two parties met in the hidden part of the mountain, no doubt with hearts beating fast from fear. But Abigail's actions, attitude, and spoken words quickly diffused this volatile situation.

When Abigail saw David, she dismounted from her donkey and fell on her face in front of him, willing to take the blame herself for not seeing David's men when they came (verse 25). Then she went on to ask God to bless David with an enduring dynasty, for she understood that David was to be the next king of Israel. It was in this context that Abigail explained, as tactfully as she could, what she understood to be the spiritual significance of the mistake David was about to make. "It shall come about when the Lord shall do for my lord according to all the good that He has spoken concerning you, and shall appoint you ruler over Israel, that this [killing members of Nabal's household] will not cause grief or a troubled heart to my lord, both by having shed blood without cause and by my lord having avenged himself."

David was impressed by Abigail's discernment, and he listened and responded to the wisdom of her words. He realized that what she was saying was true: If he did act out of uncontrolled anger, he would shed innocent blood rather than leaving vengeance up to God. At best, this would place a permanent blot on his character; at worst, it could disqualify him as a leader for the people of Israel. So he blessed her and received the provisions she had brought, turning away from his murderous intent.

Abigail must have been very relieved at the outcome of her peace-keeping mission, but when she got home, she faced another problem. Nabal had been partying and he was drunk; it was not a good time to tell him about the disaster they had so narrowly escaped (25:36). She wisely waited until the next morning to fill Nabal in, and when he heard it "his heart died within him so that he became like a stone" (verse 37). Apparently he was paralyzed by a stroke and then died ten days later. When David heard about what had become of Nabal, he was thankful that he had waited and allowed God to avenge his cause. Not surprisingly, he also sent a proposal of marriage to Abigial, and she accepted in what appears to have been a very happy ending.

Despite the fact that Abigail's marriage was probably arranged, as was the custom of the day (Nabal's wealth probably made him seem like a good catch), her situation is all too contemporary. One author describes Abigail as the perfect candidate for an Al-Anon recovery group or a support group for "women who love too much," citing Abigail's rush from an abusive marriage into a polygamous one as a foolish choice.[2] It's an interesting perspective; it could be that Abigail does give us a Biblical example of classic co-dependency, one spouse "enabling" the other's addiction by consistently covering up consequences and smoothing troubled waters.

But there was more to Abigail than that. She was not living in denial and she didn't shy away from a realistic assessment of her husband: "Please do not let my lord pay attention to this worthless man, Nabal, for as his name is, so is he. Nabal is his name and folly is with him" (verse 25). She was a woman with excellent management and interpersonal skills, as evidenced by the way she handled conflict and related with the household staff. She worked effectively for peace by clarifying the issues in a non-threatening way. And she showed tremendous spiritual discernment that bordered on prophesy. She knew that God had great plans for David. But she also knew that he was on the verge of making a critical error in judgment by taking his own revenge rather than leaving it up to God. Abigail was a master of tact and timing, choosing carefully how she would broach sensitive subjects and when she should act on her own initiative. And she chose to stay committed to Nabal rather than run from her problems.

Rather than seeing a "woman who loves too much," I see a woman with limited options who exercised the few she had quite effectively. In those days, a woman without a husband had no options. She couldn't obtain a restraining order, find a shelter for battered women, get a job and start a new life. Back then, a wife belonged to her husband in the same way that he "owned" his slaves and his cattle, and he was free to do with her as he wished. Had Abigail left Nabal, she would have been totally without support and protection and Nabal could have killed or severly punished her if he caught up with her. The option of leaving was not available to her.

However, Abigail still had the option of choosing how she would respond to her circumstances. She never used her husband's boorish behavior as an excuse to act the same way. Rather, she kept growing in a positive direction so that when the moment of crisis came, she was ready with the skills and spiritual maturity to handle it. Because she had been exercising her inner options, the moment of crisis also became a moment of opportunity—an opportunity to save her family and to be an influence for good in the life of a great man of God.

It's not only difficult marriages that cause the backdrop of some lives to be so black. For others it is chronic pain, depression, or a physical disability. A painful childhood memory. A past mistake. A child, a spouse, or an in-law who is a constant source of emotional pain. Perhaps there is something in our life that, like Paul's thorn in the flesh, hurts so badly we've begged the Lord to take it away—but it's still there. What is it for you? What can you do to insure that it becomes a backdrop to accentuate the beauty of godly character rather than a black hole from which you never return?

Talk to God About It

One thing is true: God has the power to change our circumstances. The story of Abigail tells us that. And it is perfectly acceptable for us to ask him to do just that. Paul asked the Lord three times to take away his "thorn in the flesh" (2 Corinthians 12:7-10) and Christ, the night before he was crucified, prayed, "My Father, if it is possible, let this cup pass from me; yet not what I want, but what you want" (Matthew 26:39, NRSVB). Within their willingness to do God's will was an expressed desire that God take the hard thing away. This kind of desire is not condemned or forbidden by God.

In the case of both Paul and Christ, God chose not to grant their request. But that did not lessen the importance of expressing it to him. They still needed to be in communication and know that God cared, much the same way we want to remain in communication with our children even when we have had to say no. We're not upset that they asked and we still want to talk, to know how they feel, and to tell them that we care and understand. When I want something I can't have or a particular problem seems unworkable, I find it still helps to talk to my husband or someone else who understands. It helps when he says, "Your feelings of frustration are completely natural and I understand." Sometimes he is able to offer another perspective or a ray of hope—and sometimes he isn't. But knowing that we're in this together becomes a comfort and a bond. So it is with God. We talk to him because he has the power to take our pain away. But even when he doesn't, we talk to him because he is our father and we need to know that he is with us in our pain and that he cares.

Turning to God in the midst of difficulty has a way of kicking our relationship with him into a new gear. Remembering the worst storms of her difficult marriage, one woman recalls, "I had a choice between talking to myself or talking to God so I chose to talk to God. He became like my husband, in a way, and as I look back on those times, my relationship with God seemed so much closer than it does now that I'm through the storm."

A difficult marriage or any other kind of hardship gives us the opportunity to learn to trust God and love him despite the circumstances of life. In so doing, we move beyond the honeymoon stage ("I'll follow God as long as things are going well") to a more mature relationship that transcends hardship and is able to trust even through dark times.

See It from God's Perspective

Even when God does say, "No, I'm not going to take the pain away," as we talk with him about it he gives us the opportunity to take a step back and look at the larger picture. Sometimes he even allows us to understand his reasons. Although we can never completely understand the mind of God on these matters, there are some things we do know. First of all, we know that pain and weakness keep us in touch with our vulnerability and our need for God and others. As Paul learned through his thorn in the flesh, pride lurks in dark corners of our hearts and often the greater the work that God is doing in and through our lives, the more susceptible we are: "To keep me from exalting myself, there was given me a thorn in the flesh, a messenger of Satan to buffet me—to keep me from exalting myself" (2 Corinthians 12:7, NASB).

Another thing Paul realized was that his thorn in the flesh would keep him available as a means by which God could show his power. Jim Dethmer, a pastor at Willow Creek Community Church, put it this way:

> When power is put against the backdrop of vulnerable ordinariness, it's like taking that diamond and putting it against the black velvet backdrop. As the darkness contrasts with the light, power contrasts with weakness. When we are truly in touch with our ordinariness, we become vulnerable and it becomes a black velvet background against which the stunning diamond of the power of God is seen pouring through our lives.[3]

Let It Produce Character

It would be easy for us to let the fact that God delivered Abigail from her difficult marriage take our focus off other important facets of this story. For me, the main point is not that she was delivered but that she did not allow the circumstances of her life to determine what she would become. Rather than becoming hard, bitter, cynical, or stagnate, she allowed God to chisel away at her character, making her brilliantly beautiful against the dark background of a difficult life.

Interestingly enough, the character qualities that Abigail's circumstances produced were precisely the ones she needed in order to deal with her crisis situation. These qualities were so much a part of who she was that she didn't even need to stop and think. Undoubtedly, years of living with a difficult man had given her plenty of opportunity to develop the wisdom, tact, and courage it took to approach David effectively. And years of talking with God kept her so in tune with what he was doing in her world that she could offer a spiritual perspective when it was needed. She had not allowed the negative forces in her life to shape her but rather she allowed them to produce godly character.

Just as physical muscles are developed in the hard work of pulling or pushing against weight or gravity, so our spiritual muscles are developed in the hard work of living in less-than-perfect circumstances. There is no other way for some character traits to be developed. Romans 5:3-4 says: "We exult in our tribulations; knowing that tribulations bring about perseverance; and perseverance, proven character; and proven character, hope" (NASB).

Allow It to Be a Bonding Agent Between Yourself and Others

One of the most profound experiences of my life was the opportunity to accompany a friend into the delivery room where she gave birth to a baby girl who was too young to survive outside the womb. It was an intense human drama: what is usually a life-giving process produced death. For a few suspended moments we gazed unabashedly into each other's souls, bound together by vulnerability and shared pain. Life and death were there, so closely intertwined. And the tears were there as together we grieved the loss of this baby who was already greatly loved. But there was also trust and hope in the Lord that was deeper than words. And, even in her pain, I saw beauty and strength in my friend that was different from any physical attribute I had ever seen. Her choice to allow me to be with her in that moment was one of the most valuable gifts I have ever been given.

Everyone has pain and difficulty in their life but usually we try to keep it hidden for as long as possible. What a loss that is to all of us because, when we open up our pain to others, it can level the ground between us as human beings and allow us to see each other more clearly. Tim Hansel discovered this through the ongoing physical pain he experiences as the result of a climbing accident:

> Pain, if allowed, produces an identification with the sufferings of others, and even the sufferings of Christ, that we could not experience any other way. One is allowed see dignity in the midst of human struggle and see beyond the false barriers that are oftentimes imposed between human beings.[4]

When we experience pain in our lives—whether it is the pain of a difficult marriage or any number of other hardships—we have a choice about whether to experience it in isolation or to open it up and find the bond it can create with others. If we are struggling in some area of our lives, we can be sure that others are as well. Although often our first response is to offer advice, we should keep in mind that advice isn't always the best form of support; usually what we need most is the strength and courage that comes from knowing we're not alone and that others are also struggling to hang in there. When we make the choice to share our pain, the beauty and strength we see in each other is nothing less than inspiring!

Expect God to Use It

One thing I learned early in my writing and speaking ministry is that people don't really want to hear about all the things I've got "nailed down" and no longer struggle with in life. A life that looks like it's "all put together" may be motivating to some, but to normal folks, it just seems overwhelming and unattainable. My first inklings of this came when my articles were returned because they were "too preachy." Editors would say, "Our readers want to hear what you've done right and what you've done wrong." I also noticed a pattern in people's comments about my speaking: the more I shared about my own areas of struggle, the more people could relate. They would say, "When you described some of the struggles you and your husband have, it sounded like you had been listening in at my house. I'm so glad I'm not the only one!" The understanding that we are fellow pilgrims creates a safe place to stand as we talk about what we need to do next to grow in the midst of difficulty.

I've come to accept and expect that God will often use areas of weakness and vulnerability in my life—even the areas I'm ashamed of!—for his purposes. Of course I would like to put only my strengths out there for everyone to see. Wouldn't we all? But God has a different plan. From Paul's comments regarding his own thorn in the flesh, we can understand that God wants us to boast about our weaknesses; in other words, put them right out there in plain view so that God's power can come shining through.

> Once Paul understood what he would be without it [his thorn]—a self-exalted, over-inflated, greatly blessed person who limited the display of the power of God—he decided to lead with it. He decided to say, "The greatest thing about me is that I have this difficulty that keeps me weak and vulnerable."[5]

It's not easy to let others see our difficulties and the areas where we are not strong. It seems more natural to hide those things rather than risk misunderstanding, embarrassment, or disrespect of those who don't know how to respond to the reality of human limitations—theirs and ours! Recently I spoke at a retreat about how our limitations and painful areas are part of the package God is putting together in our lives to make us of special use to him. In a discussion later, several women shared about dysfunction and abuse that took place in their homes as they were growing up and how hard it was for them to talk about it even with their closest friends. While they didn't want to rush into sharing their experiences indiscriminately, they all sensed that God would eventually want to use these experiences in the lives of others. I was impressed with their willingness to be made willing and the wisdom of waiting for God's timing.

What about you? What are the areas of weakness and pain in your life? Are you willing to put those areas "out front" so the power of God can come streaming through the prism they have created? Remember: "It's easier to take up a cause led by a fellow human being than to follow someone who covers all signs of weakness."[6]

When the Going Gets *Too* Tough

I cannot end this chapter here, for as I write about Abigail and her difficult marriage, terrible things are happening to 90s women who are in unhealthy relationships. In the past few weeks alone, one woman was gunned down by her boyfriend in the hallway of the courthouse where she had gone to get a restraining order. Another was shot to death in plain view of her teenage children by her husband who then turned the gun on himself. And another woman's estranged husband confessed to shooting her, stuffing her body in a barrel, and setting it on fire.

A cover story for *Time* magazine stated that in 1991 "some 4 million women were beaten and 1,320 murdered in domestic attacks"[7] and there is evidence that the numbers are increasing. Domestic violence is the greatest single cause of injury to American women—greater than auto accidents, rape, and mugging combined. These facts have led some to conclude that home is the most dangerous place a woman can be.

These chilling words and statistics prompt me to add: *In no way do I wish my comments in this chapter to be construed as encouragement for any woman to stay in an abusive relationship.* Battering is a sin before God and a crime in all fifty of the United States. It is, without exception, intolerable. No woman should be encouraged to think that domestic violence is normal or that it is what she deserves. The idea that if a woman would just behave better she could placate the violent man in her life is a trap because in actuality

Violence is not legislated by the wife's action; it is a specific choice made by the abusive husband. If frustrating situations offered only one option, abusers would be equally violent on the job, driving in traffic or interacting with friends; but it is simply not true. The majority of abusers direct their violence specifically and purposefully toward their wives.[8]

In many cases, the more compliant and submissive a woman becomes, the more violent her husband gets. And once a pattern of violence has been established it will continue until there is some sort of crisis (the wife leaving, an intervention, an arrest).

It would be comforting to think that in Christian marriages these problems do not exist, but this simply is not the case. In 1981 Phyllis Alsdurf prepared an article for *Family Life Today* on wife abuse in Christian homes and was stunned at the magnitude of the problem.

> Wives told of being struck in the face, kicked, bruised, dragged across the floor by their hair, and even bitten. And by whom? Ordained ministers, Christian businessmen, some well-known evangelical leaders—all men who lived a lie and perpetuated abuse that was an abomination to God.[9]

The response to Phyllis's article on wife abuse convinced Phyllis and her husband, James (a clinical and forensic psychologist), that this problem existed in greater proportion among Christians than they had ever realized. It prompted them to spend eight years researching and writing *Battered into Submission* in which they document the problem of wife abuse among Christians and trace some of its major roots to faulty theology taught in many fundamentalist homes and churches. They observe that "the distribution of power can be badly skewed in the Christian home. Fortified by preaching that accepts all sort of cultural assumptions about what 'headship' means, abusers often use Scripture as ammunition for their misuse of power."[10]

One battered wife shares how her husband's (and her own!) theology contributed to the abuse she suffered:

After marriage, my husband treated me as a nonperson with no value other than through him. He cited Scripture passages in support of his treatment of me. Any time I objected to his behavior or to his decisions, he told me that I was to submit to him just as totally as if he were Jesus Christ. He firmly believed that if I were obedient and submissive, God himself would take care of me. Therefore he was free to behave as irresponsibly as he liked without fear of hurting me or our child. He felt God wouldn't allow us to be hurt unless it was God's will.

My husband took no responsibility for his actions at all. I spent many hours in prayer and fasting, seeking to drive out every vestige of sin from my life. I believed that when I finally learned what God was trying to teach me, my husband would respond with love. But the more I submitted to him, the more arrogantly he displayed his flagrant abusive behavior. I sought counsel from pastors and friends. Many didn't believe me. It's not hard to understand why. How could such an upstanding member of the church and community be capable of such a miscarriage of God's justice? . . . Those who did believe me offered no solace; only sympathy and empty platitudes. They affirmed my submissive reaction to my husband's abusive tyranny. No one at any time went to talk to my husband about his behavior in loving correction. I was always left empty-handed to return to my own personal hell.[11]

It is easy to see how the sin of wife abuse can go unchecked in circles where wives are taught to submit blindly to husbands, where divorce is preached against without any consideration given to circumstances, and where dominance by the husband is seen as his divine right and responsibility. In fact, such teachings provide good covering for abuse under the guise of bringing one's wife "into subjection." Thus the batterer does not consider his actions abusive; he is simply fulfilling his God-given responsibilities.[12]

Wife abuse is a symptom of deeper problems in the marriage—low self-esteem, poor problem-solving and conflict resolution skills, not knowing how to cope with intense emotion, patterns of violence learned in family of origin, and so on. However, "it is too dangerous to discuss the problems of marriage until everyone is safe. Any problems with conflict resolution or communication cannot be realistically discussed while the husband is blatantly abusing power. Trust and confidence cannot be developed unless safety is achieved first."[13]

A battered woman's first step, then, is to gain safety for herself and for her children. She can do this through calling local domestic violence hotlines or women's shelters. If a hotline does not exist, calling 911 and asking for the number of a local domestic violence agency can also be effective. A woman must believe that she and her children are worth a better life (which is no small feat for a woman whose husband has been demeaning her for years) and be willing to do any or all of the following to get it: call the police, press assault charges, leave and refuse to consider returning until the abuser has completed a counselling program for offenders, or "go public" with the abuse to employers, relatives, and church community. This is the means by which "a woman offers her husband yet another opportunity to acknowledge the illegality and immorality of what he has done. These are acts of both self-preservation and love for her husband. Since he is participating in evil, forcing him to deal with it and not submitting to it is an act of love."[14]

The Alsdurfs are quick to point out, though, that once a victim has taken the first step, she holds virtually no power over whether or not the batterer will choose the path of true reconciliation. While expressing confidence in the power of God's love to redeem relationships characterized by abuse, they also acknowledge that most often reconciliation does not occur. When it does, it is not an event but a painful and slow process that involves more than will power. For the abuser, it involves facing the horror of his sin, confessing it (both privately and publicly), expressing his intent to change, and committing himself to the process of learning new patterns for loving and relating to his family. This is accomplished through professional therapy, support groups, and strong accountability within a community of Christians. For the abused, it involves forgiving, not primarily for his sake but for her own. There is no easy way back but there is a way. But it will never happen unless someone has the courage to say, "Enough."

A Fork in the Road

"Life is difficult," says Scott Peck in the opening line of *The Road Less Traveled*. He goes on to say that this is a great truth because "once we truly see this truth, we transcend it . . . Because once it is accepted, the fact that life is difficult no longer matters."[15] What does matter is what we do with it.

The difficulties and pains of our lives bring us to a fork in the road, a place where we must choose. And it's impossible to stay neutral. To allow our pain and difficulty to corrode our spirit, to make us hard and bitter, is to have chosen. To keep living for some future escape is to refuse the present. To allow God to transform us in the situation as we talk with him, look at things from his perspective, deal forthrightly with our difficulties and communicate about them with vulnerability—this is the road less travelled. And choosing that road will make all the difference.

FOR DISCUSSION

1. What is causing difficulty or pain in your life right now? What are your current patterns of coping with this difficulty?

2. Which of Abigail's character qualities do you admire most? Which would be most beneficial for you to develop in your life right now—especially as it relates to the situation you described in question one? (Remember, God doesn't expect you to work on everything at once!)

3. Describe a time when someone "let you in" on their pain in a way that was meaningful for you. What impact did that have on you? How difficult is it for you to allow others to see your pain?

4. What do you need to do to keep growing spiritually even though you have this area of difficulty in your life? What good can you see coming from it?

For Further Study

Olsen, Kathy. *Silent Pain*. Colorado Springs: NavPress, 1992.

Tada, Joni Eareckson. *A Step Further*. Grand Rapids, Mich.: Zondervan, 1990.

Yancey, Phillip. *Disappointment With God*. Grand Rapids, Mich.: Zondervan, 1988.

Regarding domestic violence and other abuse

Alsdurf, James and Phyllis Alsdurf. *Battered into Submission*. Downers Grove, Ill.: InterVarsity Press, 1989.

Johnson, David and Jeff VanVonderen. *The Subtle Power of Spiritual Abuse.* Minneapolis: Bethany House, 1991.

Rinck, Dr. Margaret J. *Christian Men Who Hate Women.* Grand Rapids, Mich.: Zondervan, 1990.

Fortune, Marie. *Keeping the Faith: Questions and Answers for the Abused Woman.* San Francisco: HarperSanFrancisco, 1989.

Scott, Catherine. *Breaking the Cycle.* Elgin, Ill.: David C. Cook, 1988.

Streeter, Carole Sanderson. *Finding Your Place After Divorce.* Wheaton, Ill.: Shaw Publishers, 1992.

Notes

1. This image was used by Jim Dethmer at Willow Creek Community Church in a message entitled "Walking with a Limp," October 18, 1990.

2. Ruth Tucker, *Multiple Choices* (Grand Rapids, Mich.: Zondervan, 1992), p. 111.

3. Jim Dethmer, "Walking with a Limp," Willow Creek Community Church, October 18, 1990.

4. Tim Hansel, *You Gotta Keep Dancin'* (Elgin, Ill.: David C.Cook, 1985), p.100.

5. Jim Dethmer, "Walking with a Limp."

6. Em Griffin, "What it Takes to Lead People," *Lay Leadership III*, p. 46.

7. Nancy Gibbs, "'Til Death Do Us Part," *Time* (January 18, 1993), p. 41.

8. James Alsdurf and Phyllis Alsdurf, *Battered Into Submission* (Downers Grove, Ill.: InterVarsity Press, 1989), p. 68.

9. Ibid., pp. 9-10.

10. Ibid., p. 17.

11. Ibid., pp. 17-18.

12. Ibid., p. 18.

13. Grant L. Martin, *Counselling for Family Violence and Abuse* (Waco, Tex.: Word Books, 1987), pp. 99-100.

14. Alsdurf, *Battered Into Submission*, p. 101.

15. M. Scott Peck, *The Road Less Travelled*, New York: Simon & Schuster, 1978, p. 1.

12

Woman to Woman: Reaching Across the Generations

If the truth be told, we today are who we are—if we are anybody—because some woman, somewhere, stooped down long enough that we might climb on her back and ride piggyback into the future.

Renita Weems

We're all familiar with doublespeak—the practice of obscuring the unpleasantness of a subject by couching it in euphemistic terms. My personal favorite is the travel newsletter that refers to the over-60 crowd not as senior citizens but as the "chronologically gifted." The reason I like this one is that, rather than obscuring the truth, this phrase actually clarifies a truth that would otherwise be lost: Older people are "chronologically gifted" with wisdom they have gained from weathering the seasons of life.

I have had the privilege of being in several life-changing relationships with women who are "chronologically gifted." In fact, as I look back over my spiritual development and try to pinpoint the factors that have contributed most significantly, I seldom think of a particular Bible study or sermon. Instead it is older women who spent time sharing their lives with me that have had the most impact on my life.

Ruth Anne was a woman who had been a close friend of our family for years. Realizing that even the best training at home needs to be supplemented by the input of other gifted Christians, my parents arranged for me to spend one of my college summers with Ruth Anne and her husband. Though I spent most of that summer working in a fast-food restaurant, it was one of the richest times of my life spiritually. Ruth Anne memorized Scripture a book at a time, so I memorized, too. She gave me a copy of A.W. Tozer's *Knowledge of the Holy*, which helped to deepen my relationship with God. Every evening we went for a three-mile walk in the Virginia hills surrounding their home and talked about everything from boyfriends to church government to the problem passages in Hebrews. She allowed me just to live and learn with her, and that summer was life-changing. More recently, I returned to her home for a week-long visit with my husband and three children. This time a lot of our conversation revolved around child rearing. I shared some of my fears and uncertainty; she made some observations and offered me encouragement, instruction, and resources. It was just the kind of challenge I needed!

Darlene shared her life with me in a different way. While I was in college, far from my own family, she took an interest in me and invited me to her home quite often. Our relationship was characterized by commitment, open sharing, and prayer. I saved all of my deep and not-so-deep questions for our get-togethers. Her perspective was a treasured source of help and encouragement. As an older woman she was able to teach me so much through the friendship she allowed to develop between us.

Titus 2:3-5: A Few Observations

Of course, the idea of older women helping younger women is not a new one. It is a biblical principle that often gets lost in the shuffle from this meeting to that Bible study. Titus 2:3-5 instructs older women to be reverent in their behavior "that they may encourage the young women to love their husbands, to love their children, to be sensible, pure, workers at home, kind, being subject to their own husbands, that the word of God may not be dishonored" (NASB).

Life experience rather than age. Paul does not define the age groups to which he is referring when he uses the words "older" and "younger." He doesn't say "Older women are those who have reached some magical age when they are suddenly deemed mature." This lack of definition indicates that all of us can be teaching and learning from each other back and forth on a continuum rather than seeing ourselves in rigid age categories. What qualifies us to teach others is maturity and life experience rather than chronological age.

Show-and-tell ministry. The apostle is speaking here of a type of ministry in which you show it with your life before you tell it with your mouth. Paul's usage of the word translated "teach what is good" indicates teaching by example as well as verbal instruction.[1] Paul's own life and writings illustrate how he helped younger Christians to maturity through relationships that were characterized by affection, tender care, and fatherly encouragement (1 Thessalonians 2:7-11). He opened up his very life so that others could learn from his example. And when it was necessary, he expressed his love through confrontation with tears (2 Corinthians 2:4). He knew that we do not necessarily need more Bible studies or preaching services; we need relationships that provide examples to follow.

Encouragement—not mothering. Most young women do not need another mother, they just need an older friend. Win Couchman gives an effective image of the role of the older woman by telling the story of her drive home one Christmas Eve night.

> A deep San Fransisco-style fog kept our car crawling blindly along the road. Suddenly another car pulled onto the road right ahead of us. Because we were now following a set of beautiful twin taillights, we could safely increase our speed from 15 to 25 miles an hour. A mentor is someone further on down the road from you who is going where you want to go and who is willing to give you some light to help you get there.[2]

There was no official relationship between the two cars—they didn't ask to get in the other car or be hooked up by a tow rope. They were just following along behind someone who was a little farther along and who could light the way. In fact, the car in front probably didn't even realize anyone was following! But unknowingly, they were providing just the amount of light that was needed.

But Can It Work Today?

This whole idea sounds so logical, so right, so comfortable. It conjures up images of a world where women share their experiences as they sit around quilting or baking bread together—a world that, for most of us, is long gone.

Our world, by contrast, is transient, fast-paced, and filled with new challenges for women. Young women today tend to move across country instead of across town, and they find themselves cut off from their mothers and other women whom they have known and learned from all their lives. And the older women find themselves with very empty nests indeed. In addition, the number of working women has increased so dramatically that there is no longer the networking that used to occur so naturally. The woman who chooses to stay at home full-time may find herself the only one home in her neighborhood during the day. In the meantime, working women find that they are barely holding themselves and their families together, without much energy and time for mutually beneficial relationships. Ironically, these very differences cause us to need helping relationships now more than ever.

Incorporating this timeless principle into contemporary life is possible if we are willing to BE FLEXIBLE AND CUSTOMIZE. There is no precise formula for helping relationships because they are friendships that are as diverse as personalities themselves. Some women get together to study the Bible and pray together while others share more spontaneously as situations arise. Sometimes a young woman may ask an older woman to share an area of expertise: some aspect of child rearing, entertaining, interior decorating, or professional advice. When a young woman is struggling with something specific, such as communication in marriage, materialism, jealousy, or job stress, she might approach an older woman to help her in that area. Or a single woman might ask a woman she respects to keep her accountable in the area of sexual purity. Some women begin with a time limit in mind; others continue indefinitely with periods of varying intensity. No matter what your stage in life, these relationships can be customized to meet the needs and lifestyles of those involved.

Setting the Tone for Cross-Generational Relationships

One of the most important things we can do to facilitate cross-generational relationship is to give some attention to our mindset.

Certain attitudes pervade our society that make it very difficult for women to encourage and learn from each other. Sometimes these attitudes exist and are conveyed to others unbeknownst to us, but their presence can greatly hinder mutually beneficial relationships.

One of the biggest barriers to relationships between women today is an attitude of self-sufficiency on the part of younger women. While it is good for them to have a sense of their own personal accountability before God so as not to be overly swayed by the opinions of others, there is a kind of independence that can be counter-productive. It is an independence rooted in pride, and it results in a disregard for the counsel of others who are older and/or wiser.

It isn't always easy for women in the baby boom and buster generations to learn from someone else; we're a pretty independent group! Never before have women been able to enjoy such success in careers and other personal achievements, and it is exhilarating. But it is easy to see how a growing self-confidence could translate itself into a false sense of control over one's life in which there is no need for anyone's help. We have allowed images of the professional woman who is out there "putting her best foot forward" to become our model for success.

For the Christian woman, these attitudes can carry over into our spiritual lives, and we find ourselves maintaining the impression that we are attractive, poised, gifted, and spiritually mature. We maintain this image even during times of great difficulty so that it becomes almost impossible for us to accept help, encouragement, or training from older women. Of course, the older women sense these attitudes and feel that we do not want or need their help. Then when times of need do cause us to be more open, the older women are nowhere to be found.

I was at such a juncture after the birth of my second child. My husband and I had withdrawn from a lot of our activities because of increased family responsibilites. I was not recovering very quickly and was feeling lonely and overwhelmed; my self-sufficiency gave way to frightening feelings of isolation. I was desperate for friendship, encouragement, and practical help from older women but none was forthcoming. At first I was angry and assumed that these women were neglecting their responsibilities. But as I began to probe for reasons I was told that people thought I had it all together and didn't need their help. Ironically enough, this is what I had wanted them to think. But now my carefully attended image of a confident, poised, self-sufficient young woman had backfired! It had made me unapproachable and beyond the reach of those who would have liked to offer encouragement.

It was through this experience that I discovered a dichotomy within. There was that part of me that recognized my need for support and encouragement; but there was also the part that wanted to continue appearing totally competent and self-assured. I believe other young women experience the same inner struggle, and it is important for us to deal with the pride that can become a barrier between us and the older women whose encouragement we need.

We must guard against "being wise in our own eyes" (Proverbs 3:7)—so wise that we disregard the wisdom of others. We need to communicate to more mature women that they have a lot to offer and that we would greatly benefit from time spent with them. We must learn to listen and be open to what they are saying even when it hurts—when our first reaction is to get defensive and clam up. Developing a teachable attitude and accepting older women as role models may require a change for some of us. However, women who are humble and teachable are the ones who are growing and learning.

Older women can also be responsible for attitudes that are hidden enemies of fruitful relationships. When they allow themselves to pass judgment on younger women—even if that judgment is unspoken—the perceptive woman will sense this and not risk opening up. Marsha has a genuine love and concern for younger women, demonstrated by her willingness to invest time and energy into relationships with them. However, she has a low tolerance for new ideas and difficulty understanding women whose struggles are different from her own. Consequently, when she reaches a point of disagreement with a younger woman, she withdraws her friendship and moves on to someone else who sees things more her way. She has had a string of friendships follow this pattern, and several women have been deeply hurt. But this unhealthy development of relationship can be avoided.

Keep clearly in mind the goal in relationships.

We who are considered more experienced are responsible to encourage others by our example and verbal instruction. We are not to make them into carbon copies of ourselves or force them to make the same choices we have made in order to win our approval. It is good to remember that they are not accountable to us but to God. As Romans 14:4 says, "Who are you to judge the servant of another? To her own master she stands or falls; and stand she will, for the Lord is able to make her stand" (NASB, feminine pronouns mine). It is our responsibility to offer ourselves in relationships; it is God's responsibility to bring about growth and change.

Don't give too much advice too soon.

Too often we offer advice before giving younger women the chance to express themselves fully. This is unfortunate because the very process of expressing feelings and talking through one's problems can be therapeutic. Learning to ask thoughtful questions will take us a long way in understanding what the other person is experiencing: "How does that make you feel? What has caused you to come to that conclusion? How do you think that decision will effect your husband, children, etc.? How do think this verse from the Bible pertains to that situation?" Many times a woman can find answers herself if she is given time to verbalize her concerns and brainstorm a little. Also, if we do not take the time to listen first, we run the risk of giving answers that are simplistic or irrelevant. It is no wonder the Bible says, "He who gives an answer before he hears, it is folly and shame to him" (Proverbs 18:13, NASB).

Mutuality

In my experience, the best cross-generational relationships are those in which both the younger and the older woman are contributing to each other. No relationship is as healthy as it could be if it remains "all taking and no giving" indefinitely. Relationships that are characterized by an awareness that each has somethng to give and something to gain are experienced as invigorating rather than draining. They tend to last long after any formal arrangements for the relationship have fallen away. The age difference is not disregarded or forgotten, but both women come to understand that chronological age does not define what we have to offer one another.

My friendship with another Ruth has been marked by this kind of mutuality. Our relationship began somewhat typically— she was an elder's wife at the church of which we were a part. Many young women were drawn to her because of her honesty, compassion, and obvious spiritual depth. She and several other women had been praying that the Lord would impassion someone to begin a women's ministry in our new and growing church. When it became clear that I was that person I determined that a team approach to leadership would be most effective in this endeavor. I asked Ruth if she would be willing to be a part of this team, because I knew her teaching and pastoral gifts would be a real asset. I asked her if she would meet with me regularly to pray, to offer her input and perspective, and to be supportive on a very personal level. I was delighted when she agreed, and thus began a friendship that has endured through challenges that neither one of us could have imagined at the outset.

Some of those challenges were related to the fact that she was an elder's wife in the church where I became a staff member. When staff and elders came down on different sides of an issue, it was awkward and stressful. Other challenges had to do with personality and generational differences. I was very direct in my communication and ready to plow ahead on issues that she needed to take more slowly. We both suffered because of gender inequities in the church, but she expressed her suffering through tears and sadness (which is generally more acceptable for women); and I expressed mine through anger, which was hard for her to deal with at times. We were at different stages in our lives so she could not take some of the risks I was free to take. This was disappointing, but we loved and respected each other enough to accept that God was leading us down our individual paths.

It took us awhile to learn that we were different—but one was not better than the other. We went through some painful transitions in our life together at church—disagreeing vehemently at times—but we learned to negotiate these rough spots with honesty, mutual respect, commitment to the relationship that transcended issues, and giving each other space when we needed it. What began as a younger woman looking to an older woman for encouragement grew into a relationship that was so valuable to both of us that we were determined not to let anything destroy it. Now that Ruth has moved away and some of the outside pressures on our relationship have been removed, I marvel at what we made it through.

What did we offer one another that was so valuable it was worth such a significant investment of time and emotional energy? For me, this relationship was honest on deeper levels than any relationship I had ever had with an older woman (other than my own mother). Ruth went through some very deep waters during the time we were sharing on a regular basis and she was remarkably vulnerable in opening them up for me. There was no attempt on her part to conceal her struggles or make them seem easier than they were. There were no simplistic solutions. The lessons I learned from seeing the unvarnished version of her experiences, from weeping with her and praying for her, are lessons that will be with me for the rest of my life. She led by her example, freeing me to share some of my most personal struggles as well. This vulnerability—which manifested itself in her friendships, her leadership style, and her teaching—had a significant impact on my own friendships and ministry style.

In addition, her graciousness in accepting and following the leadership of this young whippersnapper (which is what I was) gave me tremendous confidence. Knowing that she believed in me helped me to believe in myself. I was amazed at her willingness to learn from me even though I was her junior by about fifteen years. We shared information, and both of us were open to being stretched by the new ideas and ways of looking at the world that we were picking up in our studies and other relationships. We were also able to be open about what was going on in the relationship: feelings of competetiveness, disappointment, anger, intimidation, being misunderstood. Our honesty was painful at times but because our love and commitment was never in question, we were able to use these experiences to gain a deeper understanding of ourselves as well as each other.

It has always been obvious what I, the younger woman, gained in this friendship, but as Ruth shared in a recent letter, she experienced significant benefits as well. She says, "You have given me:

A cross-generational relationship, which I so much need to understand myself, my daughters, the world, God.

A desire for honest assessment of life and its foundational principles.

An open delving into a very difficult area of life . . . revealing your hurts, listening to and absorbing mine.

Opposite perspective or a 'different' (not wrong) way of viewing a predicament.

Patience in accepting me and trying to understand my limits of conscience and actions due to prior commitments.

Vulnerability and truth-telling.

Steadfastness to continue the relationship when we hit hard and tall barriers in the church setting and, at times, found ourselves almost on opposite sides, staring through at each other.

The largeness of spirit to admit defeat and at other times to say, "I'm sorry. Forgive me."

The example of preparing clearly (to take a stand) and then opening your mouth to verbalize it. This has given me more courage.

The joy of having another woman beside me committed to the Scriptures.

Much hope that honest relationships can be built as you have not let me go, nor have I let you go . . . because we have weathered each other's 'hard' counsel at times, asked forgiveness, explained ourselves, tried to understand each other, recognized that we are different but are both needed in the Kingdom, and that we need each other.

Maybe you can read between the lines and understand that this was not a perfect relationship. It didn't happen at the perfect time, the perfect place, in the perfect way, or with two perfect people. It was not without its mistakes. But it happened with commitment, honesty, and mutuality—some of the best stuff we as women have to give each other. Together we learned that "we women are in this thing together. And when we share information, when we console each other, encourage each other, talk to each other, we get stronger. We get powerful. Women are sisters to one another."[3]

Getting Started

All of us have someone younger than ourselves who could benefit from time spent with us and someone older than ourselves from whom we could learn. As we begin to realize our responsibility to those younger than ourselves we can ask God to show us someone in whom we can invest our time. A relatively young woman can keep her eyes open for a high school or college girl who seems open to her input. Meet somewhere for a Coke. Or, if your schedule is crowded, invite her to go along with you while you shop or take your kids to the park. All of us can be sensitive to "divine appointments" and use situations in which we are "thrown together" with a younger woman (i.e. nursery duty, committee work, travelling to a conference or retreat, etc.) as opportunities to take a special interest in them.

As younger women, we can take the initiative to identify a woman whom we respect and actively pursue a friendship with her. We can let the relationship unfold naturally or ask her to consider meeting with us on a regular basis. Taking the attitude of a learner will make it easier for that older woman to share her life with us. Realizing that we each have something to offer in relationships, regardless of our age and stage, will encourage us to search out and cultivate friendships that are mutually fulfilling.

I've heard it said, "If you can't be a good example then you'll just have to be a terrible warning." That's a frightening prospect! But God's idea is that older women be a good example of how he transforms everyday life—how he helps us build up our families by loving our husbands and children properly, how he helps us develop strong character, make right personal choices, and avoid the pitfalls that are so abundant these days. It's the real stuff of life that can't be learned in a classroom but is best learned by watching someone else. Even in our transient, fast-paced society, he wants us to be always reaching ahead to learn from those who are farther along in their journey and reaching back to those who are coming along behind. With God's help we can become the kind of encouraging, non-judgmental, teachable women who can make it happen.

FOR DISCUSSION

1. Describe a relationship with an older woman that was beneficial to you. What was it about this woman that made you willing to learn from her? What kinds of things did you learn?

2. What are some of the potential pitfalls of such relationships? How can these pitfalls be avoided?

3. In your particular setting and stage of life, how easy or difficult has it been for you to begin and maintain cross-generational relationships? Brainstorm ways that you and others can facilitate these friendships.

For Further Study
Brestin, Dee. *The Friendships of Women*. Wheaton, Ill.: Victor Books, 1988.
Clinton, J. Robert. *Connecting: The Mentoring Relationship You Need to Succeed in Life*. Colorado Springs: NavPress, 1992.
Kraft, Vicki. *Women Mentoring Women*. Chicago: Moody Press, 1992.
Ortland, Anne. *Discipling One Another*. Waco, Tex.: Word Books, 1979.

Notes
1. Gene Getz, *The Measure of a Woman* (Ventura, Calif.: Regal Books, 1977), pp. 59-61.
2. Win Couchman, "Cross-Generational Relationships," speaking at Women for Christ, 1983, Winter Break.
3. Alice Slaikeu Lawhead, *The Lie of the Good Life* (Portland, Oreg.: Multnomah, 1989), p. 144.

13

Women and Men: Working Together

There is artistry in working well together, an artistry in modeling Christ's true community—men and women functioning in tandem with mutual regard and trust. There is profound artistry in respect given, in respect received. There is artistry indeed in all the wondrous resolutions of reconciliation.

Karen Mains

When my seven-year-old daughter chose to play co-rec soccer this spring and ended up being the only girl on her team, I have to admit I had my concerns. However, I have been pleasantly surprised at the ease with which the boys and coaches have accepted her and with the lessons she has learned about being part of a team. She has tried all the positions and learned about her own abilities. She cheers the strengths of her teammates and they cheer her. And she has learned how much she and her teammates must rely on one another in order to defend their goal and move the ball down the field. When I see the teamwork and camaraderie that these little people exhibit I can't help but wonder, what happens along the way from childhood to adulthood that makes it so difficult for men and women to work together? Could it be as simple as children make it seem?

These are important questions because, as life goes on, we don't have a choice about what kind of team we are going to play on; it's co-rec all the way in marriage, ministry, and the workplace. God himself decided that the world would be a better place if women and men worked together on things. But it's gotten a little complicated lately. Some of the women on the team are dissatisfied with the positions they have been playing and would like to try something new. Others are telling them they are the wrong sex for the position they want to try. Many are struggling to hear the voice of the Coach over the din of the spectators and the advice of their teammates. And others have gotten so frustrated they have given up and gone home!

At times one wonders if it is possible for men and women to work together in the midst of such change and controversy. Yet if there is any area in which our world needs to see practical evidence of Christ's redemptive power it is in the area of gender relations. Christian men and women—of all people!—should be the ones leading the way in modeling healthy relationships that are characterized by true teamwork.

The Team Concept

One of the newest management books on the market, entitled *The Wisdom of Teams*, discusses the powerful results that can be achieved when people with complementary skills commit themselves to a common purpose, set goals together, and decide on an approach for which they hold themselves mutually accountable. That description bears an uncanny resemblance to the Body of Christ, for that is exactly what we are: a team of men and women with a variety of gifts given by God for the purpose of achieving a common goal.

When Paul described the team concept in 1 Corinthians 12 and Ephesians 4 it was much more than just a theory—it was the way the men and women in the early church had worked together from the very beginning. After Christ's death, the disciples "with one mind were continually devoting themselves to prayer, along with the women" (Acts 1:14, NASB). On the day of Pentecost when the church was born, they were all together in one place when the Holy Spirit came and filled each one of them (Acts 2:1-4). As the church grew, the presence of the Holy Spirit was further demonstrated as the women and men worked together according to the gifts he had given: some, such as Paul and Lydia, worked together in planting churches, some taught the Bible together (Priscilla and Aquilla), others such as the seven men chosen in Acts 6 and Phoebe (Romans 16:1-2) ministered as deacons, and many hosted the church in their homes. Romans 16:1-16 is a thrilling testimony to the teamwork that these men and women were able to achieve. How can we nourish that kind of teamwork today, not only in the church but also in our marriages and our working relationships?

Respect and Interdependence

Respect is a fairly intangible quality, and yet we can all sense when it is there and when it is not. For Christian women and men, mutual respect is rooted in several broad Scriptural themes, as we have noted in earlier chapters. The first is that every human being—female and male—is created in the image of God and is responsible for filling, ruling, and subduing the earth (Genesis 1:26-28). Second, the Bible teaches us that every Christian is a priest with responsibility for offering up spiritual sacrifices and proclaiming the excellencies of Christ (1 Peter 2:5, 9). Closely related to this concept of the priesthood of all believers is the reality that we as men and women are interdependent upon one another for our physical lives ("In the Lord, neither is woman independent of man, nor is man independent of woman. For as the woman originates from the man, so also the man has his birth through the woman" 1 Corinthians 11:11-12, NASB) and for our lives in the body of Christ ("to each one is given the manifestation [gift] of the Spirit for the common good" so that none of us can say to another "I have no need of you") (1 Corinthians 12:7, 21, NASB).

As we consciously remind ourselves that "This woman or man reflects the image of God to me. He/she is a royal priest just as I am and I need him/her to work alongside me in order to carry out my priestly responsiblities," it will begin to transform our own attitudes and thus our relationships.

Avoid Stereotypes

"All men ever think about is sex." "Women are so emotional you just can't take them seriously." "Real men don't cry." "All women like children." Most stereotypes are either insulting or gross generalizations!

Kaye Cook and Lance Lee, in their book, *Man and Woman: Together and Alone*, point out that stereotyping is a natural process our mind engages in as it tries to sort out reality. The problem is that

> Stereotyping (magnifying the differences between the sexes) is harmful and negative, both to women and men. Stereotyping causes us to judge or reject others without getting to know them. This process makes us respond to another based on our expectations, not on the reality of the other person's needs and personality . . . and to limit our own or another's response to God's calling.[1]

Gender stereotypes are dangerous because they go beyond what the Scriptures have to say about being created male and female. Indeed, they trap us in very small boxes created by our culture rather than freeing us to become all that we are in Christ. The more we believe the stereotypes the less chance we have of really knowing and understanding one another. True respect takes us beyond stereotypes based on gender (or anything else!) to a place where we recognize the uniqueness, the mystery, and the potential in every human being.

Deborah and Barak provide us with a refreshing example of a man and woman who were able to get beyond stereotypes so they could function as a highly effective team. Deborah was a judge in Israel who, in addition to mediating people's disagreements, provided a direct line of communication between God and his people (Judges 4:4-6). One day God gave Deborah a message for Barak, a general in Israel's army: He was to take ten thousand men and march to Mount Tabor where God would give his enemy (Sisera) into his hand. Barak accepted her instruction without hesitation and also insisted that she go with him into battle (verse 8). We are not told why Barak felt so strongly about this but we do know that Deborah went into battle with him and they won a great victory together.

Deborah's and Barak's relationship was highly unconventional, especially for that historical period. Yet one of the keys to their success was Barak's ability to see beyond Deborah's gender to her God-given strength and calling. The bottom line was that he recognized he would be more effective if he teamed with her. An entire chapter of Scripture (Judges 5) is devoted to celebrating the great victory God gave them!

We would do well to consider working according to our strengths as Deborah and Barak did. So often, when we are deciding who will keep nursery, fix food, teach, facilitate discussions, organize events, provide secretarial support, chair the building committee, or direct a new ministry, we allow gender stereotyping to inform our decisions. Who knows what strength and enthusiasm would be unleashed if we allowed gifts and ministry passion to inform us instead?

Communication and Conflict

During the time I served as director of women's ministry at our church, in that capacity I reported directly to the senior pastor. We both had strong personalities and saw things differently from time to time, but our relationship worked. As I look back on that success, I can see that, to a large extent it was due to the priority we placed on communication. We met weekly to share important information, to discuss issues relating to philosophy of ministry and organization, and to make sure that the women's ministry was on target with the overall vision for the church. Our relationship was not without its conflicts, but our regular, direct communication gave us the opportunity to deal with problems as they came up—before they got blown out of proportion.

Conflict is a normal part of any relationship; however, when two people are communicating effectively they will be able to deal with it. If people are *not* communicating effectively they will find themselves in continual conflict. That is why we cannot overstate the importance of effective communication between men and women who are working together. This communication should include frequent, informal conversation ("Say, how did your committee meeting go?" or "You did a great job organizing that social event.") as well as quality time in which more substantial matters are discussed and input is given and received. This happens in several ways.

Acceptance. Effective communication begins with simply recognizing the other person as a worthy individual entitled to his or her own experiences and opinions. Men and women often have very different perceptions of the same situation, and when one or both assume that their thoughts and feelings are the only valid ones, communication is quick to die. It is much better to acknowledge that I might learn something because you have knowledge and perspective that are worth hearing.

Careful listening. An effective communicator learns how to clarify what the other person is saying. This is the process described in Proverbs 20:5 by which a man or a woman of understanding draws out the true meaning of what is in someone else's heart. Rather than assuming that we have understood the person who is speaking, we check it out to make sure that what we heard is what they really meant: "Are you saying that . . . ?" "I heard you say . . . Did I understand you right?" "What do you mean when you use that word?" "I'm not quite clear on that. Could you explain it to me again?" The speaker then knows that he or she is being heard accurately or has the opportunity to say, "Well, not exactly. What I really meant was . . . "

Empathy. This requires us to stand in someone else's shoes, to "rejoice with those who rejoice, and weep with those who weep" (Romans 12:15, NASB). This is an especially important element in relationships between men and women because our experiences within our families, our churches, and our society are so different. Our understanding of each other will be inadaquate unless we know, to some degree, what it feels like to be in the other's situation. When a man enters into a woman's experience by asking, "What would it be like for me if I was told I couldn't do things I really wanted to do because I'm a man?" he will respond to her struggle with greater sensitivity. Likewise, when a woman understands how unsettling it would be to have all your rules for relating with the opposite sex turned upside down, she may look for more sensitive ways to approach men with the changes she is looking for.

Empathy requires us to move away from our own experience as the measure of all things and to learn about life and perhaps even ourselves from someone else's vantage point. It takes a very secure person with a lot of self-discipline to set aside her own beliefs and feelings long enough to fully enter into someone else's. It requires listening until you can see how his experience of the situation makes sense. Empathizing doesn't necessarily mean that we agree, but that we are able to say, "In the context of your experience, I can see how you would feel that way or why you have made that choice." Even when we don't agree, to know that we have been heard and understood means a great deal and keeps the relationship growing.

Direct communication. This is important between men and women, especially when we start to notice tension. It may be easier to avoid situations that involve conflict or to talk with members of our own sex, because the chances of being understood and agreed with seem higher. While these approaches may keep us within our own comfort zones, we can be assured that by choosing them we will not learn anything new about the person with whom we are dealing. Without direct communication the gulf between men and women struggling to work together will only widen. It is no wonder that the Scriptures are so consistent in telling us that the direct approach is best (Matthew 5:23-24; Ephesians 4:25-27).

Sensitivity to gender differences. In *You Just Don't Understand*, linguist Deborah Tannen states that conversation between women and men is very much like cross-cultural communication! Although each style is equally valid, misunderstandings arise because the styles are different. However,

> Learning about style differences can banish mutual mystification and blame. Being able to understand why our partners, friends, and even strangers behave the way they do is a comfort, even if we still don't see things the same way ... And having others understand why we talk and act as we do protects us from having the pain of their puzzlement and criticism."[2]

One of the most helpful insights Tannen offers is the importance of learning to distinguish between the *message* and the *metamessage* in conversation. The message is the obvious meaning of an act such as sharing a problem or giving advice. However, it is the metamessage that really counts. This is the underlying message about the relations among the people involved and their attitudes about what they are saying and the person to whom they are saying it. And it is at this level that problems usually occur.

For instance, many women complain that when they share a problem with a man, he is too quick to offer a 1-2-3 solution rather than empathy or comfort. According to Tannen, when a woman shares a problem, her underlying message is a bid for an expression of understanding ("I know how you feel" or "That must have been awful for you") or a similar complaint ("I felt the same way when . . . "). When she doesn't get this kind of reinforcement but gets advice instead, she is likely to hear the underlying message: "We're not the same. You have the problem; I have the solutions."[3] Of course, this isn't the meaningful connection she was looking for.

On the other hand, men tend to be more utilitarian in their approach to conversation. They aren't looking for connection; they are looking to get the job done. Consequently, it is easy for them to feel frustrated when, as one man put it, "women want to wallow in their problems rather than taking our advice and getting on with it." In addition, many men see themselves as problem solvers, so when a woman presents a struggle or a complaint, they offer a solution because they assume that this is what is being asked of them. Most often they offer a solution out of a sincere desire to be helpful. When that help is rejected, it hurts![4]

Once we understand that these two levels of conversation exist and begin understanding them in our conversations, we can tell each other more directly what we want and need. Now that I know about conversational styles, I preface my conversations with my husband about problems by saying, "I need to talk to you about something and I would really like to be able just to 'emote' for a while before we start discussing solutions." Chris is also free to say at any time, "I'm really frustrated because I feel like there is nothing I can do to help." To which I might reply, "I can understand how you would feel that way, but this really is helping." In this way we are being much more clear about what we want and need in the conversation and both of us are getting it more often.

A Balanced View of Emotions

I remember being told, before a meeting with a group of men about a very emotional topic: "Be sure not to cry because then they won't hear you." Well, that was a frightening prospect, so I spent most of my emotional energy that evening making sure I didn't cry. For this group of men that was probably good advice. But I couldn't help wondering, *Was that my only option or could we have found some sort of middle ground between their discomfort with emotion and my need to express it?*

Christians tend to have a deep distrust of emotions and this puts women at a disadvantage because, in general, women are more emotionally expressive than men. This can result in discomfort on the part of the men and fears about losing respect and credibility on the part of the women. The uneasiness that we experience in the face of deep emotion is puzzling to me because it isn't consistent with what we see in the Scriptures. There we learn that you can be angry and not sin (as Jesus did). You can weep over the loss of a friend (as David did). You can be beastly with jealousy and by admitting it, take the first step to getting free of it (as the Psalmist did). You can sing and dance with joy (as Moses and the Israelites did). You can weep with passion for ministry (as Paul did). Rather than reasons for not hearing or respecting an individual, emotions are signs of life and authentic relationships with God and others.

Our uneasiness in the face of deep emotion can result in some pretty significant losses to the team. Says one writer in *Harvard Business Review*:

> When an organization [including the church] either denies the validity of emotions or seeks to permit only certain kinds of emotions, two things happen. The first is that managers cut themselves off from their own emotional lives. Even more important, they cut off the ideas, solutions, and new perspectives that other people can contribute.[5]

She goes on to describe how an information systems department of a company that was undergoing a complex computer conversion acknowledged and even utilized both positive and negative emotion. Rather than denying the huge demands placed on the department and the enormous stress everyone was under, the project director had T-shirts made that said on the front "Yes, it's hard." On the back they said, "But we can do it." In addition, during biweekly meetings the team used the first fifteen minutes to "visit Pity City" and talk about their gripes and struggles. However, they were told up front that "You can visit Pity City, but you aren't allowed to move there." So, for the second fifteen minutes, the meeting became a brag session in which people would showcase their victories. Everyone was required to participate at least once a week in the griping and the bragging.

The team discovered that these sessions created a remarkable degree of camaraderie among the team members, making it easier for them to ask each other for help and give each other ideas for how to handle tough situations. As they told each other about little victories, they began to feel that they were part of a winning team. And when the pressure period was over, they felt better about themselves and their organization than they had at the beginning. Denying or disallowing "negative emotions" such as anger and frustration would have robbed them of these benefits.

Because women are traditionally more in touch with feelings and more comfortable expressing them than men, we may well be the ones to lead the way toward a healthier view of emotions. But here, as in many areas, there is a need for balance. Roger Fischer and Scott Brown, in *Getting Together*, give four suggestions for balancing emotion and reason.

Develop an awareness of emotions—yours and others'

Why? Because

> Insecurity, frustration, fear, or anger can take hold and begin to affect our actions without our realizing what is happening. [If we fail to] recognize our own feelings or the feelings of others, it will be difficult indeed to control how we express them. And if we cannot control how we express our emotions, we are unlikely to deal well with substantive issues."[6]

Emotions are experienced in our bodies as physical sensations such as a tightening of the stomach muscles, tension in the jaw, sweaty palms, quicker heartbeat, raised voice, lump in the throat, tears, etc. By paying attention to my body's signals I have the opportunity to distance myself from my emotions for a moment. Then I can analyze them and think about how I want to respond.

Take charge of your behavior instead of merely reacting.

We are able to do this once we are more practiced at recognizing our emotions. Most women would welcome the opportunity to be more confident in controlling how they express their emotions in pressured or painful situations. I realize now that my greatest fear going into the meeting I mentioned earlier had nothing to do with the content of the material I was to present (I was very well prepared) or the quality of my work up to that point (it had been very well received). My greatest fear was that I would not be able to control my responses to the emotions I usually experienced regarding the subject we were discussing. Being out of control was a very frightening prospect indeed. I had not yet learned to create a quiet space within myself from which I could observe my own emotions and then make a conscious choice about what I was going to do or say next. Without that skill, I knew I was at the mercy of some of my strongest emotions. I didn't want to rid myself of them, but to control their influence on my behavior.

Acknowledge emotion.

Fisher and Brown go on to point out that rather than ignoring or supressing emotion, the third step in achieving a balanced approach is to acknowledge it. While we may try to hide our emotions for fear of the consequences of showing them,

> denying emotions doesn't make them go away, it only makes them harder to deal with . . . Unless we reveal our emotions at least to ourselves, potentially destructive feelings like anger and resentment can fester until they flare into an outburst that causes long-term damage to a relationship. Furthermore when we hide our feelings we may be ignoring underlying substantive problems (in the relationship) that need attention.[7]

One way to deal with emotions is to talk about them. Explaining ("I am starting to feel frustrated because I keep getting interrupted.") rather than displaying or denying the way we feel actually demonstrates self-confidence, honesty, and self-control—all qualities that build trust in a relationship. Our purpose in acknowledging our emotion is not to blame the other person; it is important that we accept responsibility for our emotions and behavior. But we do want to explain them to the other person so that negative feelings will not stand in the way of a good working relationship.

Prepare for emotions before they arrive.

Whenever our emotions catch us off guard we are more likely to react rather than make a rational choice about how we want to respond. Any work we can do to anticipate our emotions and plan our response in a given situation will take us a step further toward balance. For instance, a woman who doesn't have children and finds that being asked about it dredges up feelings of pain or frustration, can plan her response ahead of time. Choosing a lighthearted response ("That's kind of personal, don't you think?") or a more serious one ("That's something I'm really struggling with right now") in advance (say, before she attends a family gathering where it always comes up) puts her more in control than if she were unprepared for the torrent of emotions and dissolved into tears at the dinner table.

The more we practice recognizing emotions such as anger or disappointment, acknowledging them to ourselves and to those with whom we are working, giving ourselves enough space to analyze them and choosing a constructive response, the more confident and effective we will be in our team-working relationships. Every time I am able to work through this process with Chris (my marriage is the most important cross-gender team I'm on), I am amazed at the difference it makes in our ability to work together. I gain confidence for other working relationships as well. It is just the help I've needed in learning to "Be angry [or sad or frustrated or disappointed] and yet do not sin" (Ephesians 4:26, NASB).

Tools for Teambuilding

Chris and I started working as a team in ministry shortly after we started working as a team in marriage, and it didn't take us long to discover that becoming an effective team doesn't happen by accident. What did happen "by accident" is that our egos collided, insecurity and competitiveness surfaced, and communication became more challenging under the pressure of tasks that needed to be accomplished. This is what often happens when women and men try to work together without intentionally working toward a sense of team—especially during these days of controversy and change in gender relations. In response to these realities, we have identified questions that help us deal with important issues before we get into the heat of tense moments. In answering these questions together, with equal regard for the other's input, we have formed a stronger foundation for our working relationship.

1. What are our goals for the area in which we are working together? How can those goals best be accomplished? Each of us has very personalized expectations as we approach different tasks and opportunities. We can envision what we would like to see happen and what we would like our role in that to be. Taking the time to put these longings into words and brainstorming ways that they can become reality gives each of us a greater sense of ownership in whatever we are doing together. "Being intent on one purpose" (Philippians 2:2) is a key to unity.

2. What are the strengths that each of us bring to this task? How can we fully utilize these in accomplishing our goals? Sometimes it is easier to feel threatened or competitive regarding the other person's gifts than to plan ways of allowing those gifts to blossom. However, when we begin our working relationships by sharing strengths and weaknesses and planning ways to help each other grow, we level the playing field and pave the way for true teamwork.

3. What values are important to us as we work together? How will we deal with difficulties that arise? Every team experiences conflicts and misunderstandings. Rather than being taken by surprise, we can prepare for the inevitable by deciding ahead of time what qualities are important in the relationship and how we will proceed when the going gets tough. We gain a great deal of trust in each other and confidence in the relationship when we have committed ourselves to: speaking directly with another about problems; listening until both of us feels heard; confessing stubbornness, competitiveness, and pride; getting help from an objective third party when necessary.

Any team that begins by discussing these issues will greatly enhance their ability to work together.

"You're on the Same Team!"

I had to smile the other day when the players on my daughter's soccer team got so intent on their own individual performance that they were actually kicking the ball away from each other. The coach had to remind them from the sidelines, "Hey! Don't forget you're on the same team!"

That statement embodies a coach's greatest challenge: to help gifted individuals learn how to work together as a single unit for greater results than they could achieve alone. That is also God's challenge to us—to learn to function as a team for greater results than men or women could achieve alone. Mutual respect and acknowledging our need for one another will help. So will effective communication, a balanced view of emotions, and an avoidance of stereotypes. But it is Christ among us, who breaks down dividing walls through the power of his blood (Ephesians 2:13-14), who will take us the rest of the way.

FOR DISCUSSION

1. What cross-gender teams are you a part of right now? How has the fact that both genders are represented enhanced the effectiveness of these teams?

2. What difficulties have you encountered? How might mutual respect, acknowledging interdependence, effective communication, or a balanced view of emotions help with these difficulties?

3. What have you learned from your experiences of being on a "co-rec" team that you might not have learned from being on a same-sex team?

For Further Study

Cook, Kaye and Lance Lee. *Man and Woman: Alone and Together.* Wheaton, Ill.: Scripture Press, 1992.

Fisher, Roger and Scott Brown. *Getting Together: Building Relationships as We Negotiate.* New York: Penguin Books, 1988.

Tannen, Deborah. *You Just Don't Understand: Women and Men in Conversation.* New York: Ballantine Books, 1990.

Notes

1. Kaye Cook and Lance Lee, *Man and Woman: Alone and Together* (Wheaton, Ill.: Scripture Press, 1992), p. 77.

2. Deborah Tannen, *You Just Don't Understand: Women and Men in Conversation* (New York: Ballantine Books, 1990), pp. 47-48.

3. Ibid., pp. 32, 50

4. Ibid., p. 52.

5. Jeanie Daniel Duck, "Managing Change: The Art of Balancing," *Harvard Business Review* (November/December, 1993), p. 113.

6. Roger Fisher and Scott Brown, *Getting Together: Building Relationships as We Negotiate* (New York: Penguin Books, 1988), pp. 48-49.

7. Ibid., pp. 54-55.

14

Today's Christian Woman: Christ-like amid Controversy

When we are fully and wholly given up to the Lord, I am sure the heart can long for nothing so much as that our time, talents, life, soul, and spirit, may become upon earth a constant and living sacrifice. How I can be most so, that is the one object of my poor heart. Therefore, to have all the light that is possible, to see my way in this matter is my prayer day and night; for worthy is the Lamb to receive all honor and glory, and blessing.

Lady Huntingdon, in a letter to John Wesley

As I bring this book to a close, I have been reading the Christian classic *In His Steps* by Charles Sheldon.[1] Although it is a work of fiction, it illustrates what can happen when Christians commit themselves to fashion their every decision after the question, "What would Jesus do?" The Christians described in this book were challenged by this "greatest question in all of human life" to be as honest as possible in trying to determine what Jesus would do in their particular situation—and then to do it.

This commitment meant entire dedication of money, talent, career, and influence to Christ. For some it caused misunderstanding and suffering, but also great joy. For those who prayed, hoped, worked, and regulated their lives by answering the question, "What would Jesus do", it became the inspiration of their conduct and a most satisfying discovery in their search for meaning in this life.

The Christian's Highest Calling

Some books are so convicting that you are tempted to put them down before they turn your life upside down! *In His Steps* has been such a book for me. It has reminded me that, amid the complexity of the issues facing women today, it is easy for our minds to be "led astray from the simplicity and purity of devotion to Christ" (2 Corinthians 11:3, NASB). It is a temptation that we must guard against vigilantly.

These are challenging days for women and the men who love them, to be sure. The controversies continue over roles of women and men in marriage, ministry, and the marketplace, and the issues that have been raised will not go away—regardless of how fervently we might wish they would. Their complexity demands that we continue in our search for insight and practical solutions. But as we take on this formidable task, our greatest challenge is to begin, continue, or return to (whichever the case may be) our quest for Christlikeness. Even as we work to right the wrongs that have been perpetrated against women in society and seek to nurture a world in which the strengths of women can fully emerge, our conformity to Christ must not be sacrificed.

It may seem simplistic or impossible, given the sophistication of our society, to think that we could proceed through life with the question "What would Jesus do?" as our guiding principle. And yet, the Scriptures are clear that the Christian's highest calling is to be like Christ. We are "predestined to become conformed to the image of his Son" (Romans 8:29), called to follow in his steps (1 Peter 2:21), given new birth for the purpose of reflecting his glory (2 Corinthians 3:18). For the committed Christian woman there is no cause or purpose greater than the call to follow Christ. It is at this point she must part company with the feminist for whom the fight for fairness and equality has become an end in itself. At the same time, the woman who is committed to "doing what Jesus would do" may also be called upon to part company with those women for whom personal comfort, "keeping the peace," or maintaining the status quo has become their highest value. Neither of these is the life that Christ modelled.

What Will It Mean for Me to Follow Christ?

In addition to committing themselves to ask "What would Jesus do?" before speaking or acting, the Christians in Sheldon's story also pledged not to judge the actions of others who were seeking to follow Christ in this way. The apostle Peter had to learn this, too, one day after the resurrection as he walked with Christ. Jesus was speaking in general terms about "the kind of death by which Peter would glorify God" (John 21:18-19). Peter turned around and saw John, the disciple whom Jesus loved, following close behind and promptly asked, "Lord, what about him?"

Jesus replied, "If it is my will that he remain until I come, what is that to you? Follow me!"

This is an important lesson for all of us, because there is something about human nature that makes it easier for us to concern ourselves with or even judge someone else's attempts at discipleship than to focus on what it means for us to follow Christ in our own situation. No one can interpret the life of Christ for another in terms of what it will mean for them to follow him. Christ's response to our over-concern about how he is leading someone else is, "That is really none of your business. You concentrate on following me."

It is with this understanding, then, that I proceed to make some observations about the life of Christ in answer to my own questioning about what Jesus would do. I realize that I cannot answer this question for anyone else but myself; those kinds of decisions are very personal. But I can offer some general observations about the life of Christ, in the context of the issues raised in this book.

Christ Came to Do God's Will

Christ was in a situation similar to that which women often face: For the most part, he was not recognized for who he was or what he had to offer. Yet it was not the main purpose of his life to prove who he was or to glorify himself. He knew who he was in relation to God and humankind, an important first step for all who want to be Christ-followers. He knew that he was here to do God's will in God's timing and that at the proper time his full identity and purpose would be revealed. In the meantime, he moved through life with singlemindedness unaffected by the opinion or persuasion of others.

Early in his ministry when Satan, the disciples, and even his family members tried to convince him to reveal his identity and set up his kingdom, Christ refused to be pushed. His answer was always some variation on the statement he made to his brothers when they encouraged him to show himself to the world at one of the Jewish festivals, "Go to the festival yourselves. I am not going to this festival, for my time has not yet fully come." (John 7:8, NRSVB)

When Peter first heard about Christ's impending death and protested the necessity of it ("God forbid it, Lord! this must never happen to you!"), Jesus refused to be sidetracked from the main purpose for which he had come. "Get behind me, Satan! You are a stumbling block to me; for you are setting your mind not on divine things but on human things" (Matthew 16:21-23, NRSVB).

When the Pharisees and religious leaders began to persecute him and try to arrest him, he was undeterred because he knew that, ultimately, God's will would be accomplished through him, regardless of human interference. Sometimes he withdrew for a while so that things could have a chance to cool off, but never for very long. He always came back, faithfully ministering, healing, and speaking the message that people needed to hear.

I am tremendously comforted and at the same time challenged by this image of an unflappable Christ walking this earth with an unwavering commitment "to do the will of him who sent me" (John 4:34, NRSVB). He expected that there would be those who didn't understand what he was trying to do and would attempt to stop him—some out of ignorance and some out of malice. But because he was in such close communion with the Father and knew he was in the center of his will, there was a peace that emanated from him.

As I observe this in Christ's life, I too rest in the fact that people—even those who try to limit the ways in which women serve God—cannot ultimately prevent God from accomplishing his will in and through my life. If he has given me spiritual gifts to use in service to others, he will give me opportunities to use them. Too often I have looked to people to recognize my gifts and give me the opportunity to use them, as if they had ultimate control. But God does not waste his gifts or his calling. As I am engaged in the process of becoming the kind of person God can use, he will place me where I can be of greatest use to him.

I am reminded of Joseph, whom God caused to find favor in the eyes of key people so that his purposes could be accomplished—despite jealous brothers who sold him to strangers, false accusations by an immoral woman, and a forgetful cup-bearer. The vision God gave Joseph while he was still a young boy, the lessons he learned while he was second-in-command at Potiphar's house, the breaking he experienced during time spent in jail, his meteoric rise to the top of Egyptian government were all part of God's plan for him that could not be thwarted. Later in his life he was able to say, without bitterness, to his brothers who had been so cruel, "You meant evil against me, but God meant it for good in order to bring about the present result" (Genesis 50:20, NASB). Like Joseph, I too can look past people and situations that seem limiting and see an all-powerful God.

Christ Learned Obedience Through the Things That He Suffered

I find this to be one of the most amazing and freeing assertions about Christ found in Scripture. It is amazing because it is hard to comprehend why Jesus needed to learn if he was already perfect. At the same time, this statement is very freeing because it helps me realize that to learn or to have need of learning is nothing to be ashamed of.

This insight into Christ's life became a particular comfort and instruction to me some years ago. I wanted badly to serve on a committee that I cared very much about, and I felt I had the qualifications to make a positive contribution. I expressed this desire to the chairman of the committee but was never invited. I was sure this was because I was a woman and that it was yet another instance where "women had to do twice as well as men to be thought half as good." That may have been partially true, but that wasn't all.

When I got up the nerve to ask the chairman about it, he described weaknesses in my character that he felt would render me ineffective on that committee. I was devastated. But as much as I wanted to run away from his words and categorically deny them, I needed to consider the truth in what he was saying— truth about pushiness and pride and being difficult to work with. I knew that God wanted me to look past the people in the situation and see him disciplining and training me. The discipline was painful, not pleasant (as it says in Hebrews 12:11), but I needed it.

While my suffering could not be compared with Christ's in terms of its intensity or the fact that mine was in connection with my own character weaknesses, it was encouraging to know that I was in very good company as I tried to remain open to learning. Hebrews 5:8 and surrounding verses make it clear that the things Christ learned through his suffering prepared him to be our perfect Savior—one who could understand what it means to suffer in obedience to God. Even though he was fully divine, there were some things he needed to learn through experience.[2] How much more true that would be for me!

Shortly after that incident, the Lord moved me to a situation where I had greater opportunities to use my gifts than I had ever expected. Of course I was much better prepared than I would have been had I not had the experience of being limited. I had not been limited by my gender or by people (as I had been tempted to believe) but by God himself because he knew I wasn't quite ready. Today I am tempted to chuckle, because some of the things people now observe as my strengths are the very qualities I lacked all those years ago and had to work so consciously to change.

I realize now that if I want to be the kind of woman who follows God courageously and lives consistently with the way he has gifted and called me, there will always be this kind of learning to be done. I will seldom "get it right" the first time and sometimes there will be consequences to suffer for my mistakes. At other times I will be called upon to suffer for doing what is right (as Christ did) and will have the opportunity to identify with Christ in new ways and grow in fellowship with him (Philippians 3:10). And so I am encouraged by Christ's example not to become hardened and immovable in my approach to life but rather to relax into the process of growing and learning.

Christ Spoke the Truth

There was nothing that got Christ into hot water more regularly than his consistency in speaking the truth. It was usually after some particularly honest moment—such as the times he revealed that he was God in the flesh or exposed the hypocrisy of the Pharisees—that crowds got violent, picked up stones to stone him, or tried to arrest him. However, to those whose hearts were open, his penetrating insight was one of the things that convinced them of his authenticity as the Son of God.

Although Christ was consistent in telling the truth, there was great variety in the way he told the truth. He had a knack for choosing a communication style that was appropriate for each situation. With the Samaritan woman, Christ was very gentle and at times even subtle in helping her understand the truth about who he was, who she was, and what she needed. With people like Nicodemus (the Pharisee who came to see Jesus by night in John 3), and the rich young ruler (Mark 10:17f) he was polite but cut right to the heart of the matter. In response to Nicodemus' lack of understanding of the fundamentals of the Gospel, he said, "You're a respected teacher of Israel and you don't know these basics? Listen carefully. I'm speaking sober truth to you. I speak only of what I know by experience; I give witness only to what I have seen with my own eyes. . . . Yet instead of facing the evidence and accepting it, you procrastinate with questions. If I tell you things that are plain as the hand before your face and you don't believe me, what use is there in telling you of things you can't see, the things of God?" (John 3:10-12, TM).

To the rich young ruler, who wanted to know what he had to do to inherit eternal life, Christ had this to say: "You lack one thing; go, sell what you own, and give the money to the poor, and you will have treasure in heaven; then come, follow me" (Mark 10:21, NRSVB). Honest. Take it or leave it. (This guy left it.)

And then there were the religious leaders and Pharisees for whom Christ reserved his strongest brand of truth-telling. It seems that politeness and subtlety would not be effective with ones who were so hard-headed: "Woe to you Pharisees! For you tithe mint and rue and herbs of all kinds [they were legalistic to the point of tithing on every last spice], and neglect justice and the love of God; it is these you ought to have practiced without neglecting the others. Woe to you Pharisees! For you love to have the seat of honor in the synagogues and to be greeted with respect in the marketplaces. Woe to you! For you are like un-marked graves, and people walk over them without realizing it" (Luke 11:42-44, NRSVB). No wonder the Pharisees and Scribes began to be very hostile toward him.

There were even times when speaking the truth was not enough, when action was needed. For instance, when opportun-ists used the spiritual yearnings of poor people as an occassion to make money in the temple courts, Christ became so indignant and impassioned for justice that he strode through the temple court overturning their tables and chasing them out (Matthew 21:12f). At that point the blind and the lame practically came out of the woodwork as though they had been waiting for someone who had pure motives to come and care for them. And Christ healed them. But where were the spiritual leaders with wisdom and courage enough to stand for what was right?

In an earlier chapter, we discussed the particular struggle that women in our culture have with telling the truth or taking a stand. And yet, in light of Christ's example, it would seem hard for us to justify cowering in a corner, cringing from telling the truth when there is hypocrisy or injustice to be be exposed. For those of us who are asking, "What would Jesus do?" part of the answer is "He would tell the truth." He would have several different styles from which to choose and he would pick the one best suited to the situation. But he would do it. And so will we if we are following in his steps.

Christ Was Moved with Compassion

The English language doesn't have a single word to describe the phenomenon of compassion in the life of Christ as he participated in the experience of being human. In fact, in its Biblical usage as it relates to Christ's experience, the concept of compassion is a verb that means "to be moved as to one's inwards, to yearn with compassion, to suffer with another, to be affected similarly."[3]

Compassion was not something Christ *had;* it was a moving within. It caused him to weep, to reach out and touch, to heal, to raise from the dead, to cast out demons, to speak the truth that would set the multitudes and the individual free.

When he saw that the crowds were hungry, he was moved with compassion to mobilize his disciples to feed them (Matthew 15:32). When he saw with spiritual eyes the crowds of people who were like sheep lost without a shepherd, it was fron a heart filled with compassion that he spoke and began to teach them many things. He then called his disciples so they too could share in this vision, giving them power, authority, and a plan so that they too could meet needs (Matthew 9:35–10:42). When the rich young ruler came for instruction on how to receive eternal life, Jesus looked at him, loved him *and then* told him the hard truth (Mark 10:17f). When he saw a widow on the way to bury her only son and envisioned what her life would be without him, he was moved with compassion to raise him from the dead.

One of the most wrenching descriptions of Christ's compassion came during his triumphal entry into Jersalem. Finally, people were getting the idea that he was the Messiah and they began waving palm branches and screaming "Hosanna!" or, "Save us, we pray!" But as Jesus approached that beloved city, in his omniscience he saw the tragedy that was in its future. Rather than being caught up in this moment of popularity and praise, he wept with compassion for what he saw, wishing with his whole heart that they could be spared: "If you, even you, had only recognized on this day the things that make for peace! But now they are hidden from your eyes. Indeed the days will come upon you, when your enemies will set up ramparts around you and surround you, and hem you in on every side. They will crush you to the ground, you and your children within you, and they will not leave within you one stone upon another; because you did not recognize the time of your visitation from God" (Luke 19:41-44, NRSVB)

Christ never lost sight of the value of people and his compassion for them—not even on the cross. Certainly it was compassion that moved him to ask God to forgive the soldiers who nailed him to the cross "for they do not know what they are doing" (Luke 23:34, NRSVB). It was out of compassion that he promised Paradise—as only he could—to a man who was dying the same death as he.

And so I am compelled to ask, How often is my teaching motivated by true compassion? When have I been perceptive enough to look past someone's material wealth and see their loneliness or their need for meaning in life? Do I look at people (husband, children, parent, fellow Christian, difficult neighbor) and really love them before I speak truth that is hard to hear? Am I willing to take a good hard look at the person (made in the image of God) who is wasting away with AIDS, the battered woman who has run for her life, the divorced woman fighting for custody of her children, the pregnant teenager who knows abortion is wrong but feels she has no other option, the child sitting next to his dying mother in a refugee camp—and look away so I can sleep at night? Am I able to extend compassion even when I am hurting and feeling mistreated? How often do I weep over anything but my own pain?

Not often enough.

Compassion is not something that can be conjured up by a mere act of the will; it happens in us as we recognize that all people suffer.

> Through compassion it is possible to recognize that the craving for love that men [and women] feel resides also in our own hearts, that the cruelty the world knows all too well is also rooted in our own impulses. Through compassion we also sense our hope for forgiveness in our friends' eyes and our hatred in their bitter mouths. When they kill, we know we could have done it; when they give life, we know we can do the same. For a compassionate man [or woman] nothing human is alien; no joy or sorrow, no way of living and no way of dying.[4]

That is why compassion is revolutionary. When we begin to discover that the weaknesses, sins, and sorrows of others are within us as well, we are changed in relation to them. It is hard to stay angry at someone when you realize that they hurt just like you do (whether they admit it or not); that they cry just like you do (whether they cry in front of you or not); that life is difficult for them, just like it is for you (no matter how trouble-free their life appears).

Yes, there is a time for anger in this world, a time to say, "This is wrong and I must stand against it." But there is also a time (perhaps it is the same time) for compassion, for looking at the person on the other side of an argument, the person who has been cruel, the person who has all the power as well as the one who has very little, and see that their struggle with the human experience is our own. Their sin is the same sin to which we are prone. Cynicism melts away when hearts are laid bare and we look inside. And condescension seems totally out of place when we realize that "there but for the grace of God go I."

Henri Nouwen makes the observation:

No one can help anyone without becoming involved, without entering with his whole person into the painful situation, without taking the risk of becoming hurt, wounded, or even destroyed in the process. Who can save a child from a burning house without taking the risk of being hurt by the flames? Who can listen to a story of loneliness without taking the risk of experiencing similar pains in his own heart and even losing his precious peace of mind? In short: who can take away suffering without entering it?[5]

No one. Not even Christ himself.

Christ Came to Serve

In the midst of rotting chicken pieces and dirty diapers, the poorest of the poor pick through the trash of Guatemala's city dump to find plastic containers to recycle, pieces of cardboard to shade them from the heat, or morsels of food to keep them alive. The dump is their home and they have little hope of ever leaving it *except* for the fact that two women, Gladys Acuna and Lisbeth Piedrasanta, have come to offer them hope in Christ. Four years ago Gladys and Lisbeth left their comfortable counseling center and founded the Casa del Alfarero ("the potter's house") fifty feet from the edge of the dump. Here, with a team of thirty, they run a medical and dental clinic, offer carpentry and sewing classes, teach Bible lessons and serve up meals. Gladys serves as spiritual director and Lisbeth as administrative director. Their dream? In addition to meeting the physical needs of those who live in this place where fresh air is an impossibility and vultures fly overhead, they long to see spiritual revival. Says Lisbeth, "I ask the Lord not let me die until I see spiritual revival here. We've been planting seeds for several years, and I would like to see kids seek the Lord sincerely. That is my desire: to see spiritual revival here, because I know that's the exit to their pain and suffering."[6]

A life spent serving people who live in a dump? Somehow it seems like something Jesus would do.

Perhaps the most difficult aspect of Christ's life for us to emulate is his passion for serving others. That is why we are surprised when we find people like Lisbeth and Gladys actually doing it. Most of us are more like the disciples who, on the very night when Christ gave an example of servanthood by washing their feet, argued over who would have the most prominent positions in the kingdom. If we are at all honest, many of us would say that we too have wasted time and energy striving for positions of prominence at times when we could have been serving. How painful it is to realize that in those moments we are utterly unlike Christ.

The more I study the Scriptures, the clearer it becomes that love (not to be confused with co-dependency), humility (not low self-esteem), and a servant's attitude (not being a doormat) are the supreme Christian virtues. Christ modeled them perfectly.[7] Conformity to Christ in these virtues must be top priority *not because I am a woman but because I am a Christian.* A few key questions can help me keep evaluating whether or not I have a servant's heart.

- Is there a true lack of opportunity to use my gifts, or am I frustrated that the opportunities God has given do not showcase my gifts in the way I would like?
- Do my frustrations in life stem from a desire for prominence and recognition, or am I satisfied to serve for the sake of the task?
- Do I believe that responsibilities with titles attached are necessarily more important than other kinds of responsibility?
- Do I insist on getting credit for what I do? Or am I happy to serve for God's eyes alone?
- In conversation do I do most of the talking or am I able to focus on others?
- Do I have ulterior motives in my relationships with others?

I cannot use discrimination or mistreatment as an excuse to be anything less than what Christ was. Anything I do without love is worthless. If I am motivated by pride, God will oppose me. And Christ demonstrated servanthood so that I could learn to serve.

Why Do We Wait?

Catherine Booth, co-founder of the Salvation Army, heard and accepted God's call upon her life to preach one Sunday morning as her husband William, a Methodist minister, finished his sermon. She later recalled her inner feelings: "It seemed as if a voice said to me, 'Now if you were to go and testify, you know I would bless it to your own soul as well as to the souls of the people.' I gasped and said to my soul . . . I cannot do it. 'And then the devil said, 'Besides, you are not prepared to speak. You will look like a fool and have nothing to say.' "

Catherine chose to accept the Holy Spirit's challenge that day rather than the doubts planted by Satan. She stood up in front of a crowd of more than a thousand packed into Bethesda Chapel and said, "I want to say a word . . . " William was as surprised as anyone when she made her sudden announcement, but he quickly recovered, and when she had finished, he announced that she would preach that evening. Catherine's only regret was that she had waited so long.[8]

Women today face the same choice as did Catherine Booth. Our choice is not necessarily whether to preach or not to preach. It is how to answer the challenge that the Holy Spirit is speaking to our soul, whatever that is. For some it is the challenge to begin seeing ourselves as God sees us so we can be in a better position to give of ourselves to others. For others, it is the challenge to pull our heads out of their comfortable position in the sand and stand for what is right. For many in affluent communities around the country, the challenge is to get a grip on our materialism so we can invest in spiritual gain. For all of us, following in Christ's footsteps will involve having a heart that breaks for the pain of those who are still searching for love and meaning because they have yet to find Christ. We too face the possiblity of regret and the inevitable question, "Why did I wait so long?"

Soon after her pulpit debut, at least one of God's reasons in calling Catherine Booth to preach became clear. William became ill. Because of his slow recovery, Catherine took over his entire preaching circuit, her dynamic and forceful speaking style drawing crowds of thousands. When William recovered they were able to work together again in a revivalistic ministry that involved preaching, rescue-mission work (especially with teenage prostitutes), founding the Salvation Army, and training their own children into the ministry. Many agree that, as important as her work with the Salvation Army was, her thirty years of preaching ministry was perhaps most significant. "No man of her era exceeded her in popularity or spiritual results, including her husband."[9]

I have heard the question asked, almost tongue-in-cheek, "Why should women be like Christ in humility and suffering, yet unlike him in authority, power, and exultation?" The answer is: There is no reason at all. Catherine Booth is a flesh-and-blood example of what happens when a woman asks the question "What would Jesus do?" and then lays down her life to follow him. Spiritual authority is born of her obedience, power is forged as she speaks the truth, and grace pours from her life as she channels her strength to serve others. The exultation comes when we hear those words, "Well done, good and faithful servant."

And what of the man who is privileged enough to have women like this in his life as wife, sister, mother, daughter, or fellow disciple? His challenge is to be like William Booth, who, after he got over his shock that God had called his wife to preach, opened his pulpit so God could speak through her as well. How he must have praised God that he had been given this woman of strength to join him so thoroughly and completely in his life and work.

I can think of no other appropriate response.

FOR DISCUSSION

1. How feasible do you think it would be for Christians today to live their lives with the question "What would Jesus do?" as their guiding principle? Explain your answer.

2. How feasible would it be for you personally to make the commitment not to do anything without first asking "What would Jesus do?" What changes could you envision if you did make such a pledge?

3. In which area of the Christ-life is it most difficult for you to "follow in his steps":

   • singleminded focus on doing God's will
   • relaxing into the process of learning and growing
   • speaking the truth and/or standing for what is right
   • moving with compassion
   • serving others

   What would be the next step of obedience for you in this difficult area?

4. In your own words, what does it mean to be "a Woman of Strength"? What is your prayer?

For Further Study

Adeney, Miriam. *A Time for Risking*. Portland, Oreg.: Multnomah Press, 1987.

Groothuis, Rebecca Merrill. *Women Caught in the Conflict: The Culture War Between Traditionalism and Feminism*. Grand Rapids, Mich.: Baker Book House/Revell, 1993.

Mains, Karen Burton. *With My Whole Heart*. Portland, Oreg.: Mult-nomah Press, 1987.

Nouwen, Henri. *The Wounded Healer*. New York: Doubleday, 1972.

Piper, John. *Desiring God*. Portland, Oreg.: Multnomah Press, 1986.

Sheldon, Charles. *In His Steps*. Uhrichsville, Ohio: Barbour and Co., 1990 (originally published in 1897).

Swindoll, Charles R. *Improving Your Serve*. Waco, Tex.: Word Books, 1981.

Tozer, A.W. *The Pursuit of God*. Harrisburg, Penn.: Christian Publications, Inc., 1948.

Winter, David. *Closer Than a Brother* (a reinterpretation of the devotional classic *Practicing the Presence of God* by Brother Lawrence). Wheaton, Ill.: Shaw Publishers, 1971.

Notes

1. Charles M. Sheldon, *In His Steps* (Uhrichsville, Ohio: Barbour and Co., 1990, originally published 1897), pp. 134-135.

2. "In a real sense, not fully comprehensible, the incarnation gave the already infinitely wise and perfect Son of God the experiential acquisition of knowledge about the human condition. He had to experience the true meaning of obedience in terms of the suffering it entailed. He was thereby made perfect for the role he would play as His people's Captain and High Priest. Suffering thus became a reality that he tasted and from it he can sympathize deeply with his followers." John F. Walvoord and Roy B. Zuch, eds., *The Bible Knowledge Commentary*, (Wheaton, Ill.: Victor Books, 1983), p. 792.

3. W. E. Vine, Merril F. Unger, William White, eds., *Vine's Expository Dictionary of Biblical Words* (Nashville: Thomas Nelson Publishers, 1985), pp. 116-117.

4. Henri Nouwen, *The Wounded Healer* (New York: Doubleday Books, 1979), p. 41.

5. Ibid.

6. Ana Gascon Ivey, "Down in the Dumps in Guatemala," *Clarity* (July/August, 1994), pp. 31-35.

7. One of the reasons Christ was able to give so much of himself was because he had a self to give. He knew who he was so he didn't have to prove it, and he replenished himself in the presence of God regularly. On the other hand, a woman who sees herself as one who is "shot full of holes" or "a total blank" doesn't have much self to give. It is hard to lay down your life if you don't have one yet. That's why the issues covered in the early chapters of this book are so important.

8. Ruth Tucker and Walter Leifeld, *Daughters of the Church* (Grand Rapids, Mich.: Zondervan, 1987), p. 264.

9. Norman H. Murdoch, "Female Ministry in the Thought and Work of Catherine Booth," *Church History* 53 (September 1984), p. 354, as quoted in *Daughters of the Church*, p. 269.